three films

three films

SMOKE, BLUE IN THE FACE,
LULU ON THE BRIDGE

Paul Auster

Picador
Henry Holt and Company
New York

www.picadorusa.com

Picador® is a U.S. registered trademark and is used by Henry Holt and Company under license from Pan Books Limited.

For information on Picador Reading Group Guides, as well as ordering, please contact the Trade Marketing department at St. Martin's Press.
Phone: 1-800-221-7945 extension 488
Fax: 212-677-7456
E-mail: trademarketing@stmartins.com

ISBN 0-312-42314-4

First Picador Edition: December 2003

10 9 8 7 6 5 4 3 2 1

contents

smoke

The Making of

smoke

Annette Insdorf: I gather that *Smoke* began with a Christmas story you wrote for *The New York Times*.

Paul Auster: Yes, it all started with that little story. Mike Levitas, the editor of the Op-Ed page, called me out of the blue one morning in November of 1990. I didn't know him, but he had apparently read some of my books. In his friendly, matter-of-fact way he told me that he'd been toying with the idea of commissioning a work of fiction for the Op-Ed page on Christmas Day. What did I think? Would I be willing to write it? It was an interesting proposal, I thought—putting a piece of make-believe in a newspaper, the paper of record, no less. A rather subversive notion when you get right down to it. But the fact was that I had never written a short story, and I wasn't sure I'd be able to come up with an idea. "Give me a few days," I said. "If I think of something, I'll let you know." So a few days went by, and just when I was about to give up, I opened a tin of my beloved Schimmelpennincks—the little cigars I like to smoke—and started thinking about the man who sells them to me in Brooklyn. That led to some thoughts about the kinds of encounters you have in New York with people you see every day but don't really know. And little by little, the story began to take shape inside me. It literally came out of that tin of cigars.

AI: It's not what I would call your typical Christmas story.

PA: I hope not. Everything gets turned upside down in "Auggie Wren." What's stealing? What's giving? What's lying? What's telling the truth? All these questions are reshuffled in rather odd and un-orthodox ways.

AI: When did Wayne Wang enter the picture?

PA: Wayne called me from San Francisco a few weeks after the story was published.

AI: Did you know him?

PA: No. But I knew of him and had seen one of his films, *Dim Sum*, which I had greatly admired. It turned out that he'd read the story in the *Times* and felt it would make a good premise for a movie. I was flattered by his interest, but at that point I didn't want to write the script myself. I was hard at work on a novel [*Leviathan*] and couldn't think about anything else. But if Wayne wanted to use the story to make a movie, that was fine by me. He was a good filmmaker, and I knew that something good would come of it.

AI: How was it, then, that you wound up writing the screenplay?

PA: Wayne came to New York that spring. It was May, I think, and the first afternoon we spent together we just walked around Brooklyn. It was a beautiful day, I remember, and I showed him the different spots around town where I had imagined the story taking place. We got along very well. Wayne is a terrific person, a man of great sensitivity, generosity, and humor, and unlike most artists, he doesn't make art to gratify his ego. He has a genuine calling, which means that he never feels obligated to defend himself or beat his own drum. After that first day in Brooklyn, it became clear to both of us that we were going to become friends.

AI: Were any ideas for the film discussed that day?

PA: Rashid, the central figure of the story, was born during that preliminary talk. And also the conviction that the movie would be about Brooklyn. . . . Wayne went back to San Francisco and started working with a screenwriter friend of his on a treatment. He sent it to me in August, a story outline of ten or twelve pages. I was with my family in Vermont just then, and I remember feeling that the outline was good, but not good enough. I gave it to my wife Siri to read, and that night we lay awake in bed talking through another story, a different approach altogether. I called Wayne the next day, and he agreed that this new story was better than the one he'd sent me. As a small favor to him, he asked me if I wouldn't mind writing up the treatment of this new story. I figured I owed him that much, and so I did it.

AI: And suddenly, so to speak, your foot was in the door.

PA: It's funny how these things work, isn't it? A few weeks later, Wayne went to Japan on other business. He met with Satoru Iseki of NDF [Nippon Film Development] about his project, and just in passing, in a casual sort of way, he mentioned the treatment I had written. Mr. Iseki was very interested. He'd like to produce our film, he said, but only if "Auster writes the script." My books are published in Japan, and it seemed that he knew who I was. But he would need an American partner, he said, someone to split the costs and oversee production. When Wayne called me from Tokyo to report what had happened, I laughed. The chances of Mr. Iseki ever finding an American partner seemed so slim, so utterly beyond the realm of possibility, that I said yes, I'll do the screenplay if there's money to make the film. And then I immediately went back to writing my novel.

AI: But they did find a partner, didn't they?

PA: Sort of. Tom Luddy, a good friend of Wayne's in San Francisco, wanted to do it at Zoetrope. When Wayne told me the news, I was stunned, absolutely caught off guard. But I couldn't back out. Morally speaking, I was committed to writing the script. I had given my word, and so once I finished *Leviathan* [at the end of '91], I started writing *Smoke*. A few months later, the deal between NDF and Zoetrope fell apart. But I was too far into it by then to want to stop. I had already written a first draft, and once you start something, it's only natural to want to see it through to the end.

AI: Had you ever written a screenplay before?

PA: Not really. When I was very young, nineteen or twenty years old, I wrote a couple of scripts for silent movies. They were very long and very detailed, seventy or eighty pages of elaborate and meticulous movements, every gesture spelled out in words. Weird, deadpan slapstick. Buster Keaton revisited. Those scripts are lost now. I wish to hell I knew where they were. I'd love to see what they looked like.

AI: Did you do any sort of special preparation? Did you read scripts? Did you start watching movies with a different eye toward construction?

PA: I looked at some scripts, just to make sure of the format. How to number the scenes, moving from interiors to exteriors, that kind of thing. But no real preparation—except a lifetime of watching movies. I've always been drawn to them, ever since I was a boy. It's the rare person in this world who isn't, I suppose. But at the same time, I also have certain problems with them. Not just with this or that particular movie, but with movies in general, the medium itself.

AI: In what way?

PA: The two-dimensionality, first of all. People think of movies as "real," but they're not. They're flat pictures projected against a wall, a simulacrum of reality, not the real thing. And then there's the question of the images. We tend to watch them passively, and in the end they wash right through us. We're captivated and intrigued and delighted for two hours, and then we walk out of the theater and can barely remember what we've seen. Novels are totally different. To read a book, you have to be actively involved in what the words are saying. You have to work, you have to use your imagination. And once your imagination has been fully awakened, you enter into the world of the book as if it were your own life. You smell things, you touch things, you have complex thoughts and insights, you find yourself in a three-dimensional world.

AI: The novelist speaks.

PA: Well, needless to say, I'm always going to come down on the side of books. But that doesn't mean movies can't be wonderful. It's another way of telling stories, that's all, and I suppose it's important to remember what each medium can and can't do . . . I'm particularly attracted to directors who emphasize telling stories over technique, who take the time to allow their characters to unfold before your eyes, to exist as full-fledged human beings.

AI: Who would you put in that category?

PA: Renoir, for one. Ozu for another. Bresson . . . Satyajit Ray . . . a whole range, finally. These directors don't bombard you with pictures, they're not in love with the image for its own sake. They tell their stories with all the care and patience of the best novelists. Wayne is that kind of director. Someone who has sympathy for the inner lives of his characters, who doesn't rush things. That was why I was happy to be working with him—to be working *for* him. A screenplay is no more than a blueprint, after all. It's not the finished product. I didn't write the script in a vacuum. I wrote it for Wayne, for a movie that he was going to direct, and I very consciously tried to write something that would be compatible with his strengths as a director.

AI: How long did it take you to write it?

PA: The first draft took about three weeks, maybe a month. Then the negotiations between NDF and Zoetrope broke down, and suddenly the whole project was left dangling. It was probably dumb of me to start without a signed contract, but I hadn't yet understood how iffy and unstable the movie business is. At that point, however, NDF decided to go ahead and "develop" the script anyway while they searched for another American partner. That meant that I'd be given a little money to continue writing, and so I kept at it. Wayne and I discussed the first draft, I tinkered with it a little more, and then we both moved on to other things. Wayne went into preproduction for *The Joy Luck Club*, and I began writing a new novel [*Mr. Vertigo*]. But we stayed in close touch, and every once in a while over the next year and a half we'd talk on the phone or get together somewhere to discuss new ideas about the script.

I did about three more versions, and each time that entailed a week or two of work—adding elements, discarding elements, rethinking the structure. There's a big difference between the first draft and the final draft, but the changes happened slowly, by increments, and I never felt that I was changing the essence of the story. Gradually finding it is probably more like it. At some point in all this, Peter Newman came in as our American producer, but the money to make the movie still had to be found. Meanwhile, I kept working on *Mr. Vertigo*, and by the time I finished it, Wayne's movie was about to be released. And so there we were, ready to tackle *Smoke* again.

By some twist of good luck, Wayne decided to show the script to Robert Altman. Altman had very nice things to say about it, but he felt it lagged a bit in the middle and probably needed one more little something before it found its definitive shape. Robert Altman is not someone whose opinion should be discounted, and so I went back and reread the script with his comments in mind, and lo and behold, he was right. I sat down to work again, and this time everything seemed to fit. The story was rounder, fuller, more integrated. It was no longer a collection of fragments. It finally had some coherence to it.

AI: A very different process from writing a novel, then. Did you enjoy it?

PA: Yes, completely different. Writing a novel is an organic process, and most of it happens unconsciously. It's long and slow and very grueling. A screenplay is more like a jigsaw puzzle. Writing the actual words might not be very time-consuming, but putting the pieces together can drive you crazy. But yes, I did enjoy it. I found it a challenge to write dialogue, to think in dramatic terms rather than narrative terms, to do something I had never done before.

AI: And then Miramax stepped in and decided to back the film.

PA: *The Joy Luck Club* turned out to be a big success, the screenplay was finished, and Peter Newman happens to be a very droll and persuasive man. I was out of the country for a couple of weeks last fall, and when I came home, it seemed that we were in business. All the arrangements were in place.

AI: And that's when the screenwriter is supposed to disappear.

PA: So they say. But Wayne and I forgot to pay attention to the rules. It never occurred to either one of us to part company then. I was the writer, Wayne was the director, but it was *our* film, and all along we had considered ourselves equal partners in the project. I understand now what an unusual arrangement this was. Writers and directors aren't supposed to like each other, and no one had ever heard of a director treating a writer as Wayne treated me. But I was naive and stupid, and I took it for granted that I was still involved.

AI: Not all that naive, though. You'd been involved in another film once before—*The Music of Chance*.

PA: Yes, but that was completely different. Philip Haas adapted a novel of mine and turned that adaptation into a movie. A different story altogether. He and his wife wrote the script, and he directed it. He had a free hand to interpret the book as he chose, to present his particular reading of the book I had written. But my work was already finished before he started.

AI: Yes, but you also wound up playing a role in that film, didn't you? As an actor, I mean.

PA: True, true. My thirty-second cameo appearance in the final scene. Never again! If nothing else, I emerged from that experience with a new respect for what actors can do. I mean trained, professional actors. There's nothing like a little taste of the real thing to teach you humility.

AI: Back to *Smoke*, then. Were you involved in the casting, for example?

PA: To some degree, yes. And Wayne and I discussed every decision very thoroughly. We had some disappointments along the way, and also some very hard decisions to make. One actor I made a very intense plea for was Giancarlo Esposito. His role is very small. He plays Tommy, the OTB Man, and appears only peripherally in two scenes. But his character gets to speak the first lines in the movie, and I knew that if he accepted, things would get off to a flying start. It was a great moment for me when he said yes. The same with Forest Whitaker. I couldn't imagine any other actor playing Cyrus, and I can't tell you how thrilled I was when he agreed to do the part. . . . Other than that, I sat in on a lot of the auditions. What a heart-breaking spectacle that can be. So many talented people marching in with their high hopes and tough skins. It takes courage to court rejection on a daily basis, and I must say that I was moved by all this. . . .

Looking back on it now, though, I would say that the single most memorable experience connected with the casting was an open call organized by Heidi Levitt and Billy Hopkins. A bitter cold Saturday in late January, snow on the ground, howling winds, and three thousand people showed up at a high school in Manhattan to try out for bit parts in *Smoke*. Three thousand people! The line went all the way down the block. What a motley collection of humanity. The large and the small, the fat and the thin, the young and the old, the white, the black, the brown, the yellow . . . everyone from a former Miss Nigeria to an ex-middleweight boxing champion, and every last one of them wanted to be in the movies. I was astonished.

AI: Well, you wound up with an extraordinary cast. Harvey Keitel, William Hurt, Stockard Channing, Forest Whitaker, Ashley Judd . . . and Harold Perrineau in his first role. It's a great line-up.

PA: They were good people to work with, too. None of the actors made a lot of money, but they all seemed enthusiastic about being in the film. That made for a good working atmosphere all around. . . . About two months before shooting began, Wayne and I started meeting with the actors to discuss their roles and examine the nuances of the script. I wound up writing "Character Notes" for many of the parts, exhaustive lists and comments to help fill in the background of each character's life. Not just biographies and family histories, but the music they listened to, the foods they ate, the books they read—anything and everything that might help the actor get a handle on his role.

AI: Marguerite Duras used precisely that approach when she wrote her script for *Hiroshima Mon Amour*, one of my favorite films of all time. There is a sense of texture about the characters, even though we aren't told very much about their backgrounds.

PA: The more you know, the more helpful it is. It's not easy pretending to be someone else. The more you have to hold on to, the richer your performance is going to be.

AI: I take it there were rehearsals for *Smoke*—something for which there isn't always time with movies.

PA: It seemed essential in this case, given that there's so much talk in the film and so little action! Rehearsals went on for several weeks in a church near Washington Square. Harvey, Bill, Harold, Stockard, Ashley . . . they all worked very hard.

AI: Were there any other aspects of preproduction that you were involved with?

PA: Involved might be too strong a word, but I did have numerous conversations with Kalina Ivanov, the production designer. Particularly about the apartment that Bill Hurt's character lives in. That was the only set constructed for the movie—on a sound stage in Long Island City. Everything else was filmed in real places. Considering that the apartment is lived in by a novelist, it made sense that Kalina should want to consult with me. We talked about everything: the books on the shelves, the pictures on the walls, the precise contents of the clutter on the desk. I think she did a remarkable job. For once, there's an authentic-looking New York apartment in a movie. Have you ever noticed how many supposedly ordinary people in Hollywood films manage to live in three-million-dollar TriBeCa lofts? The apartment that Kalina designed rings true, and a lot of work and thought went into what she did, things that often aren't even visible on screen. The little coffee-cup rings on the table, the postcard of Herman Melville over the desk, the unused word processor sitting in the corner, a thousand and one minute details. . . . Philosophically speaking, production design is a fascinating dicipline. There's a real spiritual component to it. Because what it entails is looking very closely at the world, seeing things as they really are and not as you want them to be, and then recreating them for wholly imaginary and fictitious purposes. Any job that requires you to look that carefully at the world has to be a good job, a job that's good for the soul.

AI: You're beginning to sound like Auggie Wren!

PA: (*Laughs*) Well, Auggie didn't come out of nowhere. He's a part of me—just as much as I'm a part of him.

AI: Once the shooting started, did you go to the set?

PA: Occasionally. Every now and then I'd stop by to see how things were going, especially when they were filming the cigar store scenes, since that set was within walking distance of my house. And I was up in Peekskill for the last three or four days of shooting. But in general I kept myself at a distance. The set was Wayne's territory, and I didn't want to get in his way. He didn't sit in my room with me while I wrote the script, so it seemed only right to do the same for him. . . . What I did do, however, was attend the dailies every evening at the DuArt Building on West 55th Street. That proved to be indispensable. I saw every inch of footage, and when we went into the cutting room in mid-July, I had a pretty good understanding of what the options were. . . . The dailies were also instructive in teaching me how to cope with disappointment. Every time an actor blew a line or strayed from the script, it was like a knife going through my heart. But that's what happens when you collaborate with other people, it's something you have to learn to live with. I'm talking about the smallest deviations from what I wrote, things that only I would notice, probably. But still, you work hard to get the words to scan in a certain way, and it's painful to see them come out in another way. . . . And yet, there's another side to it, too. Sometimes the actors improvised or threw in extra lines, and a number of these additions definitely improved the film. For example, Harvey yelling at the irate customer in the cigar store: "Take it on the arches, you fat fuck!" I'd never heard that expression before, and I found it hilarious. Just the kind of thing Auggie would say. . . .

AI: So, even if you didn't go to the set every day, you were prepared to contribute after the shooting was finished.

PA: I hadn't really planned to get so involved in the editing, but like so many other things connected with *Smoke*, it just seemed to happen on its own. Maysie Hoy had worked with Wayne on his last movie, Wayne and I already knew each other well, and it turned out that Maysie and I hit it off—as if we'd been friends in some previous incarnation. It was an excellent three-way relationship. We all felt free to express our opinions, to talk through every little problem that arose, and each one of us listened carefully to what the other two had to say. The atmosphere was one of respect and equality. No hierarchies, no intellectual terrorism. We worked together for weeks and months, and there was rarely any tension. Hard work, yes, but also a lot of jokes and laughter.

AI: When it comes down to it, that's where every movie is really made. In the cutting room.

PA: It's like starting all over again. You begin with the script, which establishes a certain idea of what the film should be, and then you shoot the script, and things begin to change. The actors' performances bring out different meanings, different shadings, things are lost, other things are found. Then you go into the cutting room and try to marry the script to the performances. At times, the two mesh very harmoniously. At other times, they don't, and that can be maddening. You're stuck with the footage you have, and that limits the possibilities. You're like a novelist trying to revise his book, but fifty percent of the words in the dictionary are not available to you. You're not allowed to use them. . . . So you fiddle and shape and juggle, you search for a rhythm, a musical flow to carry you from one scene to the next, and you have to be willing to discard material, to think in terms of the whole, of what is essential to the overall good of the film. . . . Then, on top of these considerations, there's the question of time. A novel can be ninety pages or nine hundred pages, and no one thinks twice about it. But a movie has to be a certain length, two hours or less. It's a fixed form, like a sonnet, and you have to get everything into that limited space. As it happened, the script I wrote was too long. I cut things from it before we started shooting, but even so, it was still too long. The first assemblage that Maysie put together was two hours and fifty minutes, which meant that we had to cut out almost a third of the story. To tell the truth, I didn't see how it could be done. From what I understand, nearly everyone who makes a movie has to face this problem. That's why it always takes longer to cut a film than to shoot it.

AI: What was the biggest surprise that turned up in the cutting room?

PA: There were many surprises, but the biggest one would have to be the last scene, when Paul tells Auggie the Christmas story. As originally written, the story was supposed to be intercut with black-

and-white footage that would illustrate what Auggie was saying. The idea was to go back and forth between the restaurant and Granny Ethel's apartment, and when we weren't watching Auggie tell the story, we would hear his voice over the black-and-white material. When we put it together that way, however, it didn't work. The words and the images clashed. You'd settle into listening to Auggie, and then, when the black-and-white pictures started to roll, you'd get so caught up in the visual information that you'd stop listening to the words. By the time you went back to Auggie's face, you'd have missed a couple of sentences and lost the thread of the story.

We had to think through the whole business from scratch, and what we finally decided to do was keep the two elements separate. Auggie tells his story in the restaurant, and then, as a kind of coda, we see a close-up of Paul's typewriter typing out the last words of the title page of the story Auggie has given him, which then dissolves into the black-and-white footage with the Tom Waits song playing over it. This was the only plausible solution, and I feel it works well. It's a rare thing in movies to watch someone tell a story for ten minutes. The camera is on Harvey's face for almost the whole time, and because Harvey is such a powerful and believable actor, he manages to pull it off. When all is said and done, it's probably the best scene in the film.

AI: The camera moves in very close in that scene, right up against Harvey's mouth. I wasn't expecting that at all.

PA: Wayne worked out the visual language of the film in a very bold and interesting way. All the early scenes are done in wide shots and masters. Then, very gradually, as the disparate characters become more involved with each other, there are more and more close shots and singles. Ninety-nine percent of the people who see the film probably won't notice this. It works in a highly subliminal way, but in relation to the material in the film, to the kind of story we were trying to tell, it was the right approach. By the time we get to the last scene in the restaurant, the camera has apparently moved in on the actors as close as it ever will. A limit has been established, the rules have been defined—and then, suddenly, the camera pushes in even closer, as close as it can get. The viewer is not at all prepared for it. It's as if the camera is bulldozing through a brick wall, breaking down the last barrier against genuine human intimacy. In some way, the emotional resolution of the entire film is contained in that shot.

AI: I like the title of the film, *Smoke*. It's catchy and evocative. Would you care to elaborate?

PA: On the word "smoke"? I'd say it's many things all at once. It refers to the cigar store, of course, but also to the way smoke can obscure things and make them illegible. Smoke is something that is never fixed, that is constantly changing shape. In the same way that the characters in the film keep changing as their lives intersect. Smoke signals . . . smoke screens . . . smoke drifting through the air. In small ways and large ways, each character is continually changed by the other characters around him.

AI: It's hard to pin down the tone of the film. Would you call it a comedy? A drama? Perhaps the French category "dramatic comedy" is more appropriate?

PA: You're probably onto something there. I've always thought of it as a comedy—but in the classical sense of the term, meaning that all the characters in the story are a little better off at the end than they were in the beginning. Not to get too high-flown about it, but when you think about the difference between Shakespeare's comedies and tragedies, it's not so much in the material of the plays as in how the conflicts are resolved. The same kinds of human problems exist in both. With the tragedies, everyone winds up dead on the stage. With the comedies, everyone is still standing and life goes on. That's how I think of *Smoke*. Good things happen, bad things happen, but life goes on. Therefore, it's a comedy. Or, if you prefer, a dramatic comedy.

AI: With some dark spots.

PA: Definitely. That goes without saying. It's not farce or slapstick, but at bottom it takes a fairly optimistic view of the human condition. In many ways, I think the screenplay is the most optimistic thing I've ever written.

AI: It's also one of the very few American films of recent years in which the characters take pleasure in smoking. And there's no one walking into the frame telling them not to do it.

PA: Well, the fact is that people smoke. If I'm not mistaken, more than a billion people light up around the world every day. I know the anti-smoking lobby in this country has grown very strong in the last few years, but Puritanism has always been with us. In one way or another, the teetotalers and zealots have always been a force in American life. I'm not saying that smoking is good for you, but compared to the political and social and ecological outrages committed every day, tobacco is a minor issue. People smoke. That's a fact. People smoke, and they enjoy it, even if it isn't good for them.

AI: You won't get an argument from me.

PA: I'm just guessing now, but maybe all this is connected to the way the characters act in the film . . . to what you might call an undogmatic view of human behavior. Does this sound too far-fetched? I mean, no one is simply one thing or the other. They're all filled with contradictions, and they don't live in a world that breaks down neatly into good guys and bad guys. Each person in the story has his strengths and weaknesses. At his best, for example, Auggie is close to being a Zen master. But he's also an operator, a wise guy, and a downright grumpy son-of-a-bitch. Rashid is essentially a good and very bright kid, but he's also a liar, a thief, and an impudent little prick. Do you see what I'm driving at?

AI: Absolutely. As I said before, you won't get an argument from me.

PA: That's the spirit.

AI: Another question—about Brooklyn. I'd like you to tell me why the film is set there. I know you live in Brooklyn, but was there any special reason—other than familiarity?

PA: I've been living there for fifteen years now, and I must say I'm fond of my neighborhood, Park Slope. It has to be one of the most democratic and tolerant places on the planet. Everyone lives there, every race and religion and economic class, and everyone pretty much gets along. Given the climate in the country today, I would say that qualifies as a miracle. I also know that terrible things go on in Brooklyn, not to speak of New York as a whole. Wrenching things, unbearable things—but by and large the city works. In spite of everything, in spite of all the potential for hatred and violence, most people make an effort to get along with one another most of the time. The rest of the country perceives New York as a hellhole, but that's only one part of the story. I wanted to explore the other side of things in *Smoke*, to work against some of the stereotypes that people carry around about this place.

AI: I'm curious why the novelist in *Smoke* is named Paul. Is there an autobiographical element in the film?

PA: No, not really. The name Paul is a holdover from the Christmas story published in the *Times*. Because the story was going to appear in a newspaper, I wanted to bring reality and fiction as close together as possible, to leave some doubt in the reader's mind as to whether the story was true or not. So I put in my own name to add to the confusion—but only my first name. The writer that Bill Hurt plays in *Smoke* has nothing to do with me. He's an invented character.

AI: Tell me a little about *Blue in the Face*. Not only did you and Wayne make this other film after *Smoke*, but you wound up as co-director

PA: Weird but true. It's a crazy project that was filmed in a total of six days. We're still in the process of putting it together, so I don't want to say too much about it, but I can give you the rough outline.

AI: Please.

PA: It all started during the rehearsals for *Smoke*. Harvey came in to work on some of the cigar store scenes with the OTB Men—Giancarlo Esposito, José Zuniga, and Steve Gevedon. As a way of warming up and getting to know one another, they launched into a few short improvisations. It turned out to be very funny. Wayne and I just about fell on the floor, and in a burst of enthusiasm he announced: "I think we should make another film with you guys after *Smoke* is finished. Let's go back into the cigar store for a few days and see what happens."

AI: It might have started out with those four, but the cast certainly grew. You had some of the other actors from *Smoke*—Jared Harris, Mel Gorham, Victor Argo, and Malik Yoba—but also Lily Tomlin, Michael J. Fox, Roseanne, Lou Reed, Jim Jarmusch, Mira Sorvino, Keith David, and Madonna. Not too shabby.

PA: No, not too shabby. Everyone worked for scale—with the best spirit in the world. They were all troupers, every last one of them.

AI: And you did it with no script?

PA: No script—and no rehearsals. I wrote out notes for all the scenes and situations, so each actor more or less knew what had to be done, but there was no script per se, no written dialogue. . . . It was shot in two stages: three days in mid-July and three days in late October. It was wild, let me tell you, pure chaos from start to finish.

AI: And fun.

PA: Oh yes, lots of fun. I enjoyed myself immensely. The finished film is sure to be one of the oddest films ever made: wall-to-wall wackiness, a lighter-than-air creampuff, an hour and a half of singing, dancing, and loopy shenanigans. It's a hymn to the great People's Republic of Brooklyn, and a cruder, more vulgar piece of work would be hard to imagine. Strangely enough, it appears to work well with *Smoke*. They're opposite sides of the same coin, I guess, and the two films seem to complement each other in mysterious ways.

AI: Now that you've caught the bug, do you have any desire to direct again?

PA: No, I can't say that I do. Working on these films has been a terrific experience, and I'm glad it happened, I'm glad I got caught up in it as fully as I did. But enough is enough. It's time for me to crawl back into my hole and begin writing again. There's a new novel calling out to be written, and I can't wait to lock myself in my room and get started.

November 22, 1994

smoke

Directed by
Wayne Wang

Written by
Paul Auster

Produced by
**Greg Johnson, Peter Newman, Kenzo Harikoshi, and
Hisami Kuroiwa**

Director of Photography
Adam Holender

Editor
Maysie Hoy

Production Designer
Kalina Ivanov

Line Producer
Diana Phillips

Costumes
Claudia Brown

Music
Rachel Portman

Executive Producers
Bob Weinstein, Harvey Weinstein, and Satoru Iseki

Still Photographer
Lorey Sebastian

CAST

(In order of appearance)

Auggie Wren	**Harvey Keitel**
Tommy	**Giancarlo Esposito**
Jerry	**José Zuniga**
Dennis	**Steve Gevedon**
Jimmy Rose	**Jared Harris**
Paul Benjamin	**William Hurt**
Book Thief	**Daniel Auster**
Rashid Cole	**Harold Perrineau, Jr.**
Waitress	**Deirdre O'Connell**
Vinnie	**Victor Argo**
Aunt Em	**Michelle Hurst**
Cyrus Cole	**Forest Whitaker**
Ruby McNutt	**Stockard Channing**
Irate Customer	**Vincenzo Amelia**
Doreen Cole	**Erica Gimpel**
Cyrus, Jr.	**Gilson Reglas**
Baseball Announcer	**Howie Rose**
Felicity	**Ashley Judd**
April Lee	**Mary Ward**
Violet	**Mel Gorham**
1st Lawyer	**Baxter Harris**
2nd Lawyer	**Paul Geier**
Charles Clemm (The Creeper)	**Malik Yoba**
Roger Goodwin	**Walter T. Mead**
Waiter	**Murray Moston**
Granny Ethel	**Clarice Taylor**

What follows is the entire shooting script of *Smoke*. In the final version of the film, a number of scenes were either shortened or eliminated.

1. EXT: DAY. ELEVATED SUBWAY TRAIN

Against the backdrop of the Manhattan skyline, we see an elevated subway train heading toward Brooklyn.

After a moment, we begin to hear voices. An animated discussion is taking place inside the Brooklyn Cigar Company.

2. INT: DAY. THE BROOKLYN CIGAR CO.

The cigar shop from within. Displays of cigar boxes, a wall of magazines, piles of newspapers, cigarettes, smoking paraphernalia. On the walls, we see framed black-and-white photographs of people smoking cigars: Groucho Marx, George Burns, Clint Eastwood, Edward G. Robinson, Orson Welles, Charles Laughton, Frankenstein's monster, Leslie Caron, Ernie Kovacs.

Words appear on the screen: SUMMER 1990.

AUGGIE WREN is behind the counter. Somewhere between forty and fifty years old, AUGGIE is a scruffy presence: unkempt hair, a two-day stubble of beard, dressed in blue jeans and a black T-shirt. We see an intricate tattoo on one arm.

It is a slow hour. AUGGIE is flipping through a photography magazine.

Near the counter are the three OTB MEN. *These are local characters who like to hang out in the store, shooting the breeze with* AUGGIE. *One is black (*TOMMY*) and the other two are white (*JERRY *and* DENNIS*).* DENNIS *wears a T-shirt with the following words printed across the front: "If life is a dream, what happens when I wake up?"*

TOMMY

I'll tell you why they're not going anywhere.

JERRY

Yeah? And why is that?

TOMMY

Management. Those guys are walking around with their heads up their asses.

DENNIS

They made some great deals, Tommy. Hernandez, Carter. Without those two, there never woulda been no World Series.

TOMMY

That was four years ago. I'm talking about now. (*Growing more intense*) Look who they got rid of. Mitchell. Backman. McDowell. Dykstra. Aguillera. Mookie. Mookie Wilson, for Chrissakes. (*Shakes his head*)

JERRY

(*Sarcastically*) And Nolan Ryan. Don't forget him.

DENNIS

(*Chiming in*) Yeah. And Amos Otis.

TOMMY

(*Shrugs*) Okay, joke about it. I don't give a shit.

JERRY

Jesus, Tommy, it ain't science, you know. You got your good trades and your bad trades. That's how it works.

TOMMY

They didn't have to do a thing, that's all I'm saying. The team was good, the best fucking team in baseball. But then they had to screw it up. (*Pause*) They traded their birthright for a mess of porridge. (*Shakes his head*) A mess of porridge.

The bells on the door jangle as someone enters. It is AUGGIE's protégé, JIMMY ROSE, a mentally retarded man in his late twenties. He has been sweeping the sidewalk outside the store and holds a broom in his right hand.

AUGGIE

How'd you do out there, Jimmy?

JIMMY

Good, Auggie. Real good. (*Proudly thrusts out broom*) All finished.

AUGGIE

(*Philosophically*) It'll never be finished.

JIMMY

(*Confused*) Huh?

AUGGIE

That's how it is with sidewalks. People come, people go, and they all drop shit on the ground. As soon as you clean up one spot and move on to the next, the first spot is dirty again.

JIMMY

(*Trying to digest AUGGIE's comment*) I just do what you tell me, Auggie. You tell me to sweep, so I sweep.

The bells on the door jangle again, and a customer enters the store: a middle-class man in his early thirties. He walks to the counter as JERRY teases

27

JIMMY. *In the background, we see him talking to* AUGGIE. AUGGIE *pulls some cigar boxes out of the display case and puts them on the counter for the* YOUNG MAN *to inspect. In the foreground we see:*

JERRY

(*Interrupting. Playfully*) Hey, Jimmy. You got the time?

JIMMY

(*Turning to the* SECOND OTB MAN) Huh?

JERRY

You still have that watch Auggie gave you?

JIMMY

(*Holds up left wrist, showing a cheap digital watch. Smiles*) Tick-tock, tick-tock.

JERRY

So what's the time?

JIMMY

(*Studying watch*) Twelve-eleven. (*Pause, marveling as the numbers change*) Twelve-twelve. (*Looks up, smiling*) Twelve-twelve.

A sudden outburst is heard from the area near the counter.

YOUNG MAN

(*Aghast*) Ninety-two dollars?

The focus of the scene shifts to AUGGIE *and the* YOUNG MAN.

AUGGIE

They don't come cheap, son. These little honeys are works of art. Rolled by hand in a tropical climate, most likely by an eighteen-year-old girl in a thin cotton dress with no underwear on. Little beads of sweat forming in her naked cleavage. The smooth, delicate fingers nimbly turning out one masterpiece after another. . . .

YOUNG MAN

(*Pointing*) And how much are these?

AUGGIE

Seventy-eight dollars. The girl who rolled these was probably wearing panties.

YOUNG MAN

(*Pointing*) And these?

AUGGIE

Fifty-six. That girl had on a corset.

YOUNG MAN

(*Pointing*) And these?

AUGGIE

Forty-four. They're on special this week from the Canary Islands. A real bargain.

YOUNG MAN

I think I'll take them. (*Takes wallet from his pocket and counts out $50— which he hands to* AUGGIE)

AUGGIE

A good choice. You wouldn't want to celebrate the birth of your firstborn with a box of stinkers, would you? Remember to keep them in the refrigerator until you hand them out.

YOUNG MAN

The refrigerator?

AUGGIE

It'll keep them fresh. If they get too dry, they'll break. And you don't want that to happen, do you? (*Putting cigar box into a bag, ringing up sale on the cash register*) Tobacco is a plant, and it needs the same loving care you'd give an orchid.

YOUNG MAN

Thanks for the tip.

AUGGIE

Any time. And congratulations to you and your wife. Just remember, though, in the immortal words of Rudyard Kipling: "A woman is just a woman, but a cigar is a smoke."

YOUNG MAN

(*Confused*) What does that mean?

AUGGIE

Damned if I know. But it has a nice ring to it, don't it?

At that moment, we hear the bells on the door jangle again. Cut to the door. Another customer enters the store: PAUL BENJAMIN. *He is in his early forties, dressed in rumpled casual clothes. As he approaches the counter, the* YOUNG MAN *brushes past him and leaves the store. The* OTB MEN *and* JIMMY *look on as* PAUL *and* AUGGIE *talk.*

PAUL

Hey, Auggie. How's it going?

AUGGIE

Hey, man. Good to see you. What'll it be today?

PAUL

Two tins of Schimmelpennincks. And throw in a lighter while you're at it.

AUGGIE

(*Reaching for cigars and lighter*) The boys and I were just having a philosophical discussion about women and cigars. Some interesting connections there, don't you think?

PAUL

(*Laughs*) Definitely. (*Pause*) I suppose it all goes back to Queen Elizabeth.

AUGGIE

The Queen of England?

PAUL

Not Elizabeth the Second, Elizabeth the First. (*Pause*) Did you ever hear of Sir Walter Raleigh?

TOMMY

Sure. He's the guy who threw his cloak down over the puddle.

JERRY

I used to smoke Raleigh cigarettes. They came with a free gift coupon in every pack.

PAUL

That's the man. Well, Raleigh was the person who introduced tobacco in England, and since he was a favorite of the Queen's— Queen Bess, he used to call her—smoking caught on as a fashion at court. I'm sure Old Bess must have shared a stogie or two with Sir Walter. Once, he made a bet with her that he could measure the weight of smoke.

DENNIS

You mean, weigh smoke?

PAUL

Exactly. Weigh smoke.

TOMMY

You can't do that. It's like weighing air.

PAUL

I admit it's strange. Almost like weighing someone's soul. But Sir Walter was a clever guy. First, he took an unsmoked cigar and put it on a balance and weighed it. Then he lit up and smoked the cigar, carefully tapping the ashes into the balance pan. When he was finished, he put the butt into the pan along with the ashes and weighed what was there. Then he subtracted that number from the original weight of the unsmoked cigar. The difference was the weight of the smoke.

TOMMY

Not bad. That's the kind of guy we need to take over the Mets.

PAUL

Oh, he was smart, all right. But not so smart that he didn't wind up having his head chopped off twenty years later. (*Pause*) But that's another story.

AUGGIE

(*Handing* PAUL *his change and putting cigar tins and lighter in a paper bag*) Seven eighty-five out of twenty. (*As* PAUL *turns to leave*) Take care of yourself now, and don't do anything I wouldn't do.

PAUL

(*Smiling*) I wouldn't think of it. (*Waves casually to the* OTB MEN) See you around, fellas.

AUGGIE *and the* OTB MEN *watch as* PAUL *leaves the store.*

TOMMY

(*Turning to* AUGGIE) What is he, some kind of wise guy?

AUGGIE

Nah. He's a good kid.

JERRY

I've seen him around. He comes in here a lot, don't he?

AUGGIE

Couple of times a week, maybe. He's a writer. Lives in the neighborhood.

TOMMY

And what kind of writer is he? An underwriter?

AUGGIE

(*Peeved*) Very funny. Some of the cracks you make, Tommy, sometimes I think you should see a doctor. You know, go in for some wit therapy or something. To clean out the valves in your brain.

TOMMY

(*A little embarrassed. Shrugs*) It was just a joke.

AUGGIE

The guy's a novelist. Paul Benjamin. You ever hear of him? (*Pause*) That's a stupid question. The only things you guys read is the *Racing Form* and the sports pages of the *Post*. (*Pause*) He's published three or four books. But nothing now for the past few years.

DENNIS

What's the matter? He run out of ideas?

AUGGIE

He ran out of luck. (*Pause*) Remember that holdup out here on Seventh Avenue a few years back?

JERRY

You talking about the bank? The time those two guys started spraying bullets all over the street?

AUGGIE

That's it. Four people got killed. One of them was Paul's wife. (*Pause*) The poor lug, he hasn't been the same since. (*Pause*) The funny thing was, she stopped in here just before it happened. To stock up on cigars for him. She was a nice lady, Ellen. Four or five months pregnant at the time, which means that when she was killed, the baby was killed, too.

TOMMY

Bad day at Black Rock, eh, Auggie?

Close-up of AUGGIE's *face. Remembering.*

AUGGIE

It was bad, all right. I sometimes think that if she hadn't given me exact change that day, or if the store had been a little more crowded, it would have taken her a few more seconds to get out of here, and then maybe she wouldn't have stepped in front of that bullet. She'd still be alive, the baby would have been born, and Paul would be sitting at home writing another book instead of wandering the streets with a hangover. (*Pensive. His expression suddenly turns to one of alarm*)

Cut to white youth in the corner of the store, shoving paperback books into the pockets of his tattered army fatigue jacket.

AUGGIE (*cont'd*)

Hey! What are you doing there, kid? Hey, cut that out!

AUGGIE *scrambles out from behind the counter, pushing his way past the* OTB MEN *as the kid takes off and runs out of the store.*

3. EXT: DAY. SEVENTH AVENUE

AUGGIE *chases the* BOOK THIEF *down the street. Eventually, he gets winded and gives up. He pauses for a moment to catch his breath, then turns around and heads back in the direction of the store.*

4. INT: DAY. PAUL'S APARTMENT. A BROWNSTONE BUILDING IN PARK SLOPE (THIRD FLOOR)

Shot of a little brown cigar, burning in an ashtray.

The camera pulls back to reveal PAUL *at his desk. He is writing in longhand, using a pad of yellow legal paper. An old Smith-Corona typewriter is also on the desk, poised for work with a half-written page in the roller. Off in the corner, we see a neglected word processor.*

The workroom is a bare and simple place. Desk, chair, and a small wooden bookcase with manuscripts and papers shoved onto its shelves. The window faces a brick wall.

As PAUL *continues to write, the camera travels from the workroom into the larger of the two rooms that make up his apartment.*

This larger room is an all-purpose space that includes a sleeping area, a kitchenette in one corner, a dining table, and a large easy chair. Crowded bookshelves occupy one wall from floor to ceiling. The bow windows face front, looking down onto the street. Near the bed, we see a framed photograph of a young woman. (This is Ellen, Paul's dead wife.)

The camera travels back into the workroom. We see PAUL *at work. Fade out.*

Fade in. We see PAUL *at his desk, eating a TV dinner while still writing in the pad. After a moment, he inadvertently knocks the food off the desk with his elbow. He begins to bend over to pick up the food, but as he does so a new idea suddenly occurs to him. Instead of cleaning up the mess, he turns back to his pad and continues writing.*

5. EXT: DAY. IN FRONT OF THE BROOKLYN CIGAR CO.

We see PAUL walking out of the cigar store. JIMMY ROSE is on the corner, observing him throughout the scene. PAUL takes three or four steps, then realizes he has forgotten something. He goes back into the store. During his brief absence, JIMMY remains on the corner, imitating PAUL's gestures: patting in pockets, looking puzzled, realizing that he has forgotten the cigars he just bought.

PAUL comes out again a moment later, holding a tin of Schimmelpenninck cigars. He pauses, takes a cigar out of the tin, and lights up. He continues walking, obviously distracted. He stops briefly at a corner, then steps out into the street, paying no attention to the traffic. A speeding tow truck is rushing toward the intersection. At the last second, a black hand reaches out, grabs PAUL by the arm, and pulls him back to the curb. If not for that timely move, PAUL would surely have been run down.

We see PAUL's rescuer: it is RASHID COLE, a black adolescent of sixteen or seventeen. He is tall and well built for his age. A nylon backpack is slung over his left shoulder.

> RASHID

Watch out, man. You'll get yourself killed like that.

> PAUL

(*Badly shaken, still clinging to RASHID's arm*) I can't believe I did that . . . Christ, I'm walking around in a fog . . .

> RASHID

No harm done. Everything's okay now. (*Looks down and notices that he and PAUL are still gripping each other's arms. Tries to pull away*) I've got to be going.

> PAUL

(*Still rattled. Begins to loosen grip, then grabs hold of RASHID's arm again*) No. Wait. You can't just walk off. (*Pause*) You saved my life.

RASHID

(*Shrugs*) I just happened to be there. The right place at the right time.

PAUL

(*Relaxing grip on* RASHID'S *arm*) I owe you something.

RASHID

It's okay, mister. No big deal.

PAUL

Yes it is. It's a law of the universe. If I let you walk away, the moon will spin out of orbit . . . pestilence will reign over the city for a hundred years.

RASHID

(*Mystified, amused. Smiles faintly*) Well, if you put it that way . . .

PAUL

You have to let me do something for you to put the scales in balance.

RASHID

(*Thinks, shakes his head*) That's all right. If I think of something, I'll send my butler over to tell you.

PAUL

Come on. At least let me buy you a cup of coffee.

RASHID

I don't drink coffee. (*Smiles*) On the other hand, since you insist, if you offered me a cold lemonade, I wouldn't say no.

PAUL

Good. Lemonade it is. (*Pause. Extends right hand*) I'm Paul.

Rashid. Rashid Cole. (*Shakes PAUL's hand*)

Cut to:

6. INT: DAY. GREEK DINER IN PARK SLOPE

PAUL and RASHID are sitting in a booth. The restaurant is nearly empty. We see RASHID finishing his second lemonade.

PAUL

(*Watching RASHID drink*) Are you sure you don't want some food to go along with it? It might help to absorb some of that liquid. You don't want to slosh around too much when you stand up.

RASHID

That's okay. I've already had lunch.

PAUL

(*Looks at clock on wall*) You must eat lunch pretty early. It's only eleven o'clock.

RASHID

I mean breakfast.

PAUL

(*Studying RASHID closely*) Yeah, sure, and I bet you had lobster last night. Along with two bottles of champagne.

RASHID

Just one bottle. I believe in moderation.

PAUL

Look, kid, it's okay with me. You don't have to play games. If you want a hamburger or something, go ahead and order it.

RASHID

(*Hesitates*) Well, maybe just one. To be polite.

PAUL

(*Turning to* WAITRESS. *She comes*) Cocktail hour is over. The young man would like to order a hamburger.

WAITRESS

(*To* RASHID) How do you want that cooked?

RASHID

Medium rare, please.

WAITRESS

Fries?

RASHID

(*Looks at* PAUL. PAUL *nods*) Yes, please.

WAITRESS

Lettuce and tomato?

RASHID

(*Looks at* PAUL. PAUL *nods*) Yes, please.

WAITRESS

(*Pointing to* RASHID'*s empty lemonade glass*) You want another one of these, too?

PAUL

Yeah, give him another one. And I'll take a cup of coffee while you're at it.

WAITRESS

Hot coffee or iced coffee?

PAUL

Do you have real iced coffee, or do you just pour hot coffee over some ice cubes?

WAITRESS

Everything is real in here, honey. (*Pause*) As real as the color of my hair.

PAUL *and* RASHID *look at her hair. It is dyed bright red.*

PAUL

(*Deadpan*) I'll take the iced coffee. (*Pause*) You only live once, right?

WAITRESS

(*Equally deadpan*) If you're lucky. (*Pause*) Then again, it depends on what you call living. (*She walks off*)

PAUL

(*To* RASHID) I don't mean to pry, but I see a kid walking around with a big knapsack on his back, and I begin to wonder if all his worldly possessions aren't stowed in there. Are you in some kind of trouble or what?

RASHID

(*Keeping up his pose*) Mostly what.

PAUL

(*Studying* RASHID) You don't have to tell me if you don't want to, but I might be able to help.

RASHID

(*Hesitating*) You don't know me from a hole in the wall.

PAUL

That's true. But I also owe you something, and I'm not sure that buying you a hamburger is going to do the job. (*Pause*) What is it? Family problems? Money problems?

RASHID

(*Imitating white upper-class accent*) Oh no, Momsie and Popsie have oodles.

PAUL

And where do Momsie and Popsie live?

RASHID

East Seventy-fourth Street.

PAUL

In Manhattan?

RASHID

Of course. Where else?

PAUL

Then what are you doing in Park Slope? It's a little far from home, isn't it?

RASHID

(*Beginning to relent*) That's where the *what* comes in.

PAUL

The what?

RASHID

The what. (*Pause*) I've kind of run away from home, you see. (*Pause*) It has nothing to do with my parents or money. I saw something I wasn't supposed to see, and for the time being it's best that I keep myself out of sight.

PAUL

You can't be more specific than that?

RASHID looks at PAUL, hesitates, then lowers his eyes.

PAUL *(cont'd)*
(Pause. Decides not to press him) So where have you been staying in the meantime?

RASHID

Here and there. Around.

PAUL

Uh-huh. One of those cozy bed and breakfast places, probably.

RASHID

Yeah, that's right.

PAUL

Except that there's no bed, is there? And no breakfast either.

RASHID

The material world is an illusion. It doesn't matter if they're there or not. The world is in my head.

PAUL

But your body is in the world, isn't it? *(Pause)* If someone offered you a place to stay, you wouldn't necessarily refuse, would you?

RASHID

(Pause. Thinks) People don't do that kind of thing. Not in New York.

PAUL

I'm not "people." I'm just me. And I do whatever I goddamn want to do. Got it?

RASHID

Thanks, but I'll manage.

PAUL

In case you're wondering, I like women, not little boys. And I'm not offering you a long-term lease—just a place to crash for a couple of nights.

RASHID

I can take care of myself. Don't worry.

PAUL

Suit yourself. But if you change your mind, here's the address. (*Takes out a pad from his pocket and scribbles down the address. Tears sheet from the pad and hands it to* RASHID)

The WAITRESS *arrives with their orders.*

WAITRESS

One burger medium rare with lettuce and tomato. (*Setting down plate in front of* RASHID) One order of fries. (*Setting down plate*) One lemonade. (*Setting down glass*) And one dose of reality. (*Setting down iced coffee in front of* PAUL)

PAUL *looks on as* RASHID *picks up hamburger and takes his first bite.*

7. INT: DAY. THE BROOKLYN CIGAR CO.

A slow hour. AUGGIE *is sitting behind the counter, looking through a magazine and eating a slice of pizza for lunch.* VINNIE *enters the frame. He is the owner of the store: a large man in his fifties.*

VINNIE

Okay, I think everything's set. (*Lights up cigar*) You've got the number for Cape Cod, right? Just in case something goes wrong.

AUGGIE

(*Chewing pizza, not looking up from magazine*) No problem, Vinnie. Everything's under control. (*Finally looking up*) I could run this store in my sleep.

VINNIE

(*Studying* AUGGIE) How long you been working for me, Auggie?

AUGGIE

(*Shrugs, looks down at magazine again*) I don't know. Thirteen, fourteen years. Something like that.

VINNIE

It's pretty crazy, don't you think? I mean, a smart guy like you. What do you want to hang on to a dead-end job like this for?

AUGGIE

(*Shrugs again*) I don't know. (*Turns pages of magazine*) Maybe because I love you so much, boss.

VINNIE

Shit. You should have been married to someone by now. You know, settled down somewhere with a kid or two, a nice steady job.

AUGGIE

I almost got married once.

VINNIE

Yeah, I know. To that girl who moved to Pittsburgh.

AUGGIE

Ruby McNutt. My one true love.

VINNIE

Sounds like another one of your stories to me.

AUGGIE

(*Shakes his head*) She upped and married some other cat after I joined the navy. By the time I got my discharge, though, she was divorced. Her husband poked out her eye in a domestic quarrel.

VINNIE

(*Puffing on his cigar*) Lovely.

AUGGIE

(*Remembering*) She made a play for me after I got back, but her glass eye kept interfering with my concentration. Every time we got into a clinch, I'd start thinking about that hole in her head, that empty socket with the glass eye in it. An eye that couldn't see, an eye that couldn't shed any tears. The minute I started thinking about it, Mr. Johnson would get all soft and small. And I can't see getting married if Mr. Johnson isn't going to be in tiptop shape.

VINNIE

(*Shaking his head*) You don't take anything seriously, do you?

AUGGIE

I try not to, anyway. It's better for your health. I mean, look at you, Vincent. You're the guy with the wife and three kids and the ranch house on Long Island. You're the guy with the white shoes and the white Caddy and the white shag carpet. But you've had two heart attacks, and I'm still waiting for my first.

VINNIE

(*Takes cigar out of his mouth and looks at it with disgust*) I should stop smoking these damn things is what I should do. The fuckers are going to kill me one day.

AUGGIE

Enjoy it while you can, Vin. Pretty soon, they're going to legislate us out of business anyway.

VINNIE

They catch you smoking tobacco, they'll stand you up against a wall and shoot you.

AUGGIE

(*Nodding*) Tobacco today, sex tomorrow. In three or four years, it'll probably be against the law to smile at strangers.

VINNIE

(*Remembering something*) Speaking of which, are you still going ahead with that deal on the Montecristos?

AUGGIE

It's all set. My guy in Miami said he'd have them within the next few weeks. (*Pause*) Are you sure you don't want to go in with me? Five thousand dollars outlay, a guaranteed ten-thousand-dollar return. A consortium of Court Street lawyers and judges. They're just drooling to get their lips around some genuine Cuban cigars.

VINNIE

No thanks. I don't care what you do, but just make sure you don't get caught, okay? The last I heard, it was still illegal to sell Cuban cigars in this country.

AUGGIE

It's the law that's buying. That's what's so beautiful about it. I mean, when was the last time you heard of a judge sending himself to jail?

VINNIE

Suit yourself. But don't keep the boxes around here long.

AUGGIE

They come in, they go out. I've got it planned to the last detail.

VINNIE

(*Looking at his watch*) I've got to get moving. Terry will bust my chops if I'm late. See you in September, Auggie.

AUGGIE

Okay, my man. Love to the wife and kids, et cetera, et cetera. Drop me a postcard if you can remember the address.

VINNIE leaves. AUGGIE turns back to his pizza and magazine.

8. EXT: EVENING. FAÇADE OF THE BROOKLYN CIGAR CO.

A shot of the darkening sky. A shot of the cigar store. We see the lights go out. AUGGIE comes outside, locks the door, and begins pulling down the metal gate in front of the windows. Cut to:

A shot of PAUL running down the street toward AUGGIE.

PAUL

(*Out of breath*) Are you closed?

AUGGIE

You run out of Schimmelpennincks?

PAUL

(*Nods*) Do you think I could buy some before you leave?

AUGGIE

No problem. It's not as though I'm rushing off to the opera or anything.

AUGGIE lifts the gate and the two of them go into the store.

9. INT: EVENING. THE BROOKLYN CIGAR CO.

PAUL and AUGGIE enter the darkened store. AUGGIE turns on the lights and then goes behind the counter to fetch PAUL's cigars. PAUL, on the other side, notices a 35-millimeter camera near the cash register.

PAUL

Looks like someone forgot a camera.

AUGGIE

(*Turning around*) Yeah, I did.

PAUL

It's yours?

AUGGIE

It's mine all right. I've owned that little sucker for a long time.

PAUL

I didn't know you took pictures.

AUGGIE

(*Handing* PAUL *his cigars*) I guess you could call it a hobby. It doesn't take me more than about five minutes a day to do it, but I do it every day. Rain or shine, sleet or snow. Sort of like the postman. (*Pause*) Sometimes it feels like my hobby is my real job, and my job is just a way to support my hobby.

PAUL

So you're not just some guy who pushes coins across a counter.

AUGGIE

That's what people see, but that ain't necessarily what I am.

PAUL

(*Looking at* AUGGIE *with new eyes*) How'd you get started?

AUGGIE

Taking pictures? (*Smiles*) It's a long story. I'd need two or three drinks to get through that one.

PAUL

(*Nodding*) A photographer . . .

48

AUGGIE

Well, let's not exaggerate. I take pictures. You line up what you want in the viewfinder and click the shutter. No need to mess around with all that *artisto* crap.

PAUL

I'd like to see your pictures some day.

AUGGIE

It can be arranged. Seeing as how I've read your books, I don't see why I shouldn't share my pictures with you. (*Pause. Suddenly embarrassed*) It would be an honor.

10. INT: NIGHT. AUGGIE'S APARTMENT

AUGGIE *and* PAUL *are sitting at the kitchen table, opened boxes of Chinese food pushed to one side. Most of the surface of the table is covered with large black photograph albums. There are fourteen in all, and the spine of each one is labeled with a year—ranging from 1977 to 1990. One of these albums (1987) is open on* PAUL's *lap.*

Close-up of one of the pages in the album. There are six black-and-white photos on the page, each one of an identical scene: the corner of 3rd Street and Seventh Avenue at eight o'clock in the morning. In the upper-right-hand corner of each photo, there is a small white label bearing the date: 8-9-87, 8-10-87, 8-11-87, etc. PAUL's *hand turns the page; we see six more similar photographs. He turns the page again: same thing. And again: same thing.*

PAUL

(*Astonished*) They're all the same.

AUGGIE

(*Smiling proudly*) That's right. More than four thousand pictures of the same place. The corner of Third Street and Seventh Avenue at eight o'clock in the morning. Four thousand straight days in all kinds of weather. (*Pause*) That's why I can never take a vacation. I've got to be in my spot every morning. Every morning in the same spot at the same time.

PAUL

(*At a loss. Turns a page, then another page*) I've never seen anything like it.

AUGGIE

It's my project. What you'd call my life's work.

PAUL

(*Puts down the album and picks up another. Flips through the pages and finds more of the same. Shakes his head in bafflement*) Amazing. (*Trying to be polite*) I'm not sure I get it, though. I mean, how did you ever come up with the idea to do this . . . this project?

AUGGIE

I don't know, it just came to me. It's my corner, after all. It's just one little part of the world, but things happen there, too, just like everywhere else. It's a record of my little spot.

PAUL

(*Flipping through the album, still shaking his head*) It's kind of overwhelming.

AUGGIE

(*Still smiling*) You'll never get it if you don't slow down, my friend.

PAUL

What do you mean?

AUGGIE

I mean, you're going too fast. You're hardly even looking at the pictures.

PAUL

But they're all the same.

AUGGIE

They're all the same, but each one is different from every other one.
You've got your bright mornings and your dark mornings. You've
got your summer light and your autumn light. You've got your
weekdays and your weekends. You've got your people in overcoats
and galoshes, and you've got your people in shorts and T-shirts.
Sometimes the same people, sometimes different ones. And sometimes the different ones become the same, and the same ones disappear. The earth revolves around the sun, and every day the light
from the sun hits the earth at a different angle.

PAUL

(*Looking up from the album at* AUGGIE) Slow down, huh?

AUGGIE

Yeah, that's what I'd recommend. You know how it is. Tomorrow
and tomorrow and tomorrow, time creeps on its petty pace.

*Close-ups of the photo album. One by one, a single picture occupies the
entire screen.* AUGGIE'*s project unfolds before us. One picture follows another:
the same place at the same time at different moments of the year. Close-
ups of different faces within the close-ups. The same people appear in
different pictures, sometimes looking into the camera, sometimes looking
away. Dozens of stills. Finally, we come to a photo of Ellen,* PAUL'*s dead
wife.*

Close-up of PAUL'*s face.*

PAUL

Jesus, look. It's Ellen.

The camera pulls away. AUGGIE *leans over* PAUL'*s shoulder. We see* PAUL'*s
finger pointing to Ellen's face.*

Yeah. There she is. She's in quite a few from that year. She must have been on her way to work.

PAUL

(*Moved, on the point of tears*) It's Ellen. Look at her. Look at my sweet darling.

Fade out.

11. INT: NIGHT. PAUL'S APARTMENT

PAUL's scribbling furiously in his legal pad, lost in his work. Behind him, we see ten or twelve index cards pinned to the wall. The cards are covered with writing. One of them reads: "The woman with brown hair and blue eyes." Another one reads: "The mind is led on, step by step, to defeat its own logic." A third one reads: "Remember the Alamo."

PAUL stands up from his desk, goes over to the wall, pulls off one of the cards, and studies it as he returns to his desk. An instant later, he begins writing again.

The intercom buzzer rings loudly in the other room. PAUL continues to work, oblivious to the noise. The buzzer sounds again. PAUL puts down his pen.

PAUL

(*Under his breath*) Shit. (*He stands up from his chair, walks to the other room, and presses the "talk" button on the intercom*) Who is it?

VOICE FROM THE INTERCOM

Rashid.

PAUL

Who?

Rashid Cole. The lemonade kid, remember?

PAUL

Oh, yeah. (*Without much enthusiasm*) Come on up. (*Pushes "door" button on the intercom*)

PAUL walks to the door and opens it, peering into the hall as he waits for RASHID *to arrive. A moment later,* RASHID *appears—dressed as before, with the backpack slung over his shoulder. He appears awkward, ill at ease.*

PAUL

I didn't expect to see you again.

RASHID

(*Making the best of it*) Same here. But I had a long talk with my accountant this afternoon. You know, to see how a move like this would affect my tax picture, and he said it would be okay.

PAUL studies him with a mixture of bafflement and curiosity, but doesn't answer. RASHID *puts down his bag and begins looking around the apartment. After a moment:*

PAUL

That's it. Just the two rooms.

RASHID

(*Continuing to study his new surroundings*) This is the first house I've been in without a TV.

PAUL

I used to have one, but it broke a couple of years ago and I never got around to replacing it. (*Pause*) I'd just as soon not have one anyway. I hate those damn things.

RASHID

But then you don't get to watch the ball games. You told me you were a Mets fan.

PAUL

I listen on the radio. I can see the games just fine that way. (*Pause*) The world is in your head, remember?

RASHID

(*Smiles. Continues to walk around. Sees a small pen-and-ink drawing hanging on the wall above the stereo cabinet: the head of a small child. He stops to examine it*) Nice drawing. Did you do that?

PAUL

My father did. Believe it or not, that little baby is me.

RASHID

(*Studying the drawing more carefully. Turns to look at* PAUL, *then turns back to the drawing*) Yeah, I can believe it.

PAUL

It's strange, though, isn't it? Looking at yourself before you knew who you were.

RASHID

Is your father an artist?

PAUL

No, he was a schoolteacher. But he liked to dabble.

RASHID

He's dead?

PAUL

Twelve, thirteen years ago. (*Pause*) Actually, he died with his sketch pad open on his lap. Up in the Berkshires one weekend, drawing a picture of Mount Greylock.

RASHID

(*Studying the picture, nodding his head. As if to himself*) Drawing's a good thing.

PAUL

Is that what you do? Draw pictures?

RASHID

(*Smiles*) Yeah, sometimes. (*Shrugs, as if suddenly embarrassed*) I like to dabble, too.

12. INT: DAY. PAUL'S APARTMENT

Two hours later. We see PAUL *writing at his desk in the workroom. After a moment, he stands up and opens the double doors a crack. From* PAUL'S POV: *we see* RASHID *sitting at the table in the main room, head resting on his arms, asleep. The backpack is still where he put it down in the previous scene.*

13. INT: DAY. PAUL'S APARTMENT

8:00 in the morning. PAUL *is sitting at the dining table drinking coffee. He looks at his watch, puts down the cup, walks to the workroom door, opens it, pokes his head inside. Shot of* RASHID *asleep on the floor; shot of the typewriter and legal pad on the desk.* PAUL *closes the door, sighs, returns to the other room and pours himself another cup of coffee. Looks at his watch. Close-up of the watch: dissolve from 8:05 to 8:35.* PAUL *puts down the cup, stands up, walks to the workroom door, knocks.*

PAUL

Time to wake up. (*Waits, listens, knocks again*) Hey, kid, time to wake up. (*Waits, listens, knocks again*) Rashid! (*Opens door.* RASHID *is groggily opening his eyes*) Up and out, I have to work in here. The slumber party is over.

RASHID

(*Sitting up, rubbing his eyes*) What time is it?

PAUL

Eight-thirty.

RASHID

(*Groans, appalled by early hour*) Eight-thirty?

PAUL

You'll find juice and eggs and milk in the refrigerator. Cereal in the cupboard. Coffee on the stove. Take whatever you want. But it's time for me to get started in here.

RASHID stands up, embarrassed. He is dressed in underpants only. He rolls up the sleeping bag and pushes it to one side. Then he gathers up his clothes and hustles out of the room.

14. INT: DAY. PAUL'S APARTMENT

Twenty minutes later. PAUL is sitting at his desk, staring at his typewriter. A loud noise comes from the other room: the clatter of dishes being put into the sink. PAUL stands up, walks to the door, opens it. He sees RASHID, now fully dressed, picking up the telephone next to the bed. He sees RASHID's knapsack opened; a brown paper bag is sitting next to it. He watches RASHID dial a number.

RASHID

(*In a low voice*) May I speak to Emily Vail, please? Yes, thank you, I'll wait. (*Silence, three or four beats. RASHID fiddles with a pillow on the bed*) Aunt Em? Hi, it's me. I just wanted you to know I'm okay. (*Pause, as he listens. The response from the other end is an angry one*) I know, I'm sorry. (*Pause, as he listens*) I just didn't want you to worry about me. (*Silence, as he listens. Begins to show irritation with Aunt Em's hostility*) Just cool it, okay? Take it easy. (*Click on the other end. He stares at the receiver for a moment, then hangs up*)

PAUL *closes the door quietly.* RASHID *does not know he has been observed. Cut back to* PAUL *in workroom. He sits down at his desk, thinks for a moment, then begins typing.*

15. INT: DAY. PAUL'S APARTMENT

Several hours later. With the sounds of PAUL's *typing continuing to come from the workroom, we see* RASHID *stand on a chair next to the bookcase in the larger room and deposit the brown paper bag behind the books on one of the upper shelves.*

16. INT: NIGHT. PAUL'S APARTMENT

A shot of RASHID *asleep in* PAUL's *bed. Lying next to him on the bed is an open, half-read copy of one of* PAUL's *books:* The Mysterious Barricades, *by Paul Benjamin.*

Cut to a shot of PAUL *sleeping on the floor of the workroom.*

17. INT: DAY. PAUL'S APARTMENT

PAUL *is in his workroom, sitting at his desk, typing. We see more index cards pinned to the wall.* PAUL *hears a loud crash from the other room. He pops up from his desk, exasperated, then walks to the door and opens it. Shot of the other room:* RASHID *is standing there, looking down at broken dishes.*

PAUL
(*Irritated*) Jesus, do you make a lot of noise. Can't you see I'm trying to work?

RASHID
(*Mortified*) I'm sorry. They just . . . they just slipped out of my hands.

PAUL

A little less clumsiness around here would be nice, don't you think?

RASHID

(*Growning defensive*) I'm a teenager. All teenagers are clumsy. It's because we're still growing. We don't know where our bodies end and the world begins.

PAUL

The world is going to end pretty soon if you don't learn fast. (*Pause. PAUL reaches into his pocket and pulls out his wallet, then removes a twenty-dollar bill*) Look, why not make yourself useful? I'm just about out of smokes. Go around the corner to the Brooklyn Cigar Company and buy me two tins of Schimmelpenninck Medias. (*Hands the bill to RASHID*)

RASHID

(*Taking the bill*) Twenty dollars is a lot of money. Are you sure you can trust me with it? I mean, aren't you afraid I might steal it?

PAUL

If you want to steal it, that's your business. At least I won't have you around here making noise. (*Pause*) It might be worth it.

RASHID, *visibly hurt by PAUL's remark, puts the money in his pocket. For once, he is unable to come up with a quick retort.*

RASHID *walks out of the apartment.* PAUL *watches the door slam. Slight pause, then he bends down and starts picking up the broken dishes.*

18. INT: DAY. PAUL'S APARTMENT

The workroom. A few minutes later. PAUL *returns to his desk and begins to type. Almost immediately, the ribbon jams. He lets out a groan, then opens the typewriter to inspect the damage.*

19. EXT: DAY. THE BROOKLYN CIGAR CO., AS SEEN FROM ACROSS THE STREET

Eight o'clock in the morning. We see AUGGIE *on the corner, getting ready to take his daily photograph. Cut to the corner as seen through the lens of the camera. Hustle and bustle, people on their way to work. Automobile traffic, buses, delivery trucks. We hear the shutter click. The picture freezes.*

20. INT: DAY. PAUL'S APARTMENT

The workroom. PAUL *is sitting at his desk, writing. A loud crash from the other room punctuates the silence. He jumps in his chair.*

> PAUL

(*Groans*) Shit.

He stands up, goes to the door, opens it. Shot of RASHID *standing precariously on the arm of a chair, his right hand groping behind the books on the top shelf of the bookcase. Several books have already fallen to the floor.*

> PAUL (*cont'd*)

Jesus Christ. Are you at it again?

RASHID *turns at the sound of* PAUL's *voice, momentarily losing his balance. As he grabs hold of the bookcase again to steady himself, more books fall off the shelf and come tumbling to the floor. An instant later, he lands on the floor as well.*

> PAUL (*cont'd*)

What is it with you, anyway? You're like a human wrecking ball.

> RASHID

(*Climbing to his feet. Ashamed*) I'm sorry. I'm really sorry . . . I was trying to reach for one of the books up there . . . (*Points*) And then, I don't know, the sky fell on top of me.

PAUL

(*With growing irritation*) It just won't do, will it? I go two and a half years without being able to write a word, and then, when I finally get started on something, when it looks as though I might actually be coming to life again, you show up and start breaking everything in my house. It just won't do, will it?

RASHID

(*Hurt, subdued*) I didn't ask to come here. You invited me, remember? (*Pause*) If you want me to leave, all you have to do is say so.

PAUL

How long have you been here?

RASHID

Three nights.

PAUL

And how long did I tell you you could stay?

RASHID

Two or three nights.

PAUL

It sounds like our time is up, doesn't it?

RASHID

(*Looking down at floor*) I'm sorry I messed up. You've been very kind to me . . . (*Walks toward the bed, picks up the backpack from the floor, and begins stuffing his things into it*) But all good things have to come to an end, right?

PAUL

No hard feelings, okay? It's a small place, and I can't get my work done with you around.

RASHID

You don't have to apologize. (*Pause*) The coast is probably clear now anyway.

PAUL

(*Softening*) Are you going to be all right?

RASHID

Absolutely. The world is my oyster. (*Pause*) Whatever that means. (*He looks up at the bookshelf, studying the spot where the bag is hidden. He makes a quick, resolute decision to leave the bag where it is*)

PAUL

Do you need some money? Some extra clothes?

RASHID

Not a penny, not a stitch. I'm cool, man. (*Hoists the backpack over his shoulder, begins walking toward the door*)

PAUL

(*A little stunned by* RASHID'S *decisiveness*) Take good care of yourself, okay?

RASHID

You too. And make sure the light is green before you cross the street. (*Reaches for the doorknob, opens the door, hesitates, turns around*) Oh, by the way, I liked your book. I think you're a hell of a good writer. (*Without waiting for a response, he opens the door again and leaves*)

Shot of PAUL *standing alone in the middle of the room. He walks to the window and looks outside. Shot of the street below. After three or four seconds,* RASHID *emerges from the building. Without glancing back, he begins walking down the street.*

Cut to PAUL *standing at the window. He lights up a cigar. Cut back to the street.* RASHID *has disappeared. An instant later, a blind man comes walking around the corner, tapping his white cane on the sidewalk.*

21. INT: NIGHT. AUGGIE'S APARTMENT

The windows are open and traffic noises can be heard from the street below.

AUGGIE alone. Jazz is playing on his tape machine. He takes a TV dinner out of the oven, then sits down at the kitchen table and begins to eat. Fade out.

The meal is over. AUGGIE pours himself a shot of bourbon. He drinks it down in one swallow and smacks his lips, exhaling loudly. Stares blankly ahead of him for a moment. Then he reaches for a paperback copy of Crime and Punishment *open on the table. As he finds his place in the book, he lights a cigarette. After one or two puffs, he begins to cough: a deep, rattling, prolonged smoker's cough. He pounds his chest. It doesn't help. He stands up, banging the table as the coughing fit continues. He begins to stagger around the kitchen, cursing between breaths. In his rage, he sweeps everything off the table: glass, bottle, book, remnants of the TV dinner. The cough subsides, then starts up again. He grabs hold of the kitchen sink and spits into the basin.*

22. INT: DAY. PAUL'S APARTMENT

The main room. We hear the sound of PAUL typing. A loud, insistent banging is heard at the front door. Cut to PAUL opening the door. RASHID'S AUNT EM is standing in the hall. She is a black woman of about forty, dressed in clothes that suggest she works in an office.

> AUNT EM
> (*Angrily*) Is your name Paul Benjamin?

> PAUL
> (*Taken aback*) What can I do for you?

> AUNT EM
> (*Barging into the apartment*) I just want to know what your game is, mister, that's all.

PAUL

(*Horrified. Watching her as she charges around the room*) How the hell did you get into the building?

AUNT EM

What do you mean, how'd I get in? I pushed the door and walked in. What do you think?

PAUL

(*Muttering to himself*) The damn lock's broken again. (*Pause, as he returns* AUNT EM's *glare. Louder*) And so you just barge in on strangers, is that what you do? Is that *your* game?

AUNT EM

I'm looking for my nephew, Thomas.

PAUL

Thomas? Who's Thomas?

AUNT EM

Don't give me any of that. I know he's been here. You can't fool me, mister.

PAUL

I'm telling you, I don't know anyone named Thomas.

AUNT EM

Thomas Cole. Thomas Jefferson Cole. My nephew.

PAUL

You mean Rashid?

AUNT EM

Rashid? *Rashid!* Is that what he told you his name was?

PAUL

Well, whatever his name is, he's not here anymore. He left two days ago, and I haven't heard from him since.

AUNT EM

And what was he doing here in the first place? That's what I want to know. What's a man like you messing around with a black boy like Thomas for? Are you some kind of pervert, or what?

PAUL

(*Losing patience*) Look, lady, that's enough. If you don't calm down, I'm going to throw you out. Do you hear me? Right now!

AUNT EM

(*Getting a grip on herself*) I just want to know where he is.

PAUL

As far as I know, he went back to his parents.

AUNT EM

(*Incredulous*) His parents? Is that what he told you? His *parents?*

PAUL

That's what he said. He told me he lived with his mother and father on East Seventy-fourth Street.

AUNT EM

(*Defeated, shaking her head*) I always knew that boy had an imagination, but now he's gone and made up a whole new life for himself. (*Pause*) Do you mind if I sit down? (PAUL *gestures to a chair; she sits down*) He's been living with me and his uncle Henry since he was a baby. And we don't live in Manhattan. We live in Boerum Hill. In the projects.

PAUL

He doesn't go to the Trinity School?

AUNT EM

He goes to John Jay High School in Brooklyn.

PAUL

(*Beginning to show concern*) And his parents?

AUNT EM

His mother's dead, and he hasn't seen his father in twelve years.

PAUL

(*Softly, almost to himself*) I shouldn't have let him go.

AUNT EM

(*Studying PAUL*) Which brings me back to my original question. What was he doing here in the first place?

PAUL

I was about to get run over by a car, and your nephew pulled me back. He saved my life. (*Pause*) I sensed he was in trouble, so I offered to put him up for a few days. Maybe I should have pressed him a little more, I don't know. I feel pretty stupid about it now.

AUNT EM

He's in trouble, all right. But I don't have any idea what it is.

PAUL

(*Sits down in a chair, lets out a sigh, thinks for a moment. Turns to AUNT EM*) Do you want something to drink? A beer? A glass of water?

AUNT EM

(*Primly*) No thank you.

PAUL

(*Lapses into thought again. After a moment*) Has anything happened lately? Anything unusual or unexpected?

AUNT EM

(*Thinks*) Well, one thing I suppose, but I don't think it has anything to do with this. (*Pause*) A friend of mine called about two weeks ago and said she'd spotted Thomas's father working at some gas station outside of Peekskill.

PAUL

And you told your nephew about it?

AUNT EM

(*Shrugs*) I figured he had a right to know.

PAUL

And?

AUNT EM

And nothing. Thomas looked at me straight in the eye and said, "I don't have a father. As far as I'm concerned, that son-of-a-bitch is dead."

PAUL

Those are pretty hostile words.

The camera slowly closes in on her face as she speaks:

AUNT EM

His father walked out on his mother a couple of months after he was born. Louisa was Henry's younger sister, and she and the baby moved in with us. Four or five years go by, and then one day Cyrus shows up out of the blue, tail between his legs, wanting to patch things up with Louisa. I thought Henry was going to tear Cyrus apart when he saw him walk through the door. They're both big men, those two, and if they ever started to tangle, you'd see some teeth jumping on the floor, I guarantee it . . . So Cyrus persuaded Louisa to go out with him to talk things over in quiet. And the poor girl never came back.

PAUL (*off*)

You mean she just ran off with him and left her little boy behind?

AUNT EM

Don't put words in my mouth. What I'm saying is she drove off in Cyrus's car and went to the Five-Spot Lounge with him for a drink. What I'm saying is that he imbibed too much in the way of alcohol and that when they finished their little talk three hours later and got back in the car, he was in no shape to drive. But he drove the car anyway, and before he could get her back to where she lived, the damn fool ran a red light and went straight into a truck. Louisa got thrown through the windshield and was killed. Cyrus lived, but he came out of it a cripple. His left arm was so mangled, the doctors had to cut it off. Small punishment for what he did, if you ask me.

PAUL (*off*)

(*Aghast*) Jesus.

AUNT EM

Jesus had nothing to do with it. If He'd been involved, He would have seen to it that things worked out the opposite from what they did.

PAUL (*off*)

It can't have been easy on him. Walking around with that on his conscience all these years.

AUNT EM

No, I don't suppose it has. He was broken up like nobody's business in that hospital when he found out Louisa was dead.

PAUL (*off*)

And he's never tried to get in touch with his son?

Henry told Cyrus he'd kill him if he ever showed his face around our house again. When Henry makes a threat like that, people tend to take him seriously.

PAUL and AUNT EM look at each other. Cut to a shot of the kitchen sink. Water is slowly dripping from the faucet. Hold for two or three beats.

23. EXT: DAY. A COUNTRY ROAD OUTSIDE OF PEEKSKILL

Early morning. Trees, shrubs, twittering birds. We see RASHID trudging down the road. Dissolve to:

The same road, a mile on. RASHID looks up. Cut to:

24. EXT: DAY. COLE'S GARAGE

The garage is a ramshackle, two-story building. Over the main door is a clumsily executed hand-painted sign that reads: COLE'S GARAGE. Two Chevron gas pumps stand alone in the front: weeds sprout through the macadam. To one side of the station is a grassy area with a weather-beaten picnic table.

The double garage doors are open. We see a man in there working on the engine of an old Chevrolet. The hood is up, which obscures the man's face, but we can see that he is wearing mechanic's overalls and that the color of his skin is black.

He is a large, burly man of about forty. Once he appears from behind the hood, we see that his left hand is missing. A metal hook juts out of his sleeve.

This is RASHID's father, CYRUS COLE.

25. EXT: DAY. THE SIDE OF THE COUNTRY ROAD, DIRECTLY OPPOSITE COLE'S GARAGE

We see RASHID *sitting on the hood of a rusted car across the road from the garage. He is motionless, hugging his knees and gazing intently in the direction of the camera. Hold for three, four beats.*

26. INT: DAY. COLE'S GARAGE

A bit later. CYRUS, *still busily at work on the Chevrolet, glances up and sees* RASHID *across the road. He studies him for a moment, then returns to his work.*

27. EXT: DAY. THE SIDE OF THE COUNTRY ROAD, DIRECTLY OPPOSITE COLE'S GARAGE

An hour later. We see RASHID *sitting on the hood of the car, as before. This time he has his sketch pad propped against his knees and is doing a pencil drawing of the garage across the way.*

28. EXT: DAY. OUTSIDE COLE'S GARAGE

An hour later. We see CYRUS *emerge from the garage carrying a brown paper bag. He walks over to the picnic table, sits down, and takes out his lunch from the bag: a ham sandwich, an apple, a can of iced tea. As he chews and drinks, he studies* RASHID *across the road. Every now and then, a car or truck passes by.*

The camera cuts between RASHID *and* CYRUS. RASHID, *working busily on his drawing, pretends not to notice he is being watched.*

At last, CYRUS *finishes his lunch. He crumples up the paper bag, gets to his feet, and tosses his garbage into a rusted metal trash can next to the picnic table. Instead of going back to work, he crosses the road.*

29. EXT: DAY. THE SIDE OF THE COUNTRY ROAD, DIRECTLY OPPOSITE COLE'S GARAGE

Master shot. As CYRUS *approaches,* RASHID *looks up, meeting the man's eyes for the first time. Before* CYRUS *can get close enough to see the drawing,* RASHID *closes the sketch pad and presses it against his chest. He makes no attempt to stand up.*

CYRUS

You going to sit here all day?

RASHID

I don't know. I haven't decided yet.

CYRUS

Why don't you pick some other spot? It gives a man the creeps to be stared at all morning.

RASHID

It's a free country, isn't it? As long as I'm not trespassing on your property, I can stay here till kingdom come.

CYRUS

(*Approaching the car.* RASHID *jumps off the hood as* CYRUS *draws closer*) Let me give you some useful information, son. There's two dollars and fifty-seven cents in that cash register over there (*gestures with his hand to the garage across the road*), and considering all the time you've put in casing the joint so far, you won't make but about fifty cents an hour for all your pains. However you slice it, that's a losing proposition.

RASHID

I'm not going to rob you, mister. (*Amused*) Do I look like a thief?

CYRUS

I don't know what you look like, boy. As far as I can tell, you sprouted up like a mushroom in this spot last night. (*Pause. Studies*

RASHID *more closely*) You live in this town—or on your way from here to there?

                                    RASHID

Just passing through.

                                    CYRUS

Just passing through. A lonesome traveler with a knapsack on his back plops himself across from my garage to admire the view. There's other places to roam, kid, that's all I'm saying. You don't want to make a nuisance of yourself.

                                    RASHID

I'm working on a sketch. That old garage of yours is so rundown, it's kind of interesting.

                                    CYRUS

It's rundown, all right. But drawing a picture won't improve the way it looks. (*Zeroing in on the sketch pad pressed against RASHID's chest*) Let's see what you did, Rembrandt.

                                    RASHID

(*Thinking fast*) It'll cost you five bucks.

                                    CYRUS

Five bucks! You mean you're going to charge me five bucks just to look at it?

                                    RASHID

Once you look at it, you're going to want to buy it from me. That's guaranteed. And that's the price: five bucks. So if you're not willing to spring for it, you might as well not bother to look. It'll just tear you up inside and make you miserable.

                                    CYRUS

(*Shaking his head*) Son-of-a-bitch. You're some piece of work, aren't you?

                                      71

RASHID

(*Shrugs*) I just tell it like it is, mister. (*Pause*) If I'm getting on your nerves, though, you might want to think about hiring me.

CYRUS

(*Growing annoyed*) Do you have eyes in your head, or are those brown things bulging out of your sockets just marbles? You've been sitting here all day, and how many cars have you seen drive up and ask for gas?

RASHID

Not a one.

CYRUS

Not a one. Not one customer all day. I bought this broken-down shit-hole of a place three weeks ago, and if business don't pick up soon, I'm going straight down the skids. What do I want to be hiring someone for? I can't even pay my own wages.

RASHID

It was just a thought.

CYRUS

Yeah, well, do your thinking somewhere else, Michelangelo. I got work to do.

CYRUS begins to leave. We see him crossing the road, shaking his head. Halfway there, he suddenly stops, turns, and shouts at RASHID:

CYRUS (*cont'd*)

Who do you think I am, the fucking State Employment Agency?

30. EXT: DAY. THE SIDE OF THE COUNTRY ROAD, DIRECTLY OPPOSITE COLE'S GARAGE

Half an hour later. We see RASHID *sitting on the hood of the car, as before. This time he is eating a sandwich, chewing slowly as he gazes ahead.*

31. INT: DAY. COLE'S GARAGE

We see CYRUS *at work on the Chevrolet. Every now and then, he glances up to look at* RASHID.

CYRUS *finishes the job he has been doing. He slams the hood of the Chevrolet shut. Quick cut to:*

32. EXT: DAY. THE SIDE OF THE COUNTRY ROAD, DIRECTLY OPPOSITE COLE'S GARAGE

CYRUS *enters the frame and hoists himself onto the hood of the car—right next to* RASHID. *A long silence.*

CYRUS
(*Trying to be friendly*) I'll tell you what. You want to work, I'll give you a job. Nothing permanent, mind you, but that upstairs room over there (*turns, points*)—the one above the office—is a hell of a mess. It looks like they've been throwing junk in there for twenty years, and it's time it got cleaned up.

RASHID
(*Playing it cool*) What's your offer?

CYRUS
Five bucks an hour. That's the going rate, isn't it? (*Looks at his wristwatch*) It's a quarter past two now. My wife's picking me up at five-thirty, so that'll give you about three hours. If you can't finish today, you can do the rest tomorrow.

RASHID

(*Getting to his feet*) Is there a benefits package, or are you hiring me on a freelance basis?

CYRUS

Benefits?

RASHID

You know, health insurance, dental plan, paid vacation. It's not fun being exploited. Workers have to stand up for their rights.

CYRUS

I'm afraid we'll be working on a strictly freelance basis.

RASHID

(*Long pause. Pretending to think it over*) Five dollars an hour? (*Another pause*) I'll take it.

CYRUS

(*Cracking a faint smile. Extends his right hand*) The name is Cyrus Cole.

RASHID

I'm Paul. Paul Benjamin.

They shake hands.

33. INT: DAY. THE BROOKLYN CIGAR CO.

It is a slow hour in the middle of the afternoon. AUGGIE *is sitting on a stool behind the counter, reading his paperback copy of Dostoyevsky's* Crime and Punishment. *JIMMY ROSE is working in silence near the far wall on the other side of the counter, diligently and awkwardly straightening the stacks of newspapers and magazines.*

The bell on the front door rattles, signaling the arrival of a customer. Shot of JIMMY stopping his work to look up in the direction of the door. From JIMMY POV: a woman enters the store. She is RUBY McNUTT (AUGGIE's old flame). Mid-forties, wearing a sleeveless summer dress, her face registering a tumult of anxiety, determination, and self-consciousness. She wears a black patch over her left eye.

Shot of JIMMY looking in wonder at the patch. Shot of RUBY looking in the direction of the counter. Shot of AUGGIE sitting behind the counter, still immersed in his book, not bothering to glance up. Close-up of RUBY's face: she is looking at AUGGIE. Her lips are trembling. She is obviously moved, but she is too afraid to speak. With the camera fixed on RUBY's face, we hear:

> JIMMY (*off*)
> (*Hesitantly*) Auggie. (*No response. Pause*) Auggie, I think there's a customer.

Close-up of AUGGIE glancing up from his book. We see his expression change from one of indifference to recognition and astonishment.

Close-up of RUBY looking at him. She smiles tentatively. As they talk, JIMMY studies them with rapt attention.

> RUBY
> Auggie?

Shot of AUGGIE's face: he is still too amazed to speak.

> RUBY (*cont'd*)
> It's really you, Auggie, isn't it?

> AUGGIE
> (*Finally*) Christ, Ruby, it's been so long. I figured you were dead.

> RUBY
> Eighteen and a half years.

AUGGIE

Is that all? I thought it was about three hundred.

RUBY

(*Shyly, hesitantly*) You're looking good, Auggie.

AUGGIE

No I'm not. I look like shit. And so do you, Ruby. You look just awful. (*Pause, with increasing bitterness*) What's with the patch, anyway? What'd you do with that old blue marble—hock it for a bottle of gin?

RUBY

(*Hurt, embarrassed*) I don't want to talk about it. (*Pause*) If you really want to know, I lost it. And I'm not sorry I did. That eye was cursed, Auggie, and it never gave me nothing but grief.

AUGGIE

And you think it looks better to go around dressed up like Captain Hook?

RUBY

(*In a low voice, trying to maintain her composure and dignity*) You always were a son-of-a-bitch, weren't you? A little weasel with a quick, dirty mouth.

AUGGIE

At least I've stayed true to myself. Which is more than I can say about some people.

RUBY

(*Again, she tries to shrug it off. Takes a deep breath*) I've got something to talk to you about, and the least you can do is listen. You owe me that much. I drove all the way from Pittsburgh to see you, and I'm not going back until you've heard me out.

AUGGIE

Fine. Talk away, lady of my dreams. I'm all ears.

RUBY

(*Glancing around the store. Sees* JIMMY *studying her*) This is private, Auggie. Just between you and I.

AUGGIE

(*Addressing* JIMMY *with unaccustomed irritation*) You heard her, pip-squeak. The lady and I have private business to discuss. Go outside and stand in front of the door. If anyone tries to come in, tell 'em we're closed. You got that?

JIMMY

Sure, Auggie, I got it. (*Pause*) The store's closed. (*Pause, thinks*) And when do I tell them it's open?

AUGGIE

(*Snaps*) When I tell you it's open. It's open when I tell you it's open!

JIMMY

(*Hurt*) Okay, Auggie, I got it. You don't have to yell.

JIMMY *goes outside and posts himself in front of the door.*

AUGGIE

(*Looking closely at* RUBY *as he lights a cigarette*) All right, sugar, what's on your mind?

RUBY

(*Pause. Self-conscious*) Don't look at me like that, Auggie. It gives me the creeps.

AUGGIE

Like what?

RUBY

Like what you're doing. I'm not going to eat you up. (*Pause*) I need your help, and if you keep staring at me like that, I might start screaming.

AUGGIE

(*With an edge of sarcasm*) Help, huh? And I don't suppose this help has anything to do with money, does it?

RUBY

Don't rush me, okay? You're jumping to conclusions before I've even said anything. (*Pause*) And besides, it's not for me. (*Pause. Realizing she's let the cat out of the bag. In desperation, she plunges on*) It's for our daughter.

AUGGIE

(*Shocked, growing belligerent*) Our daughter? Is that what you said? *Our daughter?* I mean, you might have a daughter, but I sure as hell don't. And even if I did—which I don't—she wouldn't be *our* daughter.

RUBY

Her name is Felicity, and she just turned eighteen. (*Pause*) She ran away from Pittsburgh last year, and now she's living in some shit-hole here in Brooklyn with a guy named Chico. Strung out on crack, four months pregnant. (*Pause*) I can't bear to think about that baby. Our grandchild, Auggie. Just think of it. Our grandchild.

AUGGIE

(*Waving her off, impatient*) Stop it, already. Just stop all this crap right now. (*Pause. Changing the subject. With contempt*) Was that your idea to call her Felicity?

RUBY

It means "happiness."

AUGGIE

I know what it means. That still don't make it a good name.

RUBY

I don't know who else to turn to, Auggie.

AUGGIE

You've suckered me before, darling, remember? Why should I believe you now?

RUBY

Why would I lie to you, Auggie? You think it was easy to come here and walk into this place? Why would I do it if I didn't have to?

AUGGIE

That's what you told me when I shoplifted that necklace for you. You remember, baby, don't you? The judge gave me a choice: either go to the can or enlist. So, instead of going to college, I wind up in the navy for four years, I watch men lose their arms and legs, I nearly get my head blown off, and you, sweet Ruby McNutt, you run off and marry that asshole, Bill.

RUBY

You didn't write to me for more than a year. What was I supposed to think?

AUGGIE

Yeah, well, I lost my pen. By the time I got a new one, I was clean out of paper.

RUBY

It was over with Bill before you ever came home. Maybe you don't remember it now, but you were pretty hot to see me back then.

AUGGIE

You weren't so lukewarm yourself. At least at first.

RUBY

It fizzled, baby. That's the way it goes. But we had our times, didn't we? It wasn't all bad.

AUGGIE

A couple of moments, I'll grant you that. A second or two snatched from the jaws of eternity.

RUBY

And that's how Felicity came into the picture. During one of those two seconds.

AUGGIE

You're conning me, sweetheart. I ain't responsible for no baby.

RUBY

Then why do you think I married Frank? I was already pregnant, and I didn't have much time. Say what you like, but at least he gave my kid a name.

AUGGIE

Good old Frank. And how is fat Mr. Grease Monkey these days?

RUBY

Who the hell knows? (*Shrugs*) He dropped out of sight fifteen years ago.

AUGGIE

Fifteen years ago? (*Shakes head*) It won't wash, pumpkin. No mother waits fifteen years to tell a man he's a father. I wasn't born yesterday, you know.

RUBY

(*Her lips start to tremble. We see tears falling from her one good eye*) I thought I could handle it. I didn't want to bug you. I thought I could handle it on my own, but I couldn't. She's in real bad, Auggie.

AUGGIE

Nice try, old girl. I'd like to help you out. You know, for old time's sake. But all my spare cash is tied up in a business venture, and I haven't collected my profits yet. Too bad. You caught me at the wrong time.

RUBY

(*Still crying*) You're a cold-hearted bastard, aren't you? How'd you ever get so mean, Auggie?

AUGGIE

I know you think I'm lying to you, but I'm not. Every word I told you is the God's honest truth.

Pause. Then cut to the store entrance. The door suddenly bursts open as an IRATE CUSTOMER *pushes his way past* JIMMY. *We see* JIMMY *futilely trying to hold him back.*

AUGGIE (*cont'd*)

(*Shouting at customer. Beside himself*) The store's closed! Didn't you hear what the kid told you? The goddamn store is closed!

34. INT: DAY. THE UPSTAIRS ROOM OF COLE'S GARAGE

We see RASHID *working diligently. The place is a pigsty, cluttered with all sorts of debris: rusty bicycles, rags, automotive parts, a female mannequin, broken radios, shower curtains, etc. One by one,* RASHID *drags or carries these things toward the door. At one point, he finds a small, portable black-and-white TV hidden under a rug. The rabbit ears are broken, the casing is covered with dust, but other than that it seems to be in reasonably good shape.*

35. EXT: DAY. OUTSIDE COLE'S GARAGE

RASHID and CYRUS are carrying the debris from the upstairs room and throwing it into the back of an old red pickup truck. Once they get rid of a load, they go back inside for more. Since RASHID is faster, they are working out of phase: when one is outside, the other is inside.

They work in silence. CYRUS begins to huff and puff from going up and down the stairs. Eventually, after a number of trips, he drops a load into the truck and stops. He leans against the truck, pulls out a large, cheap, half-smoked cigar from his shirt pocket, and lights up. Close-up of the hook as he strikes the match. After one or two puffs on the cigar, RASHID appears with another load and tosses it into the truck.

> CYRUS

Time for a pause.

Without further ado, RASHID promptly sits down on the rear bumper of the truck. He does it so quickly, the effect is comical. He watches CYRUS smoke. Two or three beats.

> RASHID

I don't mean to be nosy, but I was wondering what happened to your arm.

> CYRUS

(*Holds up his hook and studies it for a moment*) An ugly piece of hardware, isn't it? (*Pause*) I'll tell you what happened to my arm. (*Pause. Remembering*) I'll tell you what happened. (*Pause*) Twelve years ago, God looked down on me and said, "Cyrus, you're a bad, stupid, selfish man. First of all, I'm going to fill your body with spirits, and then I'm going to put you behind the wheel of a car, and then I'm going to make you crash that car and kill the woman who loves you. But you, Cyrus, I'm going to let you live, because living is a lot worse than death. And just so you don't forget what you did to that poor girl, I'm going to rip off your arm and replace it with a hook. If I wanted to, I could rip off both your arms and both your

82

legs, but I'm going to be merciful and just take off your left arm. Every time you look at your hook, I want you to remember what a bad, stupid, selfish man you are. Let that be a lesson to you, Cyrus, a warning to mend your ways."

RASHID
(*Impressed by the sincerity of* CYRUS's *speech*) And have you mended them?

CYRUS
I don't know. I try. Every day I keep on trying, but it's no easy task for a man to change his nature. (*Pause*) I'm off the booze, though. Haven't had a drop in six years. And now I've got me a wife. Doreen. Best damned woman I've ever known. (*Pause*) And a little boy, too. Cyrus Junior. (*Pause*) So things have definitely improved since I got fitted with this hook. If I can just turn this goddamn garage around, I'll be in pretty good shape.

RASHID
You named the kid after yourself, huh?

CYRUS
(*Smiling at the thought of his son*) That boy's one in a million. A real tiger.

Cut to close-up of RASHID's *face. He seems to be growing more and more upset.*

CYRUS (*cont'd*)
And what about you, kid? What's your story?

RASHID
(*Turning away*) Who, me? I don't have a story. I'm just a kid.

Fade out.

36. EXT: DAY. OUTSIDE COLE'S GARAGE

Late afternoon. RASHID *and* CYRUS *continue loading debris into the back of the truck. We see the black-and-white portable TV sitting on the ground outside the office.*

After a few moments, a ten-year-old blue Ford pulls up next to the truck and stops. It is driven by CYRUS's *wife,* DOREEN. *She is an attractive, self-possessed woman in her late twenties.* CYRUS JUNIOR *is sitting in a child-restraint seat in the back. He is two years old.*

CYRUS's *face lights up when he sees the car.* DOREEN *cuts off the engine and gets out smiling at her husband.* RASHID, *suddenly forgotten by* CYRUS, *watches the exchange with keen interest.*

CYRUS
Hi, baby. How'd it go today?

DOREEN
(*Joking*) If I have to wash one more old lady's hair, I think my fingers would fall off. (*She kisses him on the cheek*)

CYRUS
Busy, huh? That's good, because things around here sure were sleepy today.

DOREEN
(*Opening the back of the car, unstrapping* JUNIOR *from his seat and picking him up in her arms*) Don't worry, Cy. It's early days yet. (*Addressing* JUNIOR, *but at the same time catching sight of* RASHID) Say hello to Daddy.

JUNIOR
(*Squirming in his mother's arms, excited at seeing his father*) Dada! Dada!

CYRUS

(*Taking the boy in his arms and giving him a big kiss*) Hey there, little tiger. And what did you do today?

DOREEN

(*Addressing* RASHID *as she hands the baby to* CYRUS) Hello.

RASHID

(*Shyly*) Hello.

CYRUS

(*Noticing the exchange between* DOREEN *and* RASHID) Jesus. I almost forgot you were here. Doreen, this is Paul. My new assistant.

DOREEN *extends her right hand to* RASHID.

RASHID

(*Shaking* DOREEN'*s hand*). It's only temporary. On a freelance basis.

CYRUS

(*Turning* JUNIOR *toward* RASHID) And this one, in case you haven't guessed, is Junior.

RASHID

(*Studying* JUNIOR *carefully. Mumbles in a barely audible voice*). Hi there, little brother.

CYRUS

(*To* JUNIOR) Say hi to Paul.

JUNIOR

Hi there, little brother.

CYRUS

(*To* DOREEN) He's helping me clean out that upstairs room. Might as well get this place looking good, anyway. (*To* RASHID) I guess that's it for today, sport. Come back tomorrow morning at eight, and you can pick up where you left off. (*Starts walking to the office with* JUNIOR *in his arms*)

We see him through the window: opening the cash register, pocketing the money, turning out the lights, then coming out and closing the garage doors. In the foreground, we see RASHID *standing with* DOREEN. *He looks down at the ground, too shy to say a word to her. She studies him with a mixture of curiosity and amusement. When* CYRUS *is finished closing up, he walks toward them and says to* RASHID:

CYRUS (*cont'd*)
Do you want me to pay you now, or can you wait until tomorrow?

RASHID
Tomorrow's fine. There's no rush.

37. EXT: EARLY EVENING. OUTSIDE COLE'S GARAGE

A little later. We see RASHID *sitting next to the TV outside the office door. He is utterly still. Hold for two, three beats.*

38. INT: EARLY EVENING. INSIDE THE OFFICE OF COLE'S GARAGE

We see a pencil drawing being slid under the door. It is an excellent rendering of the garage as seen from across the road.

The camera moves in on the drawing until it occupies the entire screen. Hold for two, three beats.

Fade out.

39. INT: DAY. PAUL'S APARTMENT

PAUL opens the door. RASHID is standing in the hall, holding the black-and-white TV in his arms. The knapsack is on his back. His clothes have become a little shabbier since the last time we saw him.

PAUL

(*Surprised*) Hey, it's you.

RASHID

(*Serious*) I wanted to give you this as a token of my appreciation.

PAUL

Appreciation for what?

RASHID

I don't know. For helping me out.

PAUL

(*Eyeing TV suspiciously*) Where did you get that thing?

RASHID

I bought it. Twenty-nine ninety-five on sale at Goldbaum's TV and Radio. (*Hands TV to PAUL, who takes it in his arms. RASHID smiles*) Well, that just about takes care of it, I guess. You'll be able to watch the ball games now. You know, as a little break from your work. (*Begins to leave*)

PAUL

Where the hell do you think you're going?

RASHID

Business appointment. I'm seeing my broker at three o'clock.

PAUL

Cut it out, will you? Just cut it out and come back here.

RASHID

(*Looking at his watch. Shrugs*) I don't have much time. (*Returns to the doorway, enters the apartment*)

PAUL

(*Puts TV on the stereo cabinet*) Close the door. (RASHID *closes the door*) Sit down in that chair. (*Points.* RASHID *sits down in the chair*) Now listen carefully. Your aunt Em came here a couple of days ago. She was sick with worry, out of her mind. We had an interesting talk about you, *Thomas*. Do you understand what I'm saying? Your aunt thinks you're in trouble, and so do I. Tell me about it, kid. I want to hear all about it right now.

RASHID *realizes he is trapped. Shrugs. Smiles weakly. Looks down at floor to avoid* PAUL's *gaze. When he dares to look up again,* PAUL *is still glowering at him.*

RASHID

You don't really want to know.

PAUL

(*Impatient*) I don't, huh? And what makes you such an authority on what I want or don't want?

RASHID

(*Sighs, defeated*) Okay, okay. (*Pause*) It's all so stupid. (*Pause*) There's this guy, see. Charles Clemm. The Creeper, that's what people call him. The kind of guy you don't want to cross paths with.

PAUL

And?

RASHID

(*Hesitates*) I crossed paths with him. That's why I'm trying to stay clear of my neighborhood. To make sure I don't run into him again.

PAUL

So that's the something you weren't supposed to see, huh?

Close-up of RASHID, *becoming more animated as he talks.*

RASHID

I just happened to be walking by. . . . All of a sudden, the Creeper and this other guy come running out of this check-cashing place with masks on their faces and guns in their hands. . . . They just about ran smack into me. The Creeper recognized me, and I knew he knew I recognized him. . . . If the guy from the check-cashing place hadn't rushed out then screaming bloody murder, he would have shot me. I'm telling you, the Creeper would have shot me right there on the sidewalk. But the noise distracted him, and when he turned around to see what was happening, I took off. . . . One more second, and I would have been dead.

PAUL

Why don't you go to the police?

RASHID

You're joking, right? I mean, that's your way of trying to be funny, right?

PAUL

If they put this Creeper in jail, then you'd be safe.

RASHID

The man has friends. And they're not likely to forgive me if I testify against him.

PAUL

(*Thinking*) What makes you think you'll be any safer around here? It's only about a mile away from where you live.

RASHID

It might not be far, but it's another galaxy. Black is black and white is white, and never the twain shall meet.

PAUL

It looks like they've met in this apartment.

RASHID

That's because we don't belong anywhere. You don't fit into your world, and I don't fit into mine. We're the outcasts of the universe.

PAUL

(*Studying* RASHID) Maybe. Or maybe it's the other people who don't belong.

RASHID

Let's not get too idealistic.

PAUL

(*Pause. Breaks into a smile*) Fair enough. We wouldn't want to get carried away, would we? (*Pause*) Now call your aunt Em and let her know you're alive.

40. INT: EVENING. PAUL'S APARTMENT

PAUL *and* RASHID *are watching the Mets on television. They are both smoking little cigars.* PAUL *puffs on his calmly;* RASHID *coughs after each puff of his. He is clearly not used to smoking. The television has a defective tube: the reception is poor, and every now and then one of them stands up and bangs the top of the set to bring the picture back into focus. They watch the ball game in silence. Close-up of the TV screen: the batter swings. An announcer's voice is heard describing the action.*

41. EXT: LATE AFTERNOON. THE CORNER IN FRONT OF THE BROOKLYN CIGAR CO.

AUGGIE is alone, closing up shop, looking particularly scruffy and unshaven. Just as he finishes pulling down the last metal gate, a car with Pennsylvania license plates comes speeding down Seventh Avenue and brakes to a sudden stop in front of the store. It is a ten-year-old Pontiac in rather sorry shape: belching smoke, with a defective muffler and a dented body. AUGGIE, distracted by the commotion, turns and looks at the car.

From AUGGIE's POV: we look into the car and see that the driver is RUBY McNUTT. She leans out the open window and addresses AUGGIE in an urgent voice.

> RUBY
>
> Get in, Auggie. I've got something to show you.

> AUGGIE
>
> (*Reluctant*) You don't give up, do you?

> RUBY
>
> Just get in and shut up. I'm not asking you to do anything. I just need you to come with me.

> AUGGIE
>
> Where to?

> RUBY
>
> (*Impatient*) Dammit, Auggie, don't ask so many questions. Just get in the car.

AUGGIE shrugs. RUBY opens the right front door of the car, and he climbs in. They drive off.

42. EXT: EVENING. THE STREETS OF BROOKLYN

We see RUBY'*s car as it travels through the Brooklyn evening, making its way down Seventh Avenue to Flatbush Avenue, then turning onto Eastern Parkway and gliding past the Public Library and the Brooklyn Museum as it penetrates the slums of Crown Heights and East New York.*

RUBY

I told her she was going to meet her father.

AUGGIE

You what?

RUBY

It was the only way, Auggie. Otherwise, she wasn't going to let me see her.

AUGGIE

I think you'd better stop the car and let me out.

RUBY

Relax, okay? You don't have to do anything. Just go in there and pretend. It won't kill you to do a little favor like that. Besides, you might even learn something.

AUGGIE

Yeah, like what?

RUBY

That I wasn't bullshitting you, sweetheart. At least you'll know I've been telling the truth.

AUGGIE

Look, I'm not saying you don't have a daughter. It's just that she's not my daughter.

RUBY

Wait till you see her, Auggie.

AUGGIE

And what's that supposed to mean?

RUBY

She looks just like you.

AUGGIE

(*Irritated*) Cut it out. Just cut it out, okay? It's starting to get on my nerves.

RUBY

When I told her I was going to bring her father, she kind of melted. It's the first time Felicity's talked nice to me since she left home. She's dying to meet you, Auggie.

They drive on in silence for a few more seconds. By now they have entered one of the worst, most dangerous parts of the city. We see broken-down, boarded-up buildings, vacant lots strewn with rubble, trash scattered on the sidewalks. RUBY *turns down one of these streets, then brings the car to a halt in front of a walk-up building with spray-painted graffiti on the outer door:* KILL THE COPS. AUGGIE *and* RUBY *get out of the car and start walking toward the building. Down the street, in the distance, we see a black man pick up a metal garbage can and throw it violently to the ground. It lands with a loud crash.*

AUGGIE

Nice neighborhood you've brought me to. Full of happy, prosperous people.

43. INT: EVENING. FELICITY'S APARTMENT

Close-up of a scarred green door. A knocking is heard from the other side. Pause. The knocking is heard again. After another pause, we hear feet padding toward the door. A second later a shoulder enters the frame. This is FELICITY *from behind. She is dressed in a cheap flowered robe.*

FELICITY

Yeah? Who is it?

RUBY (*off*)

It's me, honey. It's Mom.

We see FELICITY'*s hand reach out and unbolt the lock. The door opens to reveal* AUGGIE *and* RUBY *standing in the hall. They both look nervous:* RUBY *expectant and hopeful, with a forced smile on her face,* AUGGIE *guarded and closed in on himself. Cut to a close-up of* FELICITY'*s face. She is a very pretty blonde of eighteen. Her expression is hostile, however, and there is a wasted look in her eyes. We see clumsily applied rouge on her cheeks, a slash of red lipstick on her lips. She runs her hand through her stringy, unwashed hair. Cut to a close-up of* AUGGIE'*s face. It is impossible to know what he is thinking.*

As AUGGIE *and* RUBY *enter the apartment, the camera backs up to show the room. It is a tawdry place with little furniture: a double mattress on the floor (the bed is unmade), a rickety wooden table and two chairs along the far wall (we see a box of Sugar Pops on the table), a hot plate, and an enormous color television near the mattress. The television is on, but the sound is off. Images of commercials flicker in the background during the rest of the scene. The only decoration is a large black-and-white poster of Jim Morrison Scotch-taped to one of the walls. Clothes are strewn everywhere: on the floor, on the table, on top of the television set.*

By the time RUBY *has shut the door behind her,* FELICITY *has already retreated to the other side of the room and is lighting a cigarette from a pack of Newports on the table. No one says anything. An awkward silence as* FELICITY *glares at her mother and* AUGGIE.

RUBY

(*Finally*) Well?

FELICITY

Well what?

RUBY

Aren't you going to say anything?

FELICITY

What do you want me to say?

RUBY

I don't know. Hello, Mom. Hello, Dad. Something like that.

FELICITY

(*Takes a drag on her cigarette, looking* AUGGIE *up and down. Then, turning to* RUBY) I don't got no daddy, you dig? I got born last week when some dog fucked you up the ass.

AUGGIE

(*Muttering under his breath*) Jesus Christ. This is all I need.

RUBY

(*Trying to ignore the viciousness of her daughter's remark*) You told me you wanted to meet him. Well, here he is.

FELICITY

Yeah, I might have said that. Chico told me to see what he was like, maybe there'd be some dough in it for us. Well, now I've seen him, and I can't say I'm too impressed. (*Pause. Turning to* AUGGIE) Hey, mister. Are you rich or what?

AUGGIE

(*Disgusted*) Yeah, I'm a millionaire. I walk around in disguise because I'm ashamed of all my money.

RUBY

(*To* FELICITY. *Imploringly*) Be nice, sweetie. We're just here to help you.

FELICITY

(*Snaps back*) Help? What the fuck do I need your help for? I've got a man, don't I? That's more than you can say for yourself, Hawkeye.

AUGGIE

Hey, hey, don't talk to your mother like that.

FELICITY

(*Crushing out her cigarette on the table. Ignoring AUGGIE's remark. To her mother*) You're telling me you actually went to bed with this guy? You're telling me you actually let him fuck you?

RUBY

(*Mortified, struggling not to lose her composure*) You can do whatever you want with your own life. We're thinking of the baby, that's all. We want you to get yourself cleaned up for the baby. Before it's too late.

FELICITY

Baby? And what baby is that?

RUBY

Your baby. The baby you're carrying around inside you.

FELICITY

Yeah, well, there ain't no baby in there now. You dig? There's nothing in there now.

RUBY

What are you talking about?

FELICITY

An abortion, stupid. (*Laughs bitterly*) I had an abortion the day before yesterday. So you don't have to bug me about that shit anymore. (*Laughs again. Defiantly, almost to herself*) Bye-bye, baby!

(*Taking hold of* RUBY's *arm.* RUBY *is about to break into tears*) Come on, let's get out of here. I've had enough.

RUBY *shrugs off* AUGGIE's *hand and goes on looking at her daughter. As* FELICITY *speaks, the camera closes in on her face.*

FELICITY

Yeah, that's right, you better go. Chico'll be back any minute, and I'm sure your boyfriend doesn't want to mess with him. Chico's a real man. Not some scuzzy dickhead you find in last month's garbage. Do you hear what I'm saying? He'll chop up Mr. Dad here into little pieces. That's a promise. He'll kick the living shit out of him.

44. INT: DAY. PAUL'S APARTMENT

It is morning. RASHID *is preparing a pot of coffee in the kitchenette.* PAUL *stumbles out of the bathroom, wiping his face with a towel. He has just woken up and is still groggy. He approaches the table.*

PAUL

Ah, coffee. Smells good.

RASHID

(*Handing him a cup*) One sip of this stuff and your eyes will blast open.

PAUL

(*Taking the cup and sitting down*) Thanks. (*Begins to drink*)

RASHID

What time did you get to bed last night?

PAUL

I don't know. Two or three. It was pretty late.

RASHID

You work too hard, you know that?

PAUL

Once a story gets hold of you, it's hard to let go. (*Pause*) Besides, I'm making up for lost time.

RASHID

Just so you don't overdo it. You don't want to die of sleep deprivation before you finish.

PAUL

(*Almost to himself. Looking up at the photo of Ellen on the wall*) If you don't sleep, you don't dream. If you don't dream, you don't have nightmares.

RASHID

That's logical. And if you don't sleep, you don't need a bed. Saves you money, too. (*Pause*) So what's this story you're working on, anyway?

PAUL

If I tell you, I might not be able to finish it.

RASHID

Come on, just a little hint.

PAUL

(*Smiling at* RASHID's *eagerness. Pause*) Okay, just a little hint. I can't tell you the story, but I'll tell you what gave me the idea for it.

RASHID

The inspiration.

PAUL

Yeah, right. The inspiration. It's a true story anyway, so I don't suppose it can hurt, can it?

No way.

PAUL

All right. Listen carefully. (*The camera slowly moves in for a close-up of* PAUL's *face*) About twenty-five years ago, a young man went skiing alone in the Alps. There was an avalanche, the snow swallowed him up, and his body was never recovered.

RASHID (*off*)

(*Mockingly*) The end.

PAUL

No, not the end. The beginning. (*Pause*) His son was just a little boy at the time, but the years passed, and when he grew up, he became a skier, too. One day last winter, he went out by himself for a run down the mountain. He gets halfway to the bottom and then stops to eat his lunch next to a big rock. Just as he's unwrapping his cheese sandwich, he looks down and sees a body frozen in the ice—right there at his feet. He bends down to take a closer look, and suddenly he feels that he's looking into a mirror, that he's looking at himself. There he is—dead—and the body is perfectly intact, sealed away in a block of ice—like someone preserved in suspended animation. He gets down on all fours, looks right into the dead man's face, and realizes that he's looking at his father.

Cut to RASHID's *face. We see him listening intently.*

PAUL (*cont'd*) (*off*)

And the strange thing is that the father is younger than the son is now. The boy has become a man, and it turns out that he's older than his own father.

The camera holds on RASHID's *face. After a moment:*

PAUL (*off*)

So what are you going to do today?

                            RASHID
(*Shrugs*) Read, think, do some drawings if I get in the mood.

*He points to the coffee table: we see the sketch pad and a paperback copy
of Shakespeare's* Othello.

                        RASHID (*cont'd*)
But tonight I'm going to celebrate. That's definite.

                             PAUL
Celebrate? What for?

                            RASHID
It's my birthday. I'm seventeen years old (*looks at wristwatch*) as of
forty-seven minutes ago, and I think I should celebrate having made
it this far.

                             PAUL
(*Raising coffee cup*) Hey, hey. Happy birthday. Why didn't you tell
me?

                            RASHID
(*Deadpan*) I just did.

                             PAUL
I mean earlier. We could have planned something.

Close-up of RASHID's *face.*

                            RASHID
I don't like plans. I prefer to take things as they come.

45. INT: LATE AFTERNOON. A BOOKSTORE IN
BROOKLYN

A small, cluttered independent bookshop.

The scene begins with a close-up of the clerk's face: APRIL LEE, *a Eurasian woman in her mid- to late twenties. She is sitting behind the front counter with an open book before her. Her expression is puzzled, searching, as if she has just remembered or recognized something, but can't quite figure out what it is. We see her looking toward the back of the store, straining to listen in on* PAUL *and* RASHID'S *conversation.*

RASHID (*off*)

Here we are. (*Pause*) Rembrandt's drawings. Edward Hopper. Van Gogh's letters.

PAUL (*off*)

Pick two or three. Now that the coffers are open, you might as well take advantage of me.

As PAUL *and* RASHID *start walking back in the direction of the counter,* APRIL *lowers her gaze and pretends to be reading. We see* PAUL *and* RASHID *enter the field of the camera from behind.* PAUL *puts a small pile of art books on the counter.*

PAUL

We'll take these, please.

APRIL *looks up; her eyes meet* PAUL'S. *They study each other for a brief moment—a significant exchange that does not escape* RASHID'S *notice.*

APRIL

Will that be cash or charge?

PAUL

(*Taking out his wallet and looking inside*) Better make it charge. (*Removes the credit card and hands it to* APRIL)

APRIL

(*Looking at the card, smiles*) I thought I recognized you. You're Paul Benjamin the writer, aren't you?

PAUL

(*Both pleased and surprised*) I confess.

APRIL

I keep waiting for the next novel to come out. Anything in the works?

PAUL

I, uh . . .

RASHID

(*Butting in, with enthusiasm*) It's coming along. At the rate he's going, he'll have a story finished by the end of the summer.

APRIL

Wonderful. When your next book is published, maybe you could come into the store and do a signing. I'm sure we could get a lot of people to show up.

PAUL

(*Still staring at* APRIL) Uh, actually, I tend to shy away from that kind of thing.

RASHID

(*To* APRIL) Excuse me for asking, but you aren't married, are you?

APRIL

(*Taken aback*) What!

RASHID

Perhaps I should rephrase the question. What I mean to say is, are you married or seriously involved with a significant other?

APRIL

(*Still astonished. Bursts out laughing*) No! At least I don't think I am!

RASHID

(*Smiling with satisfaction*) Good. Then may I have the honor of extending an invitation to you?

APRIL

An invitation?

Close-up of PAUL, listening to the exchange between RASHID and APRIL.

RASHID

Yes, an invitation. I apologize for springing it on you at the last minute, but Mr. Benjamin and I are attending a celebration tonight, and we would be most pleased if you chose to accompany us. (*Looking at PAUL*) Isn't that right, Mr. Benjamin?

PAUL

(*Breaking into a broad smile*) Absolutely. We would be honored.

APRIL

(*Smiling*) And what's the occasion of this celebration?

RASHID

It's my birthday.

APRIL

And how many people will be attending this birthday party?

RASHID

I wouldn't actually call it a party. It's more along the lines of a dinner in celebration of my birthday. (*Pause*) The guest list is quite restricted. So far, there's Mr. Benjamin and myself. If you accept, that would make three of us.

APRIL

(*Ironic. With a crafty smile*) Ah-hah, I see. A cozy dinner. But aren't threesomes a little awkward? How does the phrase go—

RASHID

Three's a crowd. Yes, I'm aware of that. But I have to keep an eye on Mr. Benjamin wherever he goes. To make sure he doesn't get himself into trouble.

APRIL

And what are you, his chaperone?

RASHID

(*With a straight face*) Actually, I'm his father.

APRIL bursts out laughing, amused by the mounting silliness of the conversation.

PAUL

It's true. Most people assume I'm *his* father. It's a logical assumption—given that I'm older than he is and so on. But the fact is, it's the other way around. He's my father, and I'm his son.

Close-up of APRIL's face. She is still laughing.

Cut to:

46. INT: EVENING. A CHINESE RESTAURANT IN BROOKLYN

In the background, we see a number of other customers. At one table, a Chinese family is celebrating a birthday. Toward the end of the scene, they all get up to pose for a group photograph. PAUL, RASHID, and APRIL are sitting together at a round table. They are in the middle of their meal.

PAUL

So your mother grew up in Shanghai?

APRIL

Until she was twelve. She moved here in forty-nine.

PAUL

And your father? Is he from New York?

APRIL

(*Smiling*) Muncie, Indiana. He and my mother met as students. But I'm from Brooklyn. My sisters and I were all born and bred right here.

PAUL

Just like me.

RASHID

Like me, too.

APRIL

I once read somewhere that one quarter of all the people in the United States have at least one relative who's lived in Brooklyn at one time or another.

RASHID

No wonder it's such a screwed-up place.

PAUL

(*To* APRIL) And the bookstore? Have you been working there long?

APRIL

It's just a summer job. Something to help pay the bills while I finish my dissertation.

PAUL

Your dissertation? What subject do you study?

APRIL

American literature. What else?

PAUL

What else. Of course, what else? And what are you writing about
for your thesis?

APRIL

(*With mock pomposity*) Visions of Utopia in Nineteenth-Century
American Fiction.

PAUL

Wow. You don't fool around, do you?

APRIL

(*Smiling*) Of course I fool around. But not so much when it comes
to my work, it's true. (*Pause*) Have you ever read *Pierre, or the
Ambiguities?*

PAUL

Melville, huh? (*Smiles*) It's been a while.

APRIL

That's the subject of my last chapter.

PAUL

Not an easy book.

APRIL

Which explains why this hasn't been the easiest summer of my life.

RASHID

All the more reason to let 'er rip tonight, sweetheart. (*Raises glass*)
You know, go for the gusto.

APRIL *clinks her glass with* RASHID *and laughs merrily as* PAUL *looks on
and smiles. Cut to:*

47. INT: NIGHT. A BAR IN BROOKLYN

A noisy, crowded blue-collar hangout. APRIL, PAUL, and RASHID are stand-ing together, looking rather tipsy. They are engaged in an animated three-way conversation, but we can't hear their voices over the din.

A song is playing on the jukebox ("Downtown Train," by Tom Waits). APRIL asks PAUL to dance. He agrees. As they dance, RASHID looks on. Even though the rhythm of the song is fast, PAUL and APRIL dance slowly, tentatively, not quite sure how to behave with each other.

After a moment, AUGGIE emerges from the back room with VIOLET, his flashy girlfriend, hanging on his arm. They are both plastered.

AUGGIE
(*Drunk, smiling*) Hey, man, good to see you.

PAUL
This is April Lee, Auggie. April, say hello to Auggie Wren.

APRIL
(*Smiling*) Hello, Auggie Wren.

AUGGIE
(*Affecting the voice of a cowboy, tipping an imaginary hat*) Howdy, Miss April, I'm right pleased to make your acquaintance. (*Turning to VI-OLET*) And this pretty little lady here is Miss Vi-o-let Sanchez de Jalapeño, the hottest chili pepper this side of the Rio Grande. Ain't that so, baby?

VIOLET
Ees so, Auggie. And you not so cold neither. Eh, baby?

PAUL, APRIL, and RASHID nod hello to VIOLET.

AUGGIE
So, what brings you to a dive like this?

PAUL

(*Gesturing with his thumb to* RASHID; *addressing* AUGGIE) It's his birthday today, so we decided to whoop it up a little.

AUGGIE

(*To* RASHID) How old, kid?

RASHID

Seventeen.

AUGGIE

Seventeen? I remember when I was seventeen. Christ, I was one little whacked-out son-of-a-bitch when I was seventeen. Is that what you are, son? One little whacked-out crazy fella?

RASHID

(*With feigned seriousness, nodding*) Definitely. I'd say you've hit the nail on the head.

AUGGIE

Good. Keep it up, and maybe one day you'll grow up and become a great man like me. (*Bursts out laughing*)

PAUL *puts his arm around* AUGGIE, *addressing him in quieter tones. As they talk,* APRIL *and* VIOLET *look each other up and down, smiling awkwardly.* RASHID *strains to hear what* PAUL *and* AUGGIE *are saying to each other.*

PAUL

Hey, Auggie, I've just been thinking. You wouldn't need some help around the store, would you? Some summer help while Vinnie's gone?

AUGGIE

(*Thinking*) Help? Hmm. It's possible. What did you have in mind?

PAUL

I'm thinking about the kid. I'm sure he'd do a good job for you.

AUGGIE

(*Looking up and studying* RASHID) Hey, kid. You interested in a job? I just got word from your employment agency that you're looking for a position in retail sales.

RASHID

A job? (*Pause. Looks at* PAUL) I definitely wouldn't turn down a job.

AUGGIE

Come around to the cigar store tomorrow morning at ten o'clock and we'll talk about it, okay? We'll see what we can work out.

RASHID

Ten o'clock tomorrow morning. I'll be there.

PAUL

(*Patting* AUGGIE *on the back*) I owe you one. Don't forget.

48. INT: DAY. PAUL'S APARTMENT

Morning. PAUL *and* RASHID *are sitting at the table, eating breakfast.* RASHID *is wearing a red T-shirt with the word "FIRE" emblazoned on the back in white letters. We catch them in mid-conversation.*

PAUL

It's 1942, right? And he's caught in Leningrad during the siege. I'm talking about one of the worst moments in human history. Five hundred thousand people died in that one place, and there's Bakhtin, holed up in an apartment, expecting to be killed any day. He has plenty of tobacco, but no paper to roll it in. So he takes the pages of a manuscript he's been working on for ten years and tears them up to roll his cigarettes.

RASHID

(*Incredulous*) His only copy?

PAUL

His only copy. (*Pause*) I mean, if you think you're going to die, what's more important, a good book or a good smoke? And so he huffed and he puffed, and little by little he smoked his book.

RASHID

(*Thinks, then smiles*) Nice try. You had me going for a second, but no . . . no writer would ever do a thing like that. (*Slight pause. Looking at PAUL*) Would he?

PAUL

(*Amused*) You don't believe me, huh? (*Stands up from the table and begins walking to the bookcase*) Look. I'll show you. It's all in this book.

PAUL *stands on a chair and reaches for a book on the top shelf. In doing so, he catches sight of the paper bag* RASHID *planted there in Scene 15. He studies it in bewilderment, then picks it up and dangles it in the air as he turns toward* RASHID.

PAUL (*cont'd*)

What's this?

RASHID

(*Squirming with embarrassment*) I don't know.

PAUL

Is it yours?

RASHID

Yeah, it might be.

PAUL

(*Shrugs, not wanting to make an issue of it*) Here, catch.

PAUL *tosses the bag in* RASHID's *direction. The bag breaks open in midair, and a shower of twenty-, fifty-, and hundred-dollar bills rains down from the ceiling.* PAUL *is stunned;* RASHID *is watching the world crumble before his eyes.*

Fade out.

49. INT: DAY. PAUL'S APARTMENT (LATER)

Fade in. A few minutes later. PAUL *and* RASHID *are sitting at the table again, the money stacked in neat piles between them. Again, we catch them in mid-conversation.*

PAUL

So you're saying it wasn't like that at all.

RASHID

Not exactly. I mean, there was more to it than I told you.

PAUL

Christ. You didn't just see what happened. They dropped the package on the ground and you picked it up.

RASHID

Yeah, I picked it up.

PAUL

And started to run.

RASHID

And started to run.

PAUL

(*Sarcastic*) Good thinking.

RASHID

That's just it. I didn't think. I just did it.

PAUL

You have one hell of a knack for getting into trouble, don't you?
(*Pause, gesturing to the money*) So how much does it come to?

RASHID

Six thousand dollars. Five thousand eight hundred and fourteen dollars, to be exact.

PAUL

(*Shaking his head, trying to absorb this new turn of events*) So you robbed
the robbers, and now the robbers are after you.

RASHID

That's it. In a nutshell.

PAUL

Yeah, well, you have to be nuts to do what you did. If you want
my opinion, you should give this money back to the Creeper. Just
give it back and tell him you're sorry.

RASHID

(*Shaking his head*) No way. There's no way I'm giving that money
back. It's my money now.

PAUL

A lot of good it will do you if the Creeper finds you.

RASHID

(*Stubbornly*) That money is my whole future.

Keep up with that attitude, and you won't have a future. (*Pause*) Seventeen is a hell of an age to die. Is that what you want?

Close-up of RASHID's *face. Fade out.*

50. INT: DAY. THE BROOKLYN CIGAR CO.

We see RASHID *mopping the floor. He finishes up and carries the mop to the bathroom behind the cash register and puts it a bucket that is sitting in the sink. He turns on the tap and rinses the mop. Just to the side of the sink, there are two open cardboard boxes on the floor. We catch a glimpse of the contents: boxes of Montecristos (Cuban cigars).* AUGGIE's *shipment from Miami has arrived.*

RASHID *turns off the tap, but the water continues to trickle out in a small stream into the bucket.* RASHID *doesn't notice.*

RASHID *returns to the counter.* AUGGIE *is standing by the door getting ready to go out. For the first time, he is clean-shaven, his hair is combed, and he is wearing dress-up clothes: a bright red plaid sports jacket, white slacks, etc. The effect is strange, laughable.*

AUGGIE
I'll be back in about an hour. Watch the register while I'm gone, okay?

RASHID
Sure thing. See you later.

AUGGIE *waves good-bye and leaves.*

Cut to the bathroom. Close-up of the bucket in the sink. The water is overflowing, spilling onto the boxes of Cuban cigars.

Cut to the store. RASHID is sitting behind the counter, studying a picture of a naked woman in Penthouse magazine.

Cut to bathroom. Close-up of water inundating the Cuban cigars.

Cut to store. Close-up of RASHID gaping at the photograph. We hear him groan softly.

RASHID

(*Muttering to himself*) Jesus God, save me.

Dissolve.

The jarring noise of the door opening. RASHID hastily closes the magazine and stashes it under the counter. AUGGIE enters the store with two middle-aged men in dark, pin-striped suits: his lawyer-customers for the Cuban cigars.

AUGGIE

(*Addressing the TWO LAWYERS as they enter. He is obviously keyed up. His manner is jovial, ingratiating*) It might be illegal, but it's hard to see where the crime is if there's no victim. No harm done, right?

FIRST LAWYER

This is what it must have felt like to go to a speakeasy during Prohibition.

SECOND LAWYER

Forbidden pleasures, eh?

AUGGIE

(*To RASHID*) Much business while I was gone?

RASHID

A little. Not much.

AUGGIE

(*To the* LAWYERS) This way, gentlemen. Let's retire to my office, shall we? (*He points to the bathroom behind the counter.*)

The camera stays on RASHID *as* AUGGIE *and the* LAWYERS *disappear. A second later, we hear* AUGGIE *explode with rage.*

AUGGIE (*off*)

What the fuck is going on here! Look at this. The goddamn place is flooded! Holy fucking shit! Look at this! Look at this goddamn mess!

51. INT: DAY. PAUL'S APARTMENT

Close-up of RASHID's *face. He is in tears.*

PAUL (*off*)

So you lost the job. Is that what you're telling me? He just up and fired you?

RASHID

(*Scarcely able to speak*) It was more complicated than that. There was a reason.

PAUL (*off*)

Well?

RASHID

It wasn't my fault.

PAUL (*off*)

(*Irritated*) If you don't tell me what happened, how do you expect me to know that? I need facts, not opinions.

RASHID

(*Struggling to speak, fighting back the tears*) The water was dripping, see . . . I turned it off, but it was still dripping, and then Auggie had to go out, and so I left the back room . . . And later on . . . well, later on . . . when Auggie came back . . . the whole place was flooded. His Cuban cigars got all messed up . . . You know, soaked through . . . just when he was about to sell them . . . to these rich guys in suits. . . .

Shot of PAUL *standing in the middle of the room looking at* RASHID, *who is sitting on the bed.*

PAUL

Cuban cigars. You mean he had some hanky-panky going with those guys?

RASHID

I suppose so. He never told me about it.

PAUL

No wonder he was angry.

RASHID

He was out five thousand bucks, he said. . . . He kept saying it over and over. . . . Five thousand bucks down the drain. . . . He wouldn't stop. . . . Five thousand bucks, five thousand bucks. . . . He was like out of his mind with those five thousand bucks. . . .

Silence. PAUL *paces about the room, thinking. He sits down in a chair by the table. Thinks some more.*

PAUL

Here's what you're going to do. You're going to open up your backpack, take out your bag of money, count out five thousand dollars, and hand it over to Auggie.

RASHID

(*Appalled*) What are you talking about? (*Pause*) You can't be serious.

PAUL

I'm serious, all right. You've got to square it with Auggie. Since you won't give the money back to the Creeper, you can use it to make things right with Auggie. That's probably better anyway. Better to keep your friends than to worry about your enemies.

RASHID

(*Stubbornly. Fresh tears falling down his cheeks*) I'm not going to do it.

PAUL

You'll do it, all right. You fuck up, you've got to undo the damage. That's how it works, buster. If you don't do it, I'm going to throw you out of here. Do you understand me? If you don't pay Auggie what you owe him, I'm finished with you.

RASHID

I pay Auggie, and I've got nothing. Eight hundred bucks and a ticket to Shit City.

PAUL

Don't worry about it. You've got friends now, remember? Just behave yourself, and everything will work out.

52. INT: NIGHT. A BAR IN BROOKLYN

AUGGIE *is sitting alone at the bar, smoking a cigarette and drinking a beer. He looks disgusted: muttering to himself, swearing under his breath. Business is slow, and the place is almost empty.*

PAUL *and* RASHID *enter and approach* AUGGIE *at the bar.* RASHID *is carrying a brown paper bag.* AUGGIE *gestures with his head for them to follow him into the back room. Cut to:*

The three of them taking their seats at a table in the back room. A long, awkward pause.

PAUL

The kid's sorry, Auggie.

AUGGIE

(*Scowls, fiddles with the napkin on the table*) Yeah, well, I'm sorry too. (*Pause*) It took me three years to save up those five thousand bucks, and now I'm broke. I can't hardly pay for this beer. Not to speak of having my credibility destroyed. Do you understand what I'm saying? My credibility. So yeah, I'm sorry, too. About as sorry as I've ever been in my whole fucking life.

PAUL

He's got something to tell you, Auggie.

AUGGIE

If he's got something to tell me, why don't he tell it to me himself?

Without saying a word, RASHID lifts the bag off his knees and puts it on the table in front of AUGGIE. AUGGIE eyes the bag suspiciously.

RASHID

It's for you.

AUGGIE

For me? And what am I supposed to do with a paper bag?

RASHID

Open it.

AUGGIE

(*Taking a peek inside*) What is this, some kind of joke?

RASHID

No, it's five thousand dollars.

AUGGIE

(*Disgusted*) Shit, I don't want your money, you little twerp. (*Peeking inside the paper bag again*) It's probably stolen anyway.

RASHID

What do you care where it comes from? It's yours.

AUGGIE

And why the hell would you give me money?

RASHID

So I can get my job back.

AUGGIE

Your job? You've got five thousand bucks. What do you want a piece-of-shit job like that for?

RASHID

To look at the dirty magazines. I can see all the naked women I want, and it doesn't cost me a cent.

AUGGIE

You're a dumb, whacked-out little fuck, do you know that?

AUGGIE pushes the bag toward RASHID. Without hesitating for a second, RASHID pushes the bag back toward AUGGIE.

PAUL

Don't be an ass, Auggie. He's trying to make it up to you, can't you see that?

AUGGIE

(*Sighs, shakes head, peeks into bag again*) He's crazy.

PAUL

No, he's not. You are.

AUGGIE

(*Shrugs. Begins to crack a smile*) You're right. I just wasn't sure you knew.

PAUL

It's written all over you like a neon sign. Now say something nice to Rashid to make him feel better.

AUGGIE

(*Peeking into the bag again. Smiles*) Fuck you, kid.

RASHID

(*Beginning to smile*) Fuck you, too, you white son-of-a-bitch.

PAUL

(*Pause. He laughs. Then, slapping his hands on the table*) Good. I'm glad that's settled!

53. INT: DAY. PAUL'S APARTMENT

PAUL is alone at his desk, typing. The keys suddenly stick, jam up.

PAUL

(*Spreading his hands in front of his face and addressing his fingers*) Pay attention, boys. Look sharp.

54. INT: DAY. PAUL'S APARTMENT

Several hours later. As before: PAUL alone at his desk, typing. A loud knocking is heard at the door. PAUL continues typing. Another loud knock on the door. PAUL sighs, stands up from his desk, and leaves the workroom. Shot of PAUL walking through the big room and opening the front door. Two black men are standing in the hallway. One is very large, in his mid-thirties; the other is small, in his twenties. They are Charles Clemm, THE CREEPER, and his sidekick, ROGER GOODWIN.

CREEPER

Mr. Benjamin, I presume?

Before PAUL *can respond,* CREEPER *and* GOODWIN *push their way past him into the apartment.* GOODWIN *slams the door behind him.* PAUL *backs up nervously. He positions himself by the windows that look down at the street.*

GOODWIN

You got a security problem in this building, you know that? The lock on that door downstairs is busted.

CREEPER

Not a good idea in these troubled times. You never know what kind of trash might wander in off the streets.

PAUL

(*Nervous*) I'll talk to the landlord about it tomorrow.

GOODWIN

You do that. Don't want no unpleasant surprises, do you?

PAUL

(*Looking them over*) And who do I have the pleasure of talking to now?

CREEPER

Pleasure? (*Laughs*) I wouldn't call this pleasure, funny man. I'd say it's more in the nature of business.

PAUL

It doesn't matter. I know who you are anyway. (*Pause*) You're the Creeper, aren't you?

CREEPER

(*Indignant*) The what?

GOODWIN

(*Whipping out a .45 automatic and pointing it at* PAUL) Ain't nobody calls Charles by that name to his face. (*Grabs* PAUL'*s arm and puts him in a hammerlock*) Understand?

PAUL

(*Grunting in pain*) Sure, I understand.

Before GOODWIN *can do any real violence, the* CREEPER *waves him off. At that moment,* PAUL *glances out the window. Shot of* RASHID *down on the street, approaching the building. Shot from* RASHID'*s POV: We see* PAUL *upstairs with his back to the window, moving his hand with a shooing gesture, trying to warn* RASHID *of the danger. Another shot of* RASHID'*s face, puzzled. Another shot from* RASHID'*s POV: the* CREEPER'*s head enters the picture. Another shot of* RASHID*: he takes off, running down the street. As all this happens we hear the following:*

CREEPER (*off*)

Let me tell you the business we're here about. We want your co-operation in helping us locate a certain party. We know he's been staying here, so we don't want no denials about it, understand?

PAUL

What party are you looking for?

GOODWIN (*off*)

Little Tommy Cole. A homeboy with a brain the size of a pea.

PAUL (*off*)

(*Stalling*) Tommy Cole? Never heard of him.

By now, RASHID *is gone. Shot of* PAUL'*s face. He glances over his shoulder at the street below. Shot of the street: no sight of* RASHID *anywhere. Followed by a shot of* PAUL, CREEPER, *and* GOODWIN *standing in the room.*

CREEPER

I'm not sure you heard me the first time. We know that boy's been here.

PAUL

You might think you know, but you've got the wrong information. I never heard of anyone named Tommy Cole.

GOODWIN

(*Strolling about the room. Sees* RASHID's *sketch pad on the coffee table*) Lookee here, Charles. Ain't cousin Tommy fond of doodling?

He picks up the pad, flips through it, and then starts ripping up the drawings and tossing them on the floor.

PAUL

Hey, what the hell are you doing?

Before GOODWIN *answers,* CREEPER *comes close to* PAUL *and without any warning delivers a fast, powerful punch to his stomach.* PAUL *doubles over in pain and falls to the floor.*

CREEPER

So what's it going to be, funny man? Do you cooperate, or do we send you to the hospital?

GOODWIN

(*Walking toward the bookcase, addressing* PAUL *over his shoulder*) Hope you got some good Blue Cross, baby.

GOODWIN *suddenly starts pulling books off the shelves and sweeping them violently onto the floor.*

55. EXT: DAY. IN FRONT OF THE BROOKLYN CIGAR CO.

AUGGIE is standing with his arm on JIMMY ROSE's shoulder. We catch them in mid-conversation. AUGGIE is talking; JIMMY is doing his best to follow him: looking down at the ground and nodding, surreptitiously picking his nose. As they talk, we see PAUL walking down the street in their direction. He is limping; one side of his face is bandaged; his left arm is in a sling.

AUGGIE

. . . If it happens, it happens. If it doesn't, it doesn't. Do you understand what I'm saying? You never know what's going to happen next, and the moment you think you know, that's the moment you don't know a goddamn thing. That's what we call a paradox. Are you following me?

JIMMY

Sure, Auggie, I follow. When you don't know nothing, it's like paradise. I know what that is. It's after you're dead and you go up to heaven and sit with the angels.

AUGGIE

(About to correct JIMMY when he spots PAUL approaching the corner) Jesus, man, you're one fucking mess.

PAUL

(Shrugs) It could have been worse. If the cops hadn't come, I might not be standing here now.

AUGGIE

Cops? You mean they nabbed those cruds?

PAUL

No. The . . . uh . . . the Bobbsey Twins lit out when they heard the sirens. But at least they stopped playing that marimba duet on my skull. *(Pause. Smiles) Assaultus interruptus.*

AUGGIE

(*Studying* PAUL's *wounds*) Fuckus my assus. They did some number on you.

PAUL

For once in my life I managed to keep my mouth shut. There's something to be said for that, I suppose.

JIMMY, *who has been watching* PAUL *intently since his arrival, gently and hesitantly raises his hand and touches* PAUL's *bruised face.* PAUL *winces slightly.*

JIMMY

Does it hurt?

AUGGIE

Of course it hurts. What does it look like?

JIMMY

(*Quietly*) I thought maybe he was pretending.

PAUL

(*To* AUGGIE) You haven't heard from Rashid, have you?

AUGGIE

Not a peep.

PAUL

I spoke to his aunt a couple of days ago, but she hasn't heard from him either. It's beginning to get a little scary.

AUGGIE

That could be a good sign, though. It could mean that he got away.

PAUL

Or didn't. (*Pause*) There's no way of knowing, is there?

56. EXT: DAY. A BROOKLYN STREET

We see PAUL *walking down the street, returning home. He spots a young black man from behind. He is wearing the same red "FIRE" T-shirt that* RASHID *was wearing in Scene 48.* PAUL, *growing excited, limps forward to catch up with him. Once he gets close enough, he taps the young man on the shoulder.*

> ### YOUNG MAN
> (*Wheeling around as if he had been attacked. Angrily*) What the fuck you want, mister?

> ### PAUL
> (*Embarrassed*) I'm sorry. I thought you were someone else.

> ### YOUNG MAN
> I ain't someone else, got it? You can go fuck yourself with your someone else.

57. INT: NIGHT. PAUL'S APARTMENT

PAUL, *sitting in his easy chair, continues to work on his story by hand. The apartment has more or less been put back in order, but several traces of the Creeper's visit remain: bits of broken furniture, a pile of destroyed books in one corner, etc.*

After a few moments, PAUL *gets up from his chair, walks over to the television set, and turns it on. We hear the crowd noises of a baseball game, the voice of the announcer describing the action, but there is no image: only a single white line across the black screen.* PAUL *mutters under his breath and pounds the top of the TV. An image jumps into view: a baseball game in progress.* PAUL *backs up to watch. The moment he steps back, the image vanishes. Once again we see the white line across the black screen.* PAUL *steps forward and pounds the TV again. Nothing happens. He pounds again, and still the white line remains. The camera moves in slowly for a close-up of the TV screen. The camera travels through it, into the darkness.*

After a moment, we hear the clicking of PAUL's *keyboard. The sounds of typing resonate in the void.*

58. EXT: LATE MORNING. THE BROOKLYN PROMENADE

Sunday, late morning, brilliant sunshine. Against the backdrop of lower Manhattan, we see the summer weekend crowd along the Promenade: old people on benches reading newspapers, young couples out with their babies, girls on roller skates, boys on skateboards, bag ladies, bums. Traveling camera. Amongst the bustle of bodies and colors, we see the Brooklyn Bridge off to the right, a spider web of cables set against the buildings of upper Manhattan; to the left we see the expanse of New York Harbor, the Staten Island ferry, the Statue of Liberty. AUGGIE *and* RUBY *are walking along the Promenade, deep in conversation.* AUGGIE *is clean-shaven, his hair is slicked back, and he is wearing his white pants and a bright red Hawaiian shirt.* RUBY *is wearing sunglasses, black toreador pants, and spike heels.*

AUGGIE

So you're just going to give up and go home?

RUBY

I don't have much choice, do I? It's pretty clear she doesn't want me around.

AUGGIE

(*Thinks*) Still, you can't just write her off.

RUBY

Yeah? And what else am I supposed to do? There's no baby anymore, and if she wants to throw away her life, that's her business.

AUGGIE

She's just a kid. There's time for more babies later. After she grows up.

RUBY

Dream on, Auggie. She'll be lucky to make it to her nineteenth birthday.

AUGGIE

Not if you got her into one of those rehab programs.

RUBY

I'd never be able to talk her into it. And even if I could, those things cost money. And that's just what I don't have. I'm flat out dead broke.

AUGGIE

No you're not.

RUBY

(*She stops*) Are you calling me a liar? I'm telling you I'm broke. I don't even have insurance on my goddamned car.

AUGGIE

(*Ignoring her remark*) Remember that business venture I was telling you about? Well, my tugboat came in. I'm flush.

RUBY

(*Pouting*) Bully for you.

AUGGIE

No, bully for you. (*He reaches into his pocket, pulls out a long white envelope, and hands it to* RUBY)

RUBY

What's this?

AUGGIE

Why don't you open it and find out?

RUBY

(*Opens the envelope. It is filled with cash*) Jesus God, Auggie. There's money in here.

AUGGIE

Five thousand bucks.

RUBY

(*Incredulous*) And you're giving it to me?

AUGGIE

It's all yours, baby.

RUBY

(*Moved, to the point of tears*) For keeps?

AUGGIE

For keeps.

RUBY

(*Now crying in earnest*) I can't believe it. Oh God, I can't believe it. (*Pause, to catch her breath*) You're an angel, Auggie. An angel from heaven. (*She tries to put her arms around him, but* AUGGIE *squirms away*)

AUGGIE

Fuck this angel shit. Just take the dough, Ruby. But no bawling, okay? I can't stand people who blubber.

RUBY

I'm sorry, baby. I can't help it.

RUBY pulls a handkerchief from her purse and blows her nose, honking loudly. AUGGIE lights a cigarette. After a moment, they start walking again.

AUGGIE

There's just one thing I want to know.

RUBY

(*More composed*) Anything, Auggie. Just name it.

AUGGIE stops walking.

AUGGIE

Felicity. (*Pause*) She's not my daughter, is she?

Long pause. Close-up of RUBY's face.

RUBY

I don't know, Auggie. She might be. Then again, she might not. Mathematically speaking, there's a fifty-fifty chance. It's your call.

Close-up of AUGGIE's face. After a moment, he begins to smile. Fade out.

59. EXT: DAY. SEVENTH AVENUE

We see PAUL walking down the crowded street with a manila envelope tucked under his arm.

60. INT: DAY. THE BOOKSTORE

We see APRIL behind the counter. She is ringing up a sale for a CUSTOMER, an Indian woman dressed in a sari.

PAUL enters the store and approaches the counter. When APRIL looks up and notices who it is, her face brightens—then instantly shows alarm at the sight of PAUL's wounds and bandages. She completely forgets about the customer.

APRIL

Jesus, what happened to you?

PAUL

(*Shrugging it off*) It looks worse than it is. I'm okay.

APRIL

What happened?

PAUL

I'll tell you all about it (*glancing around the store*), but not here.

APRIL

(*Pause. Shyly*) It's been a while. I thought maybe you'd be in touch.

PAUL

Yeah, well, I've sort of been out of commission. (*Pause*) How's Melville?

APRIL

Almost done. A week or ten days, and I'll be there.

CUSTOMER

(*Growing impatient*) Miss, could I have my change, please?

APRIL

Oh, I'm sorry. (*Hands the woman her change*)

CUSTOMER

And my book.

APRIL

Sorry. (*She slips the book*—Portrait of a Lady—*into a bag and gives it to the woman*)

The CUSTOMER *leaves, glancing over her shoulder with a disapproving look at* APRIL *and* PAUL.

PAUL

(*Extending the manila envelope to* APRIL) I finished my story. I thought you might want to take a look at it.

APRIL

(*Taking the envelope—and at the same moment understanding the significance of* PAUL'*s gesture. She begins to smile*) I'd love to.

PAUL

Good. I hope you like it. It was a long time in coming.

APRIL

(*Glancing at her watch*) I get off for lunch in ten minutes. Can I treat you to a hamburger?

PAUL

(*Awkwardly*) Uh . . . actually, it might be better if you read the story first. Call me when you're finished, okay?

APRIL

(*A bit mystified, but putting a good face on her disappointment*) Okay. I'll read it tonight and call you tomorrow. (*Weighing the envelope in her hand*) It doesn't seem to be too long.

PAUL

Forty-one pages.

Another CUSTOMER—*a young white man of about twenty—appears at the counter with a copy of* On the Road. PAUL *begins backing toward the door.*

PAUL (*cont'd*)

You won't forget to call?

APRIL

I won't forget. I promise.

61. INT: NIGHT. PAUL'S APARTMENT

The telephone rings—two, three, four times—but no one is there to answer it. Cut to:

62. INT: NIGHT. THE BROOKLYN CIGAR CO.

A shot of the empty store. We hear a telephone ringing in the distance.

63. INT: NIGHT. AUGGIE'S APARTMENT

AUGGIE is sitting alone at his kitchen table, removing recently developed photographs from a yellow Kodak envelope. The 1990 album lies open on the table before him. One by one, AUGGIE affixes a small white label to the lower-right-hand corner of each image, carefully marking the date on each label with a pen: 7-30-90; 7-31-90; 8-1-90; etc. Then, one by one, he slips each photo into its appropriate place in the album. AUGGIE smokes a cigarette, hums a song under his breath, sips from a glass of bourbon. He looks like a beachcomber: unshaven, tousled hair, bare-chested, wearing a pair of baggy shorts.

The telephone is ringing. Not to be rushed, AUGGIE slides another photo into its place, takes a sip of his drink, and then, finally, answers the phone.

> AUGGIE
>
> Bureau of Missing Persons. Sergeant Fosdick. (*Pause. Listens*) Well, blow me down. Peter Rabbit's alive. (*Pause. Listens*) Yeah, that's cool. No problem. (*Pause. Listens*) Danzinger Road, Peekskill. (*Pause. Listens*) Yeah, I got it. I don't need no pencil. (*Pause. Listens*) How the hell do I know? I can't help it if he's not answering his phone. (*Pause. Listens*) So you're the one who called the cops, huh? Good work. (*Pause. Listens*) Yeah, I mean it. Good work. It probably saved his skin. (*Pause. Listens*) You got that right. Bad. You owe him a lot, keemosabbe. (*Pause. Listens*) No, not tomorrow. I have to work, chuckle brain—remember? (*Pause. Listens*) No, not Saturday

either. Sunday. (*Pause. Listens*) Yeah. Right. Okay. (*Smiles*) Yeah, and kiss my ass, too. (*Pause. Listens. Smiles again*) You, too. (*Hangs up the phone*)

64. EXT: DAY. PAUL'S STREET

Sunday morning. PAUL *and* AUGGIE *are walking together on the sidewalk.* PAUL *is carrying* RASHID's *backpack.*

PAUL

So what did he say when he called?

AUGGIE

Nothing much. He said his socks and underpants were dirty, and would we mind driving up with his things. (*Pause*) Fucking kids, huh? They take you for granted every time.

AUGGIE *stops in front of a car parked at the curb: a fifteen-year-old red Coupe de Ville.*

PAUL

(*Impressed*) Nice machine, Auggie. Where'd you find it?

AUGGIE

It's Tommy's. The sucker owed me a favor.

AUGGIE *unlocks the door on the passenger side, then walks around the car to unlock the door on the driver's side.*

PAUL

(*Opening the door*) It's not a long drive. An hour, an hour and a half. We'll be back in time for dinner.

AUGGIE

We'd better be. I haven't spent a night out of Brooklyn in fourteen years, and I'm not about to break my record now. Besides, I've got to be on my corner at eight sharp tomorrow morning.

They both climb into the car. AUGGIE *starts up the engine. Cut to:*

65. INT/EXT: DAY. PEEKSKILL. COLE'S GARAGE

We see RASHID *painting the walls in the upstairs room. The room has been transformed since the last time we saw it. It is entirely bare now and neat as a pin. With each touch of white paint that* RASHID *applies to the walls, the look of the place improves. He works with care, proud of what he has accomplished so far.*

Suddenly: the noise of a car down below. RASHID *goes to the open window and looks out. Cut to:*

From RASHID'S POV: *We see* CYRUS, DOREEN, *and* JUNIOR *pull up in the blue Ford. They get out.* DOREEN *is carrying a large picnic cooler.* CYRUS *opens the back door and unbuckles* JUNIOR *from his seat.*

RASHID (*off*)

(*Mumbling, alarm in his voice*) Oh, Jesus. What are they doing here on Sunday?

DOREEN

(*Waving up to* RASHID) Hi, Paul. We decided to have a picnic. Want to join us?

Cut to RASHID *at the window:*

RASHID

Uh, yeah, sure. (*Pause*) Just a minute. I'll be down in a minute.

Cut to RASHID *in the upstairs room. He crouches down, puts the brush he has been working with on top of the open paint can, and begins wiping his hands with a rag when, suddenly, the noise of another car is heard down below.* RASHID *stands up to have a look. Cut to:*

From RASHID'S POV: *We see the red Coupe de Ville limping into the station with a flat tire. The car stops.* PAUL *and* AUGGIE *climb out. Cut to:*

Close-up of RASHID, *looking out the window. His face registers panic, alarm.*

RASHID

Jesus Christ!

He begins running toward the door, hoping to get downstairs to PAUL *and* AUGGIE *before* CYRUS *can reach them. In his haste, he kicks over the open paint bucket.*

The scene ends with a close-up of white paint oozing over the bare wood floor.

66. EXT: DAY. IN FRONT OF COLE'S GARAGE

Shot of CYRUS, DOREEN, *and* JUNIOR *by the picnic table, unpacking their lunch. The camera pans from* CYRUS—*beginning to walk toward* PAUL *and* AUGGIE—*to* PAUL *and* AUGGIE, *who are standing by the gas pumps. We see* PAUL *and* AUGGIE *looking in the direction of the office, smiles beginning to form on their faces. At the precise instant* CYRUS *gets to them,* RASHID *enters the frame, panting hard from his dash down the stairs.*

PAUL

(*To* RASHID) Hi, kid.

RASHID

(*Looking at* PAUL's *wounds and bandages. He is shocked*) Wow. They sure did a job on you.

136

PAUL

Research. I worked the scene right into my story. (*Pause*) That makes the medical bills one hundred percent tax deductible.

AUGGIE

(*Under his breath*) Try selling that one to the IRS.

CYRUS

(*Watching the exchange with a confused look on his face. To* RASHID) You know these men? (*Gesturing to the flat tire*) I thought we had some customers.

AUGGIE

Yeah, he knows us. But you've also got some customers. (*Wheels around and kicks the Coupe de Ville*) Fucking Tommy. Leave it to him to drive around with bald tires.

PAUL

We came here to deliver some clean laundry.

RASHID

(*To* CYRUS) It's all right. I really do know them.

CYRUS

(*Still confused, but trying to be friendly*) I'm the owner here. Cyrus Cole. (*Extends his right hand to* AUGGIE)

AUGGIE

(*Shaking* CYRUS's *hand*) Augustus Wren.

CYRUS *extends his right hand to* PAUL.

PAUL

(*Shaking* CYRUS's *hand*) Paul Benjamin.

Cut to close-up of RASHID's *face. The sky has just fallen on top of him.*

CYRUS

(*More confused than ever. Turning to* RASHID) That's funny. His name is the same as yours.

RASHID

(*In a panic*) Well, you and Junior have the same name, too, don't you?

CYRUS

Yeah, but he's my son. Nothing strange about that. He's my own flesh and blood. But here you got the same name as this man here, and you're not even the same *color*.

RASHID

(*Improvising*) That's how we met. We're members of the International Same Name Club. Believe it or not, there are 846 Paul Benjamins in America. But only two in the New York metropolitan area. That's how Paul and I got to be such good friends. We're the only ones who show up at the meetings.

AUGGIE

(*Disgusted*) You're full of crap, kid. Why don't you just come clean and tell the man who you are?

By now, drawn by curiosity, DOREEN *has come over to where the four men are standing. She is carrying* JUNIOR *in her arms.*

CYRUS

(*Turning to* PAUL) What the hell's going on, mister?

PAUL

(*Shrugs, gestures to* RASHID) You better ask him.

AUGGIE

Yeah, Rashid baby, spill it.

DOREEN

(*In a loud voice*) Rashid?

PAUL

(*To* DOREEN) Sometimes. It's what you'd call a *nom de guerre*.

CYRUS

(*More and more confused*) What the hell are we talking about?

AUGGIE

(*To* RASHID). Come on. Tell him your real name. The name on your birth certificate.

Close-up of RASHID'S *face. His lower lip is trembling. Tears are beginning to form in his eyes.*

RASHID

(*Almost inaudibly*) Thomas.

CYRUS

Paul. Rashid. Thomas. Which one is it?

RASHID

Thomas.

AUGGIE

(*Impatient*) Come on, come on, you yellow belly. The whole thing. First name and last name.

RASHID

(*Trying to stall. Tears begin to slide down his cheeks*) What difference does it make?

PAUL

If it doesn't make any difference, why not just say it?

RASHID

(*To* PAUL, *his voice breaking*) I was going to tell him . . . but in my own time. In my own time. . . .

AUGGIE

No time like the present, man.

CYRUS

(*To* RASHID) Well?

RASHID

(*Blinking back the tears. Looking at* CYRUS) Thomas Cole. My name is Thomas Jefferson Cole.

CYRUS

(*Thunderstruck*) Are you making fun of me? I won't be mocked. Do you hear me? I won't let no punk kid stand there and mock me!

DOREEN

(*Upset*) Cyrus!

JUNIOR

(*Reaching out to* CYRUS) Dada.

RASHID

(*Standing his ground*) Like it or not, Cyrus, that's my name. Cole. Just like yours.

PAUL

(*To* CYRUS) Now ask him who his mother was.

CYRUS

(*Beside himself*) I don't like this. I don't like it one bit.

RASHID

Louisa Vail. Remember her, Cyrus?

CYRUS

You shut your mouth! You shut your mouth now!

Unable to control his rage, CYRUS hauls off and slugs RASHID in the face. RASHID falls to the ground.

AUGGIE

(*Alarmed*) Hey, cut it out!

AUGGIE takes a wild swing and clips CYRUS in the mouth. DOREEN, seeing her husband attacked, gives AUGGIE a quick kick in the shins. AUGGIE lets out a yell and starts hopping up and down in pain.

DOREEN

(*To AUGGIE*) Damn you. There'll be none of that on my watch, you dumpy bag of shit.

DOREEN puts down JUNIOR. The little boy immediately runs over to PAUL and whacks him on his bad arm. PAUL howls in pain and drops to the ground. The whole scene is quickly degenerating into chaos.

In the meantime, RASHID has climbed back to his feet. He lines up CYRUS, rushes toward him, and tackles him to the ground. The two of them roll around on the macadam, fighting with all their strength. After a moment, it looks as though CYRUS is getting the better of the struggle. AUGGIE tries to pull them apart, but to no avail.

DOREEN (*cont'd*)

(*Pounding CYRUS on the back with her fists*) Stop it! Stop it! You'll kill him, Cyrus!

DOREEN's shrieking voice brings the fight to a momentary halt. CYRUS rolls off RASHID and stands up. RASHID stands up as well. But the hatred between them has not subsided. CYRUS raises his hook.

DOREEN *(cont'd)*

(Screaming) He's your son, goddammit! He's your son! Do you want to kill your son!

Suddenly: CYRUS *stops. He lowers his arm and buries his face in his right hand. A moment later, he breaks down and weeps. His sobbing makes a terrible sound: pure, animal misery. He staggers around, then falls to his knees, unable to stop the tears.*

Cut to RASHID. *He stands there without moving, watching* CYRUS. *He drops his arms to his sides, unclenches his fists. Tears are pouring down his cheeks; he is breathing hard. Close-up of his face.*

Fade out.

67. EXT. DAY. THE PICNIC TABLE OUTSIDE COLE'S GARAGE

Some time later.

Long shot. We see everyone from the previous scene sitting at the picnic table eating lunch: fried chicken, lemonade, potato chips, etc. The image has the effect of a still life.

DOREEN *is sitting next to* CYRUS. RASHID *is holding* JUNIOR *in his arms, gently rocking him as the child drinks milk from a bottle with his eyes closed.* AUGGIE *and* PAUL *are sitting next to each other, eating chicken and listening to* DOREEN *(who is the only one who has the energy to talk).* CYRUS *looks sullen, defeated. Every once in a while, he steals a glance at* RASHID. RASHID, *however, pretends to ignore him, keeping his eyes fixed on the sleeping* JUNIOR.

At first we hear nothing. Then the camera moves in for a closer shot and we can begin to make out what DOREEN *is saying. As she speaks, we see Paul reach into his pocket and take out a tin of his little cigars. He leans forward and offers one to* CYRUS, *but* CYRUS *reaches into his own pocket and offers* PAUL *a big cigar. Paul accepts and lights up.* CYRUS *then lights up one of his own.*

                              DOREEN
. . . It might not have been the smartest investment, but it didn't cost much, and if Cyrus can make a go of it, we'll be able to take care of our needs. The man knows his way around cars, I'll tell you that, but the problem is this road is too far off the beaten track. Ever since they put in that mall, the traffic hasn't been too heavy around here. But you take the good with the bad, right? You do your best and hope that things work out . . .

Music begins to play. Cut to:

68. BLACK SCREEN

The music continues. After a few moments, the following words appear on the screen: THREE MONTHS LATER.

69. EXT: DAY. ELEVATED SUBWAY, BROOKLYN

The music continues to play. We see an elevated subway train snaking along the tracks in the dim November light.

70. INT: DAY. THE BROOKLYN CIGAR CO.

AUGGIE *is behind the counter, wearing a flannel shirt. The three* OTB MEN *are there with him, as in Scene 2.* JIMMY *enters the store and places a paper bag on the counter in front of* AUGGIE, *then slides around the counter and takes a seat beside* AUGGIE. JIMMY *studies his watch.* AUGGIE *removes a cup of take-out coffee from the bag. He lifts off the cover and steam rises from the cup. In the meantime, we see and hear the* OTB MEN *talking.*

TOMMY

Of course there's gonna be a war. You think they'd send five hundred thousand troops over there just to lie in the sun? I mean, there's plenty of beach, but not a hell of a lot of water. Half a million soldiers. It ain't no seaside holiday, you can bet on that.

JERRY

I don't know, Tommy. You think anyone gives a rat's ass about Kuwait? I read something about the head sheik over there. He marries a different virgin every Friday and then divorces her on Monday. You think we want to have our kids dying for a guy like that?

DENNIS

That's one way of upholding American values, eh, Tommy?

TOMMY

Laugh all you want. I'm telling you there's gonna be a war. With things in Russia falling apart, those slobs in the Pentagon'll be out of work unless they find a new enemy. They got this Saddam character now, and they're going to hit him with all they've got. Mark my words.

PAUL enters the store wearing a scarf and leather jacket. The OTB MEN stop talking and study him as he approaches the counter.

AUGGIE

(*To PAUL*) Hey, man, how's it going?

PAUL

Hi, Auggie.

Without waiting for PAUL to ask, AUGGIE turns around, pulls out two tins of Schimmelpennincks from the cigar cabinet, and places them on the counter.

AUGGIE

Two, right?

PAUL

Uh, better make it one.

AUGGIE

You usually get two.

PAUL

Yeah, I know, but I'm trying to cut down. (*Pause*) Somebody's worried about my health.

AUGGIE

(*Twitching his eyebrows playfully*) Ah-hah.

PAUL shrugs with embarrassment, then slowly breaks into a warm smile.

AUGGIE (*cont'd*)

And how's the work going these days, maestro?

PAUL

(*Still grinning. Absent-mindedly*) Fine. (*Pause. Pulling himself together*) Or it was until a couple of days ago. A guy from *The New York Times* called and asked me to write a Christmas story. They want to publish it on Christmas Day.

AUGGIE

That's a feather in your cap, man. The paper of record.

PAUL

Yeah, great. The problem is, I have four days to come up with something, and I don't have a single idea. (*Pause*) You know anything about Christmas stories?

AUGGIE

(*Blustering*) Christmas stories? Sure, I know a ton of 'em.

PAUL

Anything good?

AUGGIE

Good? Of course. Are you kidding? (*Pause*) I'll tell you what. Buy me lunch, my friend, and I'll tell you the best Christmas story you ever heard. How's that? And I guarantee every word of it is true.

PAUL

(*Smiling*) It doesn't have to be true. It just has to be good.

AUGGIE

(*Turning to* JIMMY ROSE) Take over the register while I'm gone, okay, Jimmy? (*Begins to extricate himself from behind the counter*)

JIMMY ROSE

You want me to do it, Auggie? You sure you want me to do it?

AUGGIE

Sure I'm sure. Just remember what I taught you. And don't let any of these kibbitzers cause you trouble. (*Gestures to* OTB MEN) You got a problem, you come and see me. I'll be down the block at Jack's. (*To* PAUL) Jack's okay?

PAUL

Jack's is fine.

PAUL *and* AUGGIE *leave the store together.*

71. INT: DAY. JACK'S RESTAURANT

A cramped and boisterous kosher delicatessen with sports photographs on the walls: old Brooklyn Dodger teams, the 1969 Mets, a portrait of Jackie Robinson. PAUL *and* AUGGIE *are sitting at a table in the back, studying the menus.*

PAUL

(*Closing menu*) I have to pee. If the waiter comes, order me a corned beef on rye and a ginger ale, okay?

AUGGIE

You got it.

PAUL stands up and leaves to go to the men's room. Alone at the table, AUGGIE glances down at the empty chair next to him and sees a copy of The New York Post. *The paper is open to an article with a headline that reads: "SHOOTOUT IN BROOKLYN." AUGGIE bends over to inspect the article more closely. Close-up of the article. We see photographs of CHARLES CLEMM (the CREEPER) and ROBERT GOODWIN and their names in the captions. A secondary headline reads: "ROBBERS KILLED IN JEWEL HEIST." In the meantime, as AUGGIE continues to study the article, the WAITER arrives to take his order. He is a round, balding, middle-aged man with a weary expression on his face.*

WAITER (*off*)

What'll it be, Auggie?

AUGGIE

(*Looking up*) Uh . . . (*pointing to PAUL's empty place*) my friend over here would like a corned beef on rye and a ginger ale.

Shot of WAITER holding pencil and order pad.

WAITER

And what about for you?

AUGGIE

(*Reading the paper again. Suddenly remembers the WAITER is there*) Huh?

WAITER

What about for you?

AUGGIE

For me? (*pause*) I'll have the same thing. (*Looks down at the article again*)

147

WAITER

Do me a favor, will you?

AUGGIE

(*Glancing up again*) What's that, Sol?

WAITER

Next time, when you want two corned beef sandwiches, say, "Two corned beef sandwiches." When you want two ginger ales, say, "Two ginger ales."

AUGGIE

What's the difference?

WAITER

It's simpler, that's what. It makes things go faster.

AUGGIE

(*Mystified. Humoring the* WAITER) Uh, sure, Sol. Anything you say. Instead of saying, "One corned beef sandwich," and then, "Another corned beef sandwich," I'll say, "Two corned beef sandwiches."

WAITER

(*Deadpan*) Thanks. I knew you'd understand.

The WAITER *leaves.* AUGGIE *looks down at the article again.* PAUL *returns and sits down in his chair across from* AUGGIE.

PAUL

(*Settling in*) So. Are we ready?

AUGGIE

Ready. Any time you are.

PAUL

I'm all ears.

AUGGIE

Okay. (*Pause. Thinks*) You remember how you once asked me how I started taking pictures? Well, this is the story of how I got my first camera. As a matter of fact, it's the only camera I've ever had. Are you following me so far?

PAUL

Every word.

AUGGIE

(*Close-up of* AUGGIE's *face*) Okay. (*Pause*) So this is the story of how it happened. (*Pause*) Okay. (*Pause*) It was the summer of seventy-six, back when I first started working for Vinnie. The summer of the bicentennial. (*Pause*) A kid came in one morning and started stealing things from the store. He's standing by the rack of paperbacks near the front window stuffing skin magazines under his shirt. It was crowded around the counter just then, so I didn't see him at first. . . .

AUGGIE's *face dissolves into* PAUL's. *Black-and-white footage begins: we see* AUGGIE *acting out the events he describes to* PAUL. *This scene exactly duplicates the events shown earlier in Scenes 2 and 3—with one difference. The thief is now* ROGER GOODWIN, *the same person who beat up* PAUL *in Scene 54, the same person whose picture* AUGGIE *has just noticed in the newspaper. The events unfold in silence, accompanied by* AUGGIE's *voice-over narration.*

AUGGIE (*voice-over*)

But once I noticed what he was up to, I started to shout. He took off like a jackrabbit, and by the time I managed to get out from behind the counter, he was already tearing down Seventh Avenue. I chased after him for about half a block, and then I gave up. He'd dropped something along the way, and since I didn't feel like running anymore, I bent down to see what it was.

We see AUGGIE *chasing the kid, giving up, and bending down for the wallet. He starts walking back to the store.*

AUGGIE (*voice-over*)

It turned out to be his wallet. There wasn't any money inside, but his driver's license was there, along with three or four snapshots. I suppose I could have called the cops and had him arrested. I had his name and address from the license, but I felt kind of sorry for him. He was just a measly little punk, and once I looked at those pictures in his wallet, I couldn't bring myself to feel very angry at him . . .

We see AUGGIE *examining the pictures. Close-ups of the pictures.*

AUGGIE (*voice-over*)

Roger Goodwin. That was his name. In one of the pictures, I remember, he was standing next to his mother. In another one, he was holding some trophy he got from school and smiling like he just won the Irish Sweepstakes. I just didn't have the heart. A poor kid from Brooklyn without much going for him, and who cared about a couple of dirty magazines, anyway? . . .

Cut to Jack's Restaurant. The WAITER *arrives at the table with their orders.*

WAITER

Here you go, boys. Two corned beef sandwiches. Two ginger ales. The fast way. The simple way. (*He leaves*)

PAUL

(*Putting mustard on his sandwich*) And?

AUGGIE

(*Taking a sip of his drink*) So I held onto the wallet. Every once in a while I'd get a little urge to send it back to him, but I kept delaying and never did anything about it. (*Puts mustard on his sandwich*) Then Christmas rolls around, and I'm stuck with nothing to do. Vinnie was going to invite me over, but his mother got sick, and he and his wife had to go down to Florida at the last minute. (*Takes a bite of the sandwich, chews*) So I'm sitting in my apartment that morning, feeling a little sorry for myself, and then I see Roger Goodwin's wallet lying on a shelf in the kitchen. I figure what the hell, why not do something nice for once, and I put on my coat and go out to return the wallet. . . .

Cut to black-and-white footage: the housing projects in Boerum Hill. We see AUGGIE *wandering alone among the buildings, bundled up against the cold. At the same time, we hear:*

AUGGIE (*voice-over*)

The address was over in Boerum Hill, somewhere in the projects. It was freezing out that day, and I remember getting lost a few times trying to find the right building. Everything looks the same in that place, and you keep going over the same ground thinking you're somewhere else. Anyway, I finally get to the apartment I'm looking for and ring the bell. . . .

Shot of AUGGIE *walking down a corridor in the housing projects; graffiti on the cinder-block walls. He stops in front of a door and pushes the buzzer.*

AUGGIE (*voice-over*)

Nothing happens. I assume no one's there, but I try again just to make sure. I wait a little longer, and just when I'm about to give up, I hear someone shuffling to the door. An old woman's voice asks, "Who's there?" and I say I'm looking for Roger Goodwin. "Is that you, Roger?" the old woman says, and then she undoes about fifteen locks and opens the door. . . .

Shot of a very old black woman, GRANNY ETHEL, *opening the door. A rapturous, expectant smile is on her face. Even though the scene unfolds in silence, we see* AUGGIE *and* GRANNY ETHEL *mouthing the dialogue that* AUGGIE *repeats to* PAUL.

AUGGIE (*voice-over*)

She has to be at least eighty, maybe ninety years old, and the first thing I notice about her is she's blind. "I knew you'd come, Roger," she says. "I knew you wouldn't forget your Granny Ethel on Christmas." And then she opens her arms as if she's about to hug me.

We see AUGGIE *hesitate for a second. As he reports the next little part of the story, we see him giving in, opening his arms, and hugging* GRANNY ETHEL. *The hug is then repeated in somewhat slower motion; then again in slow motion; then again, in very slow motion; then again in motion so slow that it appears as a sequence of still photographs.*

AUGGIE (*voice-over*)

I don't have much time to think, you understand. I had to say something real fast, and before I knew what was happening, I could hear the words coming out of my mouth. "That's right, Granny Ethel," I said. "I came back to see you on Christmas." Don't ask me why I did it. I don't have any idea. It just came out that way, and suddenly this old woman's hugging me there in front of the door, and I'm hugging her back. It was like a game we both decided to play—without having to discuss the rules. I mean, that woman *knew* I wasn't her grandson. She was old and dotty, but she wasn't so far gone that she couldn't tell the difference between a stranger and her own flesh and blood. But it made her happy to pretend, and since I had nothing better to do anyway, I was happy to go along with her. . . .

AUGGIE *and* GRANNY ETHEL *enter the apartment and sit down in chairs in the living room. We see them talking, laughing. Meanwhile, we hear:*

AUGGIE (*voice-over*)

So we went into the apartment and spent the day together. Every time she asked me a question about how I was, I would lie to her. I told her I'd found a good job in a cigar store, I told her I was about to get married, I told her a hundred pretty stories, and she made like she believed every one of them. "That's fine, Roger," she would say, nodding her head and smiling. "I always knew things would work out for you. . . ."

The camera pans slowly through GRANNY ETHEL's *apartment, lingering momentarily on various objects. Among other things, we see portraits of Martin Luther King, Jr., John F. Kennedy, family photographs, balls of yarn, knitting needles. By the time this visual tour is completed, we see* AUGGIE *entering the apartment again, wearing his coat and carrying a large bag of groceries. As described in the simultaneous narration:*

AUGGIE (*voice-over*)
After a while, I started getting hungry. There didn't seem to be much food in the house, so I went out to a store in the neighborhood and brought back a mess of stuff. A precooked chicken, vegetable soup, a bucket of potato salad, all kinds of things. Ethel had a couple of bottles of wine stashed in her bedroom, and so between us we managed to put together a fairly decent Christmas dinner. . . .

We see AUGGIE *and* GRANNY ETHEL *at the dining-room table: eating the food, drinking the wine, talking.*

AUGGIE (*voice-over*)
We both got a little tipsy from the wine, I remember, and after the meal was over we went out to sit in the living room where the chairs were more comfortable. . . .

We see AUGGIE *leading* GRANNY ETHEL *by the arm and helping her into a chair. Then* AUGGIE *leaves the living room and walks to the bathroom down the hall.*

AUGGIE (*voice-over*)
I had to take a pee, so I excused myself and went to the bathroom down the hall. That's where things took another turn. It was ditsy enough doing my little jig as Ethel's grandson, but what I did next was positively crazy, and I've never forgiven myself for it. . . .

We see AUGGIE *in the bathroom. As he pees, we see the boxes of cameras, just as he describes them.*

AUGGIE (*voice-over*)

I go into the bathroom, and stacked up against the wall next to the shower, I see a pile of six or seven cameras. Brand-new, thirty-five-millimeter cameras, still in their boxes. I figure this is the work of the real Roger, a storage place for one of his recent hauls. I've never taken a picture in my life, and I've certainly never stolen anything, but the moment I see those cameras sitting in the bathroom, I decide I want one of them for myself. Just like that. And without even stopping to think about it, I tuck one of the boxes under my arm and go back to the living room. . . .

We see AUGGIE return to the living room with the camera. GRANNY ETHEL is sleeping soundly in her chair. AUGGIE puts the camera down, clears the table, and washes the dishes in the kitchen.

AUGGIE (*voice-over*)

I couldn't have been gone for more than three minutes, but in that time Granny Ethel had fallen asleep. Too much Chianti, I suppose. I went into the kitchen to wash the dishes, and she slept on through the whole racket, snoring like a baby. There didn't seem to be any point in disturbing her, so I decided to leave. I couldn't even write a note to say good-bye, seeing that she was blind and all, so I just left. I put her grandson's wallet on the table, picked up the camera again, and walked out of the apartment. . . .

We see AUGGIE bending over the sleeping GRANNY ETHEL and deciding not to wake her. We see him put the wallet on the table and pick up the camera. We see him walking out of the apartment. Shot of the closing door.

AUGGIE (*voice-over*)

And that's the end of the story.

Cut to PAUL's face. PAUL and AUGGIE are sitting at the table, eating the last bites of their sandwiches.

Did you ever go back to see her?

AUGGIE

Once, about three or four months later. I felt so bad about stealing the camera, I hadn't even used it yet. I finally made up my mind to return it, but Granny Ethel wasn't there anymore. Someone else had moved into the apartment, and he couldn't tell me where she was.

PAUL

She probably died.

AUGGIE

Yeah, probably.

PAUL

Which means that she spent her last Christmas with you.

AUGGIE

I guess so. I never thought of it that way.

PAUL

It was a good deed, Auggie. It was a nice thing you did for her.

AUGGIE

I lied to her, and then I stole from her. I don't see how you can call that a good deed.

PAUL

You made her happy. And the camera was stolen anyway. It's not as if the person you took it from really owned it.

AUGGIE

Anything for art, eh, Paul?

PAUL

I wouldn't say that. But at least you've put the camera to good use.

AUGGIE

And now you've got your Christmas story, don't you?

PAUL

(*Pause. Thinks*) Yes, I suppose I do.

PAUL looks at AUGGIE. A wicked grin is spreading across AUGGIE's face. The look in his eyes is so mysterious, so fraught with the glow of some inner delight, that PAUL begins to suspect that AUGGIE has made the whole thing up. He is about to ask AUGGIE if he has been putting him on—but then stops, realizing that AUGGIE would never tell him. PAUL smiles.

PAUL (*cont'd*)

Bullshit is a real talent, Auggie. To make up a good story, a person has to know how to push all the right buttons. (*Pause*) I'd say you're up there among the masters.

AUGGIE

What do you mean?

PAUL

I mean, it's a good story.

AUGGIE

Shit. If you can't share your secrets with your friends, what kind of friend are you?

PAUL

Exactly. Life just wouldn't be worth living, would it?

AUGGIE is still smiling. PAUL smiles back at him. AUGGIE lights a cigarette; PAUL lights a little cigar. They blow smoke into the air, still smiling at each other.

156

The camera follows the smoke as it rises toward the ceiling. Close-up of the smoke. Hold for three, four beats.

The screen goes black. Music begins to play.

Final credits.

auggie wren's christmas story

I heard this story from Auggie Wren. Since Auggie doesn't come off too well in it, at least not as well as he'd like to, he's asked me not to use his real name. Other than that, the whole business about the lost wallet and the blind woman and the Christmas dinner is just as he told it to me.

Auggie and I have known each other for close to eleven years now. He works behind the counter of a cigar store on Court Street in downtown Brooklyn, and since it's the only store that carries the little Dutch cigars I like to smoke, I go in there fairly often. For a long time, I didn't give much thought to Auggie Wren. He was the strange little man who wore a hooded blue sweatshirt and sold me cigars and magazines, the impish, wisecracking character who always had something funny to say about the weather or the Mets or the politicians in Washington, and that was the extent of it.

But then one day several years ago he happened to be looking through a magazine in the store, and he stumbled across a review of one of my books. He knew it was me because a photograph accompanied the review, and after that things changed between us. I was no longer just another customer to Auggie, I had become a distinguished person. Most people couldn't care less about books and writers, but it turned out that Auggie considered himself an artist. Now that he had cracked the secret of who I was, he embraced me as an ally, a confidant, a brother-in-arms. To tell the truth, I found it rather embarrassing. Then, almost inevitably, a moment came when he asked if I would be willing to look at his photographs. Given his enthusiasm and goodwill, there didn't seem to be any way I could turn him down.

God knows what I was expecting. At the very least, it wasn't what Auggie showed me the next day. In a small, windowless room at the back of the store, he opened a cardboard box and pulled out twelve identical black photo albums. This was his life's work, he said, and it didn't take him more than five minutes a day to do it. Every morning for the past twelve years, he had stood at the corner of Atlantic Avenue and Clinton Street at precisely seven o'clock and had taken a single color photograph of precisely the same view. The project now ran to more than four thousand photographs. Each album represented a different year, and all the pictures were laid out in sequence, from January 1 to December 31, with the dates carefully recorded under each one.

As I flipped through the albums and began to study Auggie's work, I didn't know what to think. My first impression was that it was the oddest, most bewildering thing I had ever seen. All the pictures were the same. The whole project was a numbing onslaught of repetition, the same street and the same buildings over and over again, an unrelenting delirium of redundant images. I couldn't think of anything to say to Auggie, so I continued turning pages, nodding my head in feigned appreciation. Auggie himself seemed unperturbed, watching me with a broad smile on his face, but after I'd been at it for several minutes, he suddenly interrupted me and said, "You're going too fast. You'll never get it if you don't slow down."

He was right, of course. If you don't take the time to look, you'll never manage to see anything. I picked up another album and forced myself to go more deliberately. I paid closer attention to details, took note of shifts in the weather, watched for the changing angles of light as the seasons advanced. Eventually, I was able to detect subtle differences in the traffic flow, to anticipate the rhythm of the different days (the commotion of workday mornings, the relative stillness of weekends, the contrast between Saturdays and Sundays). And then, little by little, I began to recognize the faces of the people in the background, the passers-by on their way to work, the same people in the same spot every morning, living an instant of their lives in the field of Auggie's camera.

Once I got to know them, I began to study their postures, the way they carried themselves from one morning to the next, trying to discover their moods from these surface indications, as if I could imagine stories for them, as if I could penetrate the invisible dramas locked inside their bodies. I picked up another album. I was no longer bored, no longer puzzled as I had been at first. Auggie was photographing time, I realized, both natural time and human time, and he was doing it by planting himself in one tiny corner of the world and willing it to be his own, by standing guard in the space he had chosen for himself. As he watched me pore over his work, Auggie continued to smile with pleasure. Then, almost as if he had been reading my thoughts, he began to recite a line from Shakespeare. "Tomorrow and tomorrow and tomorrow," he muttered under his breath, "time creeps on its petty pace." I understood then that he knew exactly what he was doing.

That was more than two thousand pictures ago. Since that day, Auggie and I have discussed his work many times, but it was only last week that I learned how he acquired his camera and started taking pictures in the first place. That was the subject of the story he told me, and I'm still struggling to make sense of it.

Earlier that same week, a man from the *New York Times* called me and asked if I would be willing to write a short story that would appear in the paper on Christmas morning. My first impulse was to say no, but the man was very charming and persistent, and by the end of the conversation I told him I would give it a try. The moment I hung up the phone, however, I fell into a deep panic. What did I know about Christmas? I asked myself. What did I know about writing short stories on commission?

I spent the next several days in despair, warring with the ghosts of Dickens, O. Henry, and other masters of the Yuletide spirit. The very phrase "Christmas story" had unpleasant associations for me, evoking dreadful outpourings of hypocritical mush and treacle. Even at their best, Christmas stories were no more than wish-fulfillment dreams, fairy tales for adults, and I'd be damned if I'd ever allowed myself to write something like that. And yet, how could anyone propose to write an unsentimental Christmas story? It was a contradiction in terms, an impossibility, an out-and-out conundrum. One might just as well try to imagine a racehorse without legs, or a sparrow without wings.

I got nowhere. On Thursday I went out for a long walk, hoping the air would clear my head. Just past noon, I stopped in at the cigar store to replenish my supply, and there was Auggie, standing behind the counter as always. He asked me how I was. Without really meaning to, I found myself unburdening my troubles to him. "A Christmas story?" he said after I had finished. "Is that all? If you buy me lunch, my friend, I'll tell you the best Christmas story you ever heard. And I guarantee that every word of it is true."

We walked down the block to Jack's, a cramped and boisterous delicatessen with good pastrami sandwiches and photographs of old Dodgers teams hanging on the walls. We found a table at the back, ordered our food, and then Auggie launched into his story.

"It was the summer of seventy-two," he said. "A kid came in one morning and started stealing things from the store. He must have been about nineteen or twenty, and I don't think I've ever seen a more pathetic shoplifter in my life. He's standing by the rack of paperbacks along the far wall and stuffing books into the pockets of his raincoat. It was crowded around the counter just then, so I didn't see him at first. But once I noticed what he was up to, I started to shout. He took off like a jackrabbit, and by the time I managed to get out from behind the counter, he was already tearing down Atlantic Avenue. I chased after him for about half a block, and then I gave up. He'd dropped something along the way, and since I didn't feel like running anymore, I bent down to see what it was.

"It turned out to be his wallet. There wasn't any money inside, but his driver's license was there along with three or four snapshots. I suppose I could have called the cops and had him arrested. I had his name and address from the license, but I felt kind of sorry for him. He was just a measly little punk, and once I looked at those pictures in his wallet, I couldn't bring myself to feel very angry at him. Robert Goodwin. That was his name. In one of the pictures, I remember, he was standing with his arm around his mother or grandmother. In another one, he was sitting there at age nine or ten dressed in a baseball uniform with a big smile on his face. I just didn't have the heart. He was probably on dope now, I figured. A poor kid from Brooklyn without much going for him, and who cared about a couple of trashy paperbacks anyway?

"So I held onto the wallet. Every once in a while I'd get a little urge to send it back to him, but I kept delaying and never did anything about it. Then Christmas rolls around and I'm stuck with nothing to do. The boss usually invites me over to his house to spend the day, but that year he and his family were down in Florida visiting relatives. So I'm sitting in my apartment that morning feeling a little sorry for myself, and then I see Robert Goodwin's wallet lying on a shelf in the kitchen. I figure what the hell, why not do something nice for once, and I put on my coat and go out to return the wallet in person.

"The address was over in Boerum Hill, somewhere in the projects. It was freezing out that day, and I remember getting lost a few times trying to find the right building. Everything looks the same in that place, and you keep going over the same ground thinking you're somewhere else. Anyway, I finally get to the apartment I'm looking for and ring the bell. Nothing happens. I assume no one's there, but I try again just to make sure. I wait a little longer, and just when I'm about to give up, I hear someone shuffling to the door. An old woman's voice asks who's there, and I say I'm looking for Robert Goodwin. 'Is that you, Robert?' the old woman says, and then she undoes about fifteen locks and opens the door.

"She has to be at least eighty, maybe ninety years old, and the first thing I notice about her is that she's blind. 'I knew you'd come, Robert,' she says. 'I knew you wouldn't forget your Granny Ethel on Christmas.' And then she opens her arms as if she's about to hug me.

"I didn't have much time to think, you understand. I had to say something real fast, and before I knew what was happening, I could hear the words coming out of my mouth. 'That's right, Granny Ethel,' I said. 'I came back to see you on Christmas.' Don't ask me why I did it. I don't have any idea. Maybe I didn't want to disappoint her or something, I don't know. It just came out that way, and then this old woman was suddenly hugging me there in front of the door, and I was hugging her back.

"I didn't exactly say that I was her grandson. Not in so many words, at least, but that was the implication. I wasn't trying to trick her, though. It was like a game we'd both decided to play—without having to discuss the rules. I mean, that woman *knew* I wasn't her grandson Robert. She was old and dotty, but she wasn't so far gone that she couldn't tell the difference between a stranger and her own flesh and blood. But it made her happy to pretend, and since I had nothing better to do anyway, I was happy to go along with her.

"So we went into the apartment and spent the day together. The place was a real dump, I might add, but what else can you expect from a blind woman who does her own housekeeping? Every time she asked me a question about how I was, I would lie to her. I told her I'd found a good job working in a cigar store, I told her I was about to get married, I told her a hundred pretty stories, and she made like she believed every one of them. 'That's fine, Robert,' she would say, nodding her head and smiling. 'I always knew things would work out for you.'

"After a while, I started getting pretty hungry. There didn't seem to be much food in the house, so I went out to a store in the neighborhood and brought back a mess of stuff. A precooked chicken, vegetable soup, a bucket of potato salad, a chocolate cake, all kinds of things. Ethel had a couple of bottles of wine stashed in her bedroom, and so between us we managed to put together a fairly decent Christmas dinner. We both got a little tipsy from the wine, I remember, and after the meal was over we went out to sit in the living room, where the chairs were more comfortable. I had to take a pee, so I excused myself and went to the bathroom down the hall. That's where things took yet another turn. It was ditsy enough doing my little jig as Ethel's grandson, but what I did next was positively crazy, and I've never forgiven myself for it.

"I go into the bathroom, and stacked up against the wall next to the shower, I see a pile of six or seven cameras. Brand-new thirty-five-millimeter cameras, still in their boxes, top-quality merchandise. I figure this is the work of the real Robert, a storage place for one of his recent hauls. I've never taken a picture in my life, and I've certainly never stolen anything, but the moment I see those cameras sitting in the bathroom, I decide I want one of them for myself. Just like that. And without even stopping to think about it, I tuck one of the boxes under my arm and go back to the living room.

"I couldn't have been gone for more than a few minutes, but in that time Granny Ethel had fallen asleep in her chair. Too much Chianti, I suppose. I went into the kitchen to wash the dishes, and she slept on through the whole racket, snoring like a baby. There didn't seem to be any point in disturbing her, so I decided to leave. I couldn't even write a note to say good-bye, seeing that she was blind and all, and so I just left. I put her grandson's wallet on the table, picked up the camera again, and walked out of the apartment. And that's the end of the story."

"Did you ever go back to see her?" I asked.

"Once," he said. "About three or four months later. I felt so bad about stealing the camera, I hadn't even used it yet. I finally made up my mind to return it, but Ethel wasn't there anymore. I don't know what happened to her, but someone else had moved into the apartment, and he couldn't tell me where she was."

"She probably died."

"Yeah, probably."

"Which means that she spent her last Christmas with you."

"I guess so. I never thought of it that way."

"It was a good deed, Auggie. It was a nice thing you did for her."

"I lied to her, and then I stole from her. I don't see how you can call that a good deed."

"You made her happy. And the camera was stolen anyway. It's not as if the person you took it from really owned it."

"Anything for art, eh. Paul?"

"I wouldn't say that. But at least you've put the camera to good use."

"And now you've got your Christmas story, don't you?"

"Yes," I said. "I suppose I do."

I paused for a moment, studying Auggie as a wicked grin spread across his face. I couldn't be sure, but the look in his eyes at that moment was so mysterious, so fraught with the glow of some inner delight, that it suddenly occurred to me that he had made the whole thing up. I was about to ask him if he'd been putting me on, but then I realized he would never tell. I had been tricked into believing him, and that was the only thing that mattered. As long as there's one person to believe it, there's no story that can't be true.

"You're an ace, Auggie," I said. "Thanks for being so helpful."

"Any time," he answered, still looking at me with that maniacal light in his eyes. "After all, if you can't share your secrets with your friends, what kind of a friend are you?"

"I guess I owe you one."

"No you don't. Just put it down the way I told it to you, and you don't owe me a thing."

"Except the lunch."

"That's right. Except the lunch."

I returned Auggie's smile with a smile of my own, and then I called out to the waiter and asked for the check.

blue in the face

"this is brooklyn.
we don't go by numbers."

Blue in the Face is not a sequel to *Smoke*. Although it draws on settings and characters from that film, it sprints off in an entirely new direction. Its spirit is comic; its engine is words; its guiding principle is spontaneity. As producer Peter Newman aptly put it when first presented with the idea: it's a project in which the inmates take over the asylum.

The original plan for *Blue in the Face* was far simpler than the swirling free-for-all it eventually became. The premise was to go back into the cigar store that appears at the beginning and end of *Smoke* and create a little portrait of Auggie Wren's world. Minor characters from the first film would become major characters in the second. Besides Auggie, just one other major character from *Smoke* would participate—but only in a minor role.

Our approach to all this was primitive in the extreme. We would invent situations for these characters and have each one last the length of a roll of film, approximately ten minutes. Two takes per scene would be sufficient, we felt. One to warm up and then another to get it right. We would present each skit as a chapter, continuous and uncut, and add musical interludes between the chapters for the sake of variety. With only three days of filming available to us, we didn't see how there would be time for much else.

The notes I prepared for the actors were written in extreme haste, literally dashed off in the time it took to put the words on paper. Their sole purpose was to rough out the general contents of each scene, and they were never meant to be anything more than crude signposts, a rapid shorthand to remind us of what we thought we were supposed to be doing. Even as I typed them up, I knew that everything was subject to change.

Not only were we asking the actors to improvise their lines, we were counting on them to create entire scenes without any rehearsals. The success or failure of the film was in their hands, and we had to give them absolute freedom to go where they wanted to go.

Most of the situations were cooked up in the back seat of a car—riding downtown in evening traffic after the *Smoke* dailies. Wayne and I would throw out ideas to each other at random: What if? . . . How about? . . . What do you think of? . . . We figured that we would need eleven or twelve scenes, both as a minimum and a maximum. As a minimum because we knew in advance that much of what we shot wouldn't work, and we didn't want to get caught with too little material. As a maximum because we didn't think it would be possible to shoot more than four scenes a day.

Miramax gave the go-ahead in early June. *Smoke* was in the middle of production then, and so while Wayne went to the set every day to work on that film, I met with the actors in restaurants and offices around town to prepare for the other. Little by little, new actors joined the cast and new roles had to be devised for them (Dot, Pete, Bob, et al.), but our basic approach remained the same: give the performers their marks, turn on the camera, and see what happened.

What happened proved to be fairly extraordinary. Some scenes failed, some actors were better at improvising than others, but by and large everyone performed at an astonishingly high level. We accumulated nine or ten hours of footage during those three days (July 11, 12, 13), and the minute we saw the results, we knew that we would have to throw our original conception of the film out the window. Situations would have to be broken up, a new and complex order of scenes would have to be found, and when normal editing devices didn't work, we would have to resort to jumpcuts, dissolves, and other little tricks to keep the action moving.

It was at this point that editor Chris Tellefsen became a full partner in the enterprise. Working closely with Wayne and myself, he shaped the material we gave him into the wild and wooly film it now is. There was no script to follow, no plot to rely on, no preordained structure to help simplify decisions. It was all a matter of instinct, of understanding the strengths and weaknesses of the original footage, and then drawing on those strengths to assemble the finished movie. Wayne and I spent countless hours in the cutting room with Chris, trying out scores of different ideas in an ongoing triangular conversation, and his energy and patience were unflagging. In every sense of the word, he is a co-author of the film.

What this film is, however, is difficult to pin down. Yes, it's funny. Yes, it's vulgar and rambunctious and silly—and to see it as anything other than a high-spirited celebration of daily life in Brooklyn would be a serious mistake. And yet, for all its nonsense, I believe there's something in *Blue in the Face* that makes it more than just a frivolous diversion. A certain rawness, perhaps. A certain way of rolling with the punches that's best summed up in the line Giancarlo Esposito delivers to Lily Tomlin: "This is Brooklyn. We don't go by numbers." People smoke like chimneys, people argue, people get in each other's faces. They roll up their sleeves and yell, they insult each other, they say obnoxious things. Nearly every scene in *Blue in the Face* is about conflict. The characters are embattled, highly opinionated, relentless in their anger. And yet, when all is said and done, the film is genuinely amusing, and one walks away from it with a feeling of great human warmth. I find that interesting. Perhaps that means a certain degree of conflict is good for us. Perhaps we need an occasional release from all the high-minded pieties that tell us how we're supposed to talk to each other. I'm not saying this is so, but it's definitely a question worth pondering.

However you want to describe it, the film we put together from those three days of shooting turned out to be much richer and funnier than we were expecting. There were obvious weak spots, but all in all the experiment had paid off. When we screened it in October for our backers, Harvey and Bob Weinstein, they responded enthusiastically. Good as they felt it was, however, they were convinced it could be even better. It was hard to disagree with them. They offered to finance another three days of shooting, and the moment we left their office, the mad scramble to go back into production began. The actors and crew had to be reassembled, new actors had to be hired, replacements for certain jobs had to be found, and it all had to be done in no time flat. Our main actor, Harvey Keitel, was leaving the country in nine days to begin work on another film, and he wouldn't be returning to New York for several months. It was now or never.

Somehow, we managed to pull it off, and on October 27 we all went back to the cigar store for another round of shooting. We wrapped the following Monday, Halloween. By the time we were ready to leave the set, it was dark outside, and the Brooklyn streets were filled with children dressed in costumes. Some of them, mistaking the Brooklyn Cigar Company for an actual store, wandered in to ask for candy. The store itself might have been make-believe, but it had real candy in it, and so we filled the kids' trick-or-treat bags with chewing gum and chocolate bars from the shelves. It seemed like a fitting way to say good-bye to our imaginary world, the perfect ending for *Blue in the Face*.

December 29, 1994

blue in the face

Situations created by
Paul Auster and Wayne Wang

Directed by
Wayne Wang and Paul Auster

Produced by
Greg Johnson, Peter Newman, and Diana Phillips

Director of Photography
Adam Holender

Editor
Christopher Tellefsen

Production Designer
Kalina Ivanov

Costumes
Claudia Brown

Executive Producers
Harvey Keitel, Bob Weinstein, and Harvey Weinstein

Still Photographers
Barry Wetcher and K.C. Baily

CAST

(In order of appearance)

Man with Unusual Glasses	**Lou Reed**
Auggie Wren	**Harvey Keitel**
Violet	**Mel Gorham**
Boy	**Sharif Rashed**
Young Woman	**Mira Sorvino**
Jerry	**José Zuniga**
Dennis	**Steve Gevedon**
Vinnie	**Victor Argo**
Sue	**Peggy Gormley**
Jimmy Rose	**Jared Harris**
Tommy	**Giancarlo Esposito**
Dot	**Roseanne**
Bob	**Jim Jarmusch**
Waffle Man	**Lily Tomlin**
Rapper	**Malik Yoba**
Pete	**Michael J. Fox**
Jackie Robinson	**Keith David**
Messenger	**Madonna**
Musicians	**John Lurie, Billy Martin, Calvin Weston**
Dancer	**RuPaul**
Brooklyn Residents	**Rusty Kanokogi, Sasalina Gambino, Cheif Bey, Ian Frazier, Luc Sante, Robert Jackson**

notes for the actors

July

1. PHILOSOPHERS

Cast: the Macanudo Lady, Auggie, Jimmy Rose, Tommy, Jerry, Dennis

Dennis walks into the store and tells the following, story: "Yesterday afternoon, I was walking down Seventh Avenue and saw this little twelve-year-old kid snatch a woman's purse. He just grabbed it off her shoulder and started tearing down the street. A lot of people were around, but nobody did anything, and there's this woman (not a bad-looking chick, I might add) screaming her lungs out on the sidewalk: 'Thief! Thief! He stole my purse!' So, upstanding citizen that I am, I take off after the kid. I finally nab the sucker a couple of blocks down the avenue . . . and then drag him back to the woman. At the very least, I figure I'll get a date with her for my act of heroism. At least a little hug or a kiss on the goddam cheek. By now a big crowd has gathered around the woman to see what all the fuss is about. 'Here he is,' I say to her, giving her back her purse, 'here he is, now let's call the cops.' But the bitch takes one look at him and says, 'I can't do it. He's too young. I can't be responsible for sending him to jail. He's just a baby.'

"This really pisses me off. After all I've done for her! Not only have I worked myself into a sweat, but I tore my goddamn shirt reaching for the kid . . . (points to his armpit) right here. Brand-new shirt

175

that was, one hundred percent silk. Cost me eighty-eight fucking dollars. 'Listen, lady,' I say to her, 'it's your duty as a citizen to call the cops. Is this the kind of city you want to live in? Where little kids are ripping off people's purses—and getting away with it? It's people like you who are turning New York into such a shit-hole. You won't take responsibility!' But she wouldn't back down. 'I won't do it,' she kept saying. 'I won't do it. He's just a child.'

"I was feeling pretty burned by now. Not only was I not going to see any action with this broad, but I'd chased the kid for nothing. So you know what I did? I ripped the purse out of the woman's hands and gave it back to the thief. Talk about a confused look. The kid was so frightened and mixed up by then, I thought he was going to shit his pants. 'Go on,' I said to him, 'it's yours. Get out of here. Just take it and go.' And, believe it or not, the kid went. He took off running down the street, just like before, and this time no one ran after him."

The others react and give their opinions. Auggie thinks Dennis did exactly the right thing. Tommy thinks Dennis should have gone to the cops himself. Jerry, expressing sympathy for the thief, says Dennis never should have chased him in the first place.

The men argue back and forth. The situation becomes more and more heated. Just when it is about to degenerate into a full-scale shouting match, an elegant woman in her thirties or forties enters the store . . .

WOMAN (*To AUGGIE*) A tin of Macanudos, please.
AUGGIE Your husband must like this brand a lot. This is about the tenth time you've come in this summer for Macanudos.
WOMAN My husband?
AUGGIE I don't mean to be nosy.
WOMAN Of course not. But my husband doesn't smoke. And besides, I'm not married to him anymore. Just to keep the record straight.

176

AUGGIE Oh.

WOMAN Just to keep the record straight, these babies are for me.

Jimmy Rose watches this exchange with growing wonder. He is smitten, head-over-heels in love with the Macanudo Lady. Just as she is about to leave:

JIMMY Miss . . . can I ask you a question?

WOMAN Of course . . .

JIMMY Would you let me kiss you . . . on the lips?

WOMAN What!

JIMMY Don't worry. We'll get married later. But first I want to see if you kiss good.

Just as Auggie begins to scold Jimmy for his crude behavior, the Macanudo Lady recovers her poise and gives Jimmy a kiss. Then she leaves the store.

A long discussion follows about sex and love. Everyone puts in his two cents, including Jimmy, who keeps repeating, "But that's what you guys always say." Tommy is the most amused. He commends Jimmy on his ability to say what he means. "I've wanted to say that to a hundred women on the street. I just haven't had the guts."

> The incident described in this scene is based on a real event. I heard it from my wife more than ten years ago, and it has stayed with me ever since: the quintessential New York tale, a story that embodies the social and moral dilemmas of contemporary urban life . . . with a weirdly comic twist.
>
> From the very start, we knew that this would be the first scene in the film. Not only would it capture the tone we wanted, but it would present the basic cast of characters and give a taste of everyday life in the cigar store. Unfortunately, this scene was shot early on the first day, before we abandoned our arbitrary rule of two takes per

177

scene. The actors were still warming up, and even though much good work was generated by the performances, the story of the woman's purse never emerged with sufficient clarity. *Philosophers* was edited in fifty-seven different ways, and no one was ever satisfied with the results. The failure of this episode was the primary reason for shooting again in October.

As for the Macanudo Lady, we filmed that bit as a separate scene—but the results were equally disappointing. The Macanudo Lady had been a minor character in *Smoke*, but I had cut her out of the script in the final draft. It seemed like a good idea to resurrect her for *Blue in the Face*, but whatever it was we were hoping for never quite materialized on screen.

2. BELGIAN WAFFLES

Cast: the Belgian Waffle Man, Jerry, Tommy, Dennis, Violet, John Lurie and his two drummers

A scruffy panhandler is posted outside the door of the Brooklyn Cigar Company. One by one, Auggie and the three OTB Men come out, and one by one he asks them the same question: "Excuse me, sir. Could you spare four dollars and ninety-five cents? That's how much I need for a Belgian waffle and one scoop of pistachio ice cream. Right now, that's the only thing in the world I want. I want it so bad, I can't stand it anymore. A Belgian waffle . . . with one big scoop of pistachio ice cream."

First encounter: Jerry. He's sympathetic, but he doesn't have a penny. Turns his pockets inside out to prove it.

Second encounter: Tommy. He tells him to get lost.

Third encounter: Dennis. He lectures the bum on the evils of sugar. "I'll give you a couple of bucks for a Big Mac," he says, "but I know you'll use them to buy that waffle, and I don't want to contribute to diabetes and heart disease."

Fourth encounter: Auggie. At first he resists, but the bum's appeal is so strange and his manner so bizarre that he eventually gives in and hands the guy a buck. The Waffle Man is very touched and grateful. "Thank you, kind sir," he says. "A few more people like you, and maybe my dream will come true. (*Pause*) Hey, that rhymes, doesn't it? (*Recites*): A few more people like you/And maybe my dream will come true!"

He wanders off, reciting the poem to himself.

A moment later, Violet appears. She kisses Auggie on the cheek.

AUGGIE Hey, Violet. You like Belgian waffles?
VIOLET Belgian waffles? You think I want to eat that crap and mess up a body like this? Forget those Belgian waffles, Auggie. I give you a French kiss instead.
AUGGIE Right here?
(They kiss).
VIOLET You remember those steps I taught you last week, Auggie?
AUGGIE Sure, sure. One-two-three, one-two-three.
VIOLET Let's see.
(He demonstrates; she instructs)

John Lurie and his two drummers are sitting in chairs on the sidewalk with their instruments. Lurie is grinning from ear to ear.

AUGGIE What are you smiling about?
LURIE You're about the worst dancer I ever saw.
AUGGIE Yeah, well, it's hard to dance without any music. Gotta feel the beat.
VIOLET Yeah. Can you guys play a rhumba?

179

They start playing. Violet and Auggie dance. After a few moments, the musicians stop. Lurie says to Auggie: "Music or no music, you're still the worst dancer I ever saw."

The Belgian Waffle Man was another minor character cut from the screenplay of *Smoke*—and, once again, the scene is based on a real event. I met the Waffle Man on a Brooklyn street corner about five years ago. The pitch he delivered to me was precisely the one I put in the notes, word for word.

What impressed me most about him was his determination, the absolute specificity of what he was after. Here was a man who knew what he wanted, and no matter how many people he had to beg from, no matter how many hours or days it took him, he was going to get that Belgian waffle. Since then, the words "Belgian waffle" have been fraught with meaning for me. They are a metaphor for patience and single-mindedness, for daydreams and the pursuit of pleasure, for the irreducible quirkiness of human desires.

However simple the Waffle Man's role might have been, we had a great deal of trouble finding an actor to play it. One person said yes and then backed out, and then a couple of other performers turned us down. Time was running short, and it began to look as if we would have to scratch the scene. Then, just days before we were supposed to start filming, Lily Tomlin accepted the role. Over the course of one weekend, I must have talked on the telephone with her four or five times. The first idea was for her to play it as a woman, but when I told her that wasn't strictly necessary, she decided to do it as a man. Everything about her character she prepared herself: the costume, the voice, the hair, everything. She flew in from Los Angeles the night before she was scheduled to work, arrived on the set early in the morning, and immediately went to the wardrobe trailer to put on her costume. And once she was in costume, she was in character. She wasn't Lily Tomlin anymore, she was the Waffle Man—even between takes. Looking back on it now, I'm astonished by what she was able to do with such skimpy material—a few little hints, really. What I gave her was no more than a nursery song, and she turned it into a full-scale aria.

The last part of the scene, when Violet appears and dances with Auggie, was wholly successful. Mel Gorham never made a false move in any of her scenes, and when the film consisted of just the three days from July, that segment was part of it. It was cut out later for reasons of overall structure, not performance.

3. WAR WOUNDS

Cast: Tommy, Auggie

Tommy walks into the store just as Auggie is closing up for the day. He says he has some bad news and didn't want to break it over the phone. Auggie invites him in. . . .

Tommy says that his brother Chuck died last night. "I got the news this morning. Heart attack. He was drinking a glass of beer and just keeled over."

Auggie is stunned. "But he's only 46, 47 years old. People don't die at that age."

Over the course of the conversation, we learn that Auggie and Chuck were good friends in the navy—which explains how Tommy and Auggie know each other.

Auggie reminisces about the old days: about how Chuck once busted someone in the face for calling him a nigger; about his luck at poker, his laugh, his fondness for girls named Wanda. Then Auggie launches into a story about how Chuck saved him one night in a bar in Manila.

Tommy talks about how Chuck never really recovered from the war; about how fat he became; about his trouble holding a job; about his broken marriage. "My big brother," he says over and over again. "My big brother. . . ."

Tommy asks Auggie if he'll get up and say a few words at the funeral. Auggie agrees. . . .

> One take only. It came at the end of the last day, and everyone was hot, exhausted, ready to fall on the ground. Given the other material we had filmed, it seemed clear that this scene wouldn't survive the final cut—but we decided to film it anyway. It turned out to be a harrowing twelve or fourteen minutes. Harvey and Giancarlo both wept, and the emotional intensity of their performances moved everyone who was there. But (as predicted) the tone didn't match up with the other scenes in the movie, and the entire effort wound up on the cutting-room floor.

4. RHUMBA RUMBLE

Cast: Auggie, Dot, Violet

Auggie is alone in the store, doing inventory. Dot (Vinnie's wife) enters. She complains about Vinnie . . .

DOT He don't talk to me no more.
AUGGIE You've been married to him for fifteen years—and you still expect him to talk to you?
DOT I've given him fifteen years of my life, and all I get for it is cold, blank stares.

AUGGIE And a ranch house in Massapequa. And a white Caddy. And those doodads arounds your neck.

DOT It's not worth it. I'm sorry you ever introduced me to him, Auggie. It was the biggest mistake of my life.

AUGGIE (*Playful*) Well, you had your chance with me, but you went with the bucks . . . and not with the buck!

DOT Come on, Auggie, this is serious. I've got to talk to you.

AUGGIE Listen, Dot, Vinnie's my friend. I don't want to get involved in this. It's not right for me to start choosing sides.

Before they can go any farther, Violet enters . . . and Dot exits the store.

Violet reminds Auggie of their date to go dancing on Saturday night. Auggie has forgotten and made other plans.

AUGGIE I thought it was *next* Saturday.

VIOLET Bullshit, Auggie. We said the sixteenth. What kind of number you trying to pull on me?

AUGGIE I promised Tommy I'd help him clean out his brother's apartment. Chuck. We were in the navy together. He died a couple of days ago.

VIOLET I don't know what you're talking about. Chuck, Chuck. Who the fuck is Chuck?

AUGGIE Come on, we'll do it next week.

VIOLET You two-timing, baby, ain't you? Who is it? Dot? Sally? Or maybe that little waitress with the fat ass.

Auggie grows increasingly irritated, defensive . . . but then, suddenly, Violet begins to turn on the charm. She dances a rhumba for Auggie, and after a while he joins in. One thing leads to another, and they wind up on the floor behind the counter. . . .

> Roseanne was the first "outside" actor we asked to be in
> *Blue in the Face*. Until then, our plan had been to limit
> the cast to people who had been in *Smoke*, but when we

heard that she might be interested in playing a role for us, we didn't hesitate to ask her in. That was how Dot was born—literally overnight.

Roseanne was out of the country just then, but I talked with her on the phone a couple of times to discuss her role. Right from the start, she seemed to have a strong intuitive grasp of the kind of film we were proposing to make. Wayne and I had dinner with her in New York the night before shooting began (just two days after *Smoke* was finished), and even though Roseanne wasn't scheduled to work until the second day, she came to the set the next morning and wound up staying through lunch—getting the lay of the land, so to speak, soaking up the atmosphere. That same night, she got together with Harvey Keitel and Victor Argo, and the three of them worked out many of the major issues they would be wrestling with in *Blackjack*. By the next day, she was ready to go, and her first scene went extremely well in every take.

5. IT'S A STEAL

Cast: Charles Clemm, Auggie, Tommy, Vinnie

Charles Clemm enters the store. In his present guise, he is working as a fence. He carries a briefcase filled with stolen watches, which he tries to sell to Auggie and Tommy at bargain prices.

But things don't go well. Tommy doubts the watches are authentic and taunts Clemm. After keeping up a good face, Clemm begins to get annoyed. He launches into a diatribe against smoking. "You're killing people in this store, you know that? You call me a thief, but you guys are murderers."

The tension mounts. Race becomes an issue. In his anger. Clemm turns on Tommy and says, "What are you doing here, man? You think you're white or something?"

Just when it looks as if the argument might come to blows, Vinnie enters the store and asks what the trouble is. "Nothing," Auggie says. "We were waiting for you to show up and sing us a song."

After some prompting, Vinnie takes out his guitar and sings a sad country-western ballad.

> Nothing went quite as planned, but everything worked out better than expected. Malik Yoba is a whirlwind, and at first I was thrown off by the bluster and contentiousness of his performance. I doubted it would play well on screen, but I was wrong. That bluster and contentiousness lie at the very heart of the film.
>
> Incredibly enough, the little song Malik sings with the guitar was made up *on the spot*.

6. THE BOSCO FOUNDATION

Cast: Tommy, Pete

Tommy is sitting alone in a chair outside the cigar store, idly perusing a newspaper. A man walks by carrying a briefcase. He is Peter Malone, a former high school classmate of Tommy's. They haven't seen each other in fifteen or twenty years. . . .

PETE Tommy Fratello, right?
TOMMY Right. And you're . . . you're . . . (snaps fingers) Peter Malone. The whiz kid of Midwood High.

They begin to talk. Tommy asks Pete what he's been up to all these years, and Pete tells his story. Little by little, it becomes clear that Pete is out of his mind.

PETE I got my B.A. at Harvard, and then I went to Yale for my Ph.D. Interdisciplinary studies: philosophy and biology.

TOMMY (*Impressed*) Wow. And then what?

PETE Uh. I went away.

TOMMY Away?

PETE Yeah. Government research. Top-secret stuff. Uh, I'm not really supposed to talk about it.

(It's beginning to dawn on Tommy that Pete was in a mental hospital.)

Tommy asks Pete what he's doing now, and Pete tells him that he's working as a consultant for the Bosco Foundation.

TOMMY Bosco? Isn't that the chocolate milk we used to drink as kids?

PETE That's a different Bosco. You never heard of Giuseppe Bosco, the industrialist from Milan? You're half Italian, aren't you?

TOMMY Yeah, well, I'm a little out of touch with things in the old country.

PETE Bosco invented the electronic Bible. He made millions with it, and after he died, his children set up an international social research foundation. Basically, we're out to explore people's attitudes about themselves and the world and see if we can't help to make them happier.

TOMMY And how do you do that?

PETE Well, for one thing we ask people to answer questions.

TOMMY Interesting. What kind of questions?

(Pete opens his briefcase and begins removing folders filled with sloppily arranged papers.)

PETE Look, if you're not too busy, maybe you wouldn't mind doing one of the questionnaires with me now.

TOMMY Right here?

PETE Sure, right here. It won't take long.

TOMMY Okay, why not? Fire away, Pete.

During the course of the questioning, Pete becomes increasingly overwrought. The ten questions are:

1. Do you believe there is life on other planets—or that we are alone in the universe?
2. Is there anyone you hate enough to want dead? If someone told you he could kill that person for you and the crime would never be discovered, would you allow him to go ahead and do it?
3. Do you think professional athletes are overpaid?
4. Are you satisfied with the size and shape of your penis?
5. Do you believe in God?
6. Do you look at your bowel movements before you flush the toilet?
7. If a genie came to you and offered to grant you one wish, what would that wish be?
8. Where is the most unusual place you have had sex?
9. If you were President of the United States, name three changes you would make.
10. How much money would it take for you to eat a bowl of shit?

As Tommy answers, Pete frantically transcribes what he says in a notebook. Tommy understands that Pete is not right in his head and that there is no such thing as the Bosco Foundation, but he nevertheless answers the questions seriously. He feels sorry for Pete and does his best to play along. When he hears the last question, he smiles and shakes his head.

TOMMY Every man has his price, huh? Well, it won't work with me, Pete. Eating shit is against my religion.
PETE Oh? And what religion is that?
TOMMY The religion of sanity. You should think about converting. It would make your life a hell of a lot easier.
PETE Oh, I used to belong. But they excommunicated me. (*Laughs, then grows serious. Starts putting the papers back in the briefcase*) Thank you for your cooperation, Tommy. (*Stands up and shakes Tommy's hand*) You've been a great help in the cause of truth and happiness.

And don't worry about a thing. Your answers will be kept in strictest confidence.

Pete bounces off with zest. Tommy remains in his chair, watching his old high school friend walk down the street.

This scene was a last-minute addition, an afterthought. The production was already set, the notes had been written, all the actors had been talked to (except the Waffle Man, who still had to be found), when all of a sudden I was told that Michael J. Fox had joined the cast. Would it be possible for me to write a role for him? To tell the truth, I didn't think so. I was dead tired, and whatever crazy impulse had driven me to concoct the other situations had long since vanished. I was a novelist, not a gag writer, and I was in no mood to whip up another dumb comedy sketch. The only thing I wanted was to spend a quiet Fourth of July weekend at home with my family, catching up on my sleep.

But it had to be done, and Saturday and Sunday were both ruined for me. I felt burned out, disgusted, and couldn't come up with a single idea. All the scenes had been mapped out, the balance of characters had been established, and adding another player to the mix threatened to throw everything out of whack. On Monday, my wife Siri patiently listened to my complaints. We discussed several possibilities, none of them very promising, and then, out of the blue, she tossed me the idea of the questionnaire. That got me going again, and a few hours later the Bosco Foundation scene was finished.

A couple of days later, Michael J. Fox drove up to the set of *Smoke* in Garrison, New York, where the last week of shooting was under way. I was impressed by his enthusiasm for the project, his intelligence, his goodwill. Whatever reluctance I felt about adding the scene had completely vanished by the time he drove off. That night, I spoke to Giancarlo Esposito on the phone, and the Bosco Foundation was slotted in as the first scene to be shot on the second day.

As chance would have it, the second day turned out to be my first day as director. Wayne had come down with bronchitis in Garrison during the last days of *Smoke*. He stayed in bed over the weekend (coming out only briefly on Sunday night for dinner with Roseanne) and showed up on the set Monday morning. All the scenes for that day were to be shot indoors. The air conditioner had to be turned off for the sound recording, and with temperatures outside close to a hundred degrees, it was utterly stifling inside the store. By the afternoon, it was becoming difficult to breathe in there. Wayne pushed on through the day, but he clearly wasn't up to par, and by the end of the afternoon he had lost his voice and was sick as a dog. He called Peter Newman from home that evening and said that he wouldn't be able to make it on Tuesday. "Paul can do it," he said to Peter, "there won't be a problem."

He couldn't possibly have known that, of course, but it was nice of him to say it. So I stepped in for the next two days and did what I could. The first scene up was *The Bosco Foundation*, and all three takes went like gangbusters. I was lucky. Fox, Esposito, and Harris were a great combination, and everyone on the crew was very kind to me, especially Adam Holender (the director of photography) and Todd Pfeiffer (the assistant director). The only problem was my inability to say the word "cut." For the first couple of takes, when I wanted Adam to stop shooting I lowered my arm in a kind of quick chopping motion. Adam didn't see this, of course, so the film kept rolling. It took a couple of shoves from Todd to get me to open my mouth. As I told Peter Newman after the scene was over, it was difficult for me to use an old word in a new way. Until that morning, the only time I had ever said "cut" was when I looked down at my finger and saw blood trickling out of it.

7. BLACKJACK

Cast: Auggie, Dot, Vinnie

Outline: Auggie is alone in the store when Dot enters. She unburdens herself to him and tells of her plan to leave Vinnie and run off to Las Vegas to become a blackjack dealer. She tries to entice Auggie to go with her. Eventually, Vinnie enters. It turns out that the deed for the store is made out in Dot's name, which makes her the legal owner of the Brooklyn Cigar Company. Vinnie and Dot get into a shouting match. Auggie throws them both out.

Suggestions:

DOT Listen, Auggie, you've really got to hear me out. No funny business this time.

AUGGIE Give me a break, Dot. I don't want to get involved.

DOT Well, like it or not, you are involved, and I'm not leaving this store until you listen to me.

AUGGIE Okay, okay. But make it short. I've got work to do. There's a big shipment coming within the hour.

DOT I'm leaving Vinnie.

AUGGIE I've heard that one before.

DOT This time I'm serious. I'm leaving Vinnie.

AUGGIE And what about the kids? You're just going to leave them behind?

DOT They don't need me. They're old enough to take care of themselves. And besides, they don't even like me. Goddamn brats, they can live with their father. Let him take care of them for a change.

AUGGIE And where are you going to go?

DOT That's what I want to talk to you about.

AUGGIE Me? What's this got to do with me?

DOT I want you to come with me, Auggie. We'll go out West and start a new life together.

AUGGIE What!

DOT I've got it all planned out. We'll go to Vegas and work as blackjack dealers. Enough of Brooklyn, enough of Long Island. It's time for a little glitz.

AUGGIE (*Looking at her as if she's crazy*) And you've told Vinnie about this plan of yours?

DOT Not yet. I wanted to hear what you said first.

AUGGIE Yeah, well, I say you're nuts.

DOT Come on, Auggie, just stop and think about it a little. (*Growing flirtatious, seductive*) Just because I made the wrong choice when I was young, that don't mean I can't make the right choice when I'm . . . when I'm . . . mature.

AUGGIE I'm already seeing someone. You know that. If Violet ever gets wind of this conversation, she'll scratch your eyes out. And my eyes, too.

DOT Don't be a wuss, Auggie. Forget that floozy chiquita. I know you've still got the hots for me.

AUGGIE Come on, Dot. Cut it out. You and Vinnie are in a lull, that's all. You'll get back on track.

DOT Don't make me laugh. We've been in a "lull" for the past fifteen years.

AUGGIE He's crazy about you. He tells me that all the time. "I love that chubby broad as much as I did the day I married her." He tells me that all the time.

DOT Bullshit, Auggie. Any moron could see through that one.

VINNIE enters the store.

VINNIE (*To DOT*) There you are. I've been looking all over for you.

DOT I'm having a private conversation with Auggie, Vin. Scram.

VINNIE This is my store, ain't it? I can come in here whenever I want.

DOT Think again, o beloved spouse. The papers for this place are in my name. Don't you remember that little tax scam you set up with your accountant two years ago? It's my store now, and I want you out.

Dot and Vinnie start to argue. Auggie tries to stop them, but with no success. At last, he yells at them both and tells them to leave. He has work to do, and if they want to have a domestic quarrel, they should do it at home. Dot and Vinnie head for the door, but then Dot rushes back and kisses Auggie passionately on the lips.

DOT (*To AUGGIE*) Too bad, pal. You just said good-bye to the opportunity of a lifetime. I hope you live to regret it.

> This scene was a struggle. We went through seven takes, trying out a different approach each time, all of us sweltering in the mid-afternoon heat. The pressure to come up with something usable was enormous, and there were moments in the beginning when I felt close to desperation. Nothing seemed to be developing as I'd hoped it would. By the third or fourth take, however, things took a turn for the better, and good material slowly started to emerge: Roseanne's shrieks, the kiss, the argument about listening and communication, Vic's anger and confusion, Harvey's magnificent smile at the end. Something real was happening in that room, and much of what is good about the scene crystalized as the camera was turning. The original idea was that Dot would go off to Las Vegas alone, but Roseanne's performance was so persuasive, her need to go there so powerful, that she actually talked Vic into going with her. No one was prepared for that, which probably explains why that moment is so convincing. It just happened, in the same way that most of life just happens.
>
> All three actors worked extremely hard, but of all the scenes I directed, this was the one I felt least in control of. I look back on the experience as a kind of mental

slugfest. Nevertheless, in its finished form, it stands as one of the strongest sequences in the film.

8. SWEET FAREWELL

Cast: Bob, Auggie, Jimmy Rose

Bob enters the store. Auggie asks him where he's been: he hasn't seen him in a couple of months. In Japan, Bob says: there was an exhibition of his photographs in Tokyo. Auggie asks Bob if he wants a pack of Luckies (Bob's usual brand). No, Bob says. What's the matter, Auggie answers, you switch to something else after all these years? No, Bob says, he's trying to quit. In fact, he's down to his last cigarette—and that's why he's come into the store: to smoke his last cigarette with Auggie.

Bob sits down, takes the cigarette out of the pack, and holds it in his hand. For the rest of the scene, he alternately addresses Auggie, Jimmy, and the cigarette.

A monologue follows. Memories of smoking. From the first cigarette as a kid to the final puff as an adult. Smoking and sex. Smoking and food. Smoking and work. As Schoenberg once said when asked why he kept a cigarette burning on his desk while he worked: "Composition is a lonely business, and I like it there for the companionship." Smoking and tension. Smoking and relaxation. There's never a bad time for a smoke: you celebrate with a smoke, you mourn with a smoke. Smoke as thought, as contemplation, as action. Smoking as danger: sneaking smokes in the school bathroom, smoking as a constant reminder of your own mortality. Smoking as comaraderie, as love: sharing a cigarette with your woman in bed. Smoking as the last act: the last puff before they blindfold the man about to be executed by the firing squad. Each puff is a human breath. Each puff is a thought. Each puff is another reminder that to live is also to die.

Bob strikes a match and lights the cigarette.

The part of the man who comes into the store to smoke his last cigarette was originally conceived for William Hurt. Unfortunately, he wasn't available on the day we needed him, so Paul the novelist exited the scene, and Bob the photographer (Jim Jarmusch) stepped into his shoes.

Jim and I went out for dinner one night in a restaurant near the *Smoke* production office on Lafayette Street, and in a couple of hours we came up with dozens of additional ideas for his part. The fact that Jim is a dyed-in-the-wool cigarette smoker lent an unforced authenticity and conviction to his performance. Not only is he a fine director, he is a complete natural in front of the camera.

I had always thought of this scene as a pure monologue, but Jim and Harvey played it more as a conversation. This led to a number of interesting digressions, particularly Harvey's memory of *A Walk in the Sun*, which in turn led us to find a clip from the old Richard Conte movie and weave it into the film. . . .

9. COWBOYS AND INDIANS

Cast: Sue, Dennis, Auggie, Tommy, Jerry, Jimmy Rose

Background: Sue is a waitress in a diner down the street. Dennis goes out with Sue's younger sister, Mary. Sue is divorced from Phil. Phil and Dennis occasionally work together (scalping tickets).

Sue comes into the store and asks Auggie for a pack of Kools. She spots Dennis.

SUE Don't you have anything better to do than hang around here all day?
DENNIS (*Sarcastically*) Hi, Sue.

SUE Mary told me you stood her up last night. Good work, pea brain. I still can't figure out why a sister of mine would hang out with a low-life like you.

The insults go back and forth, gradually gaining in intensity. At one point, DENNIS mentions that Phil complained that she was frigid.

SUE Yeah, well, you try going to bed with someone who hasn't taken a bath since the first Nixon administration.
DENNIS That's not the way I heard it.

Sue becomes so upset that she walks over to Dennis and slaps him. Auggie and Tommy scold Dennis for being a putz.

Jimmy Rose, feeling sorry for Sue, walks over to her and gives her a hug. "Don't feel bad," he says. "I'm rigid, too. Just like him." He points to the cigar store Indian standing by the door. Jimmy's comment is so loopy, so off the mark, that Sue begins to laugh through her tears.

Dennis leaves in disgust.

The scene ends with Jimmy doing imitations of the wooden Indian.

One of our tactics in preparing *Blue in the Face* was to give each of the actors secrets, private information that was withheld from the other actors in the scene. The hope was to inspire spontaneity in the performances, to make the action seem as "real" as possible. There were times when this method backfired on us and the actors were unintentionally working at cross-purposes, but there were other times when it was crucial to the success of the scene. *Cowboys and Indians* is probably the best example of what happens when the secret is a good one. Dennis (Steve Gevedon) had no idea that Sue (Peggy Gormley) was going to slap him. Since Dennis is the most obnoxious character in the film, Steve was instructed to insult Peggy without mercy, to go at her with every ounce of his unsavory Brooklyn manhood—but that was all he was told. When the slap came, it took him utterly by surprise. The look on his face was genuine, and yet somehow or other Steve managed to stay in character, even as he registered his shock.

10. THREADS

Cast: Tommy, Jerry

Tommy and Jerry are sitting in chairs outside the store. Tommy is disgusted with Jerry. "You're turning into a loser," he says, "a vacant lot with weeds growing in it." Jerry says he's doing his best. "I'm not a sharp guy like you."

Tommy looks at Jerry's vest. It's a complicated fisherman's thing, with a hundred little pockets. Strings of different colors are hanging out of the pockets and safety-pinned to the shoulders. "What's with this vest?" he says.

Jerry explains. He keeps forgetting things. So now he has a special compartment for each object he carries: a pocket for sunglasses, a pocket for cigarettes, a pocket for his lighter, his penknife, his chewing gum, etc.—with a different string attached to each object. It's all color-coded, he says. Once you know that blue means cigarettes and red means lighter, you can't make a mistake and reach into the wrong pocket. He gives a long-winded, infinitely detailed exegesis on the system he has developed.

Tommy, growing bored and frustrated, breaks in and lectures him on how to dress well and the importance of looking good.

This scene was essentially a holdover from the first idea for the film, before we decided to open up the cast to include actors who had not appeared in *Smoke*. Giancarlo

gave a splendid performance as a man expatiating on the values of dressing well. He looked like a million dollars in his bright yellow jacket, and from start to finish he radiated strength, happiness, and self-assurance. Alas, this scene did not fit into the overall design of the film, but one can catch a glimpse of Giancarlo and his jacket in the credit sequence at the end.

11. OY VEGAS

Cast: Auggie, Tommy, Jerry, Dennis, Jimmy Rose, Vinnie

Absolute silence. Auggie is reading a book behind the counter. Tommy is reading a newspaper. Jerry is playing with the strings on his vest. Dennis is dozing off. Jimmy Rose is dusting the wooden Indian. A long moment. Vinnie enters the store in a foul mood. He reprimands Auggie for letting the OTB Men hang out in the store without buying anything. He shoos them out. Jimmy goes on with his dusting.

Once they're alone, Auggie asks Vinnie what's wrong. Dot's disappeared, that's what's wrong. Did she leave a note? Yeah, one word: Good-bye.

AUGGIE What'd you do to her, Vin?
VINNIE I didn't do nothing. She's crazy, that woman. Sick in the head.
AUGGIE Then maybe you're lucky to be rid of her.
VINNIE She's my wife. And besides, I can't take care of the kids myself. They're driving me nuts.
AUGGIE Call around. Maybe she's at her mother's.
VINNIE I did. I called her mother, her sister, her brother, her goddamn aunts and uncles, her mah-jongg partners . . . and no one's heard from her.
AUGGIE Try Vegas.
VINNIE You mean Las Vegas?

AUGGIE Oy Vegas.

VINNIE Shit, Auggie, that's not funny.

AUGGIE No, I mean it. That's where she told me she wanted to go. To become a blackjack dealer.

The conversation continues. Eventually:

VINNIE Well, I guess I'm going to Vegas, then.

AUGGIE Don't forget to take your guitar, Vinnie. Maybe you can get a gig or two while you're out there.

VINNIE (*Thinks*) You know, that's not a bad idea. Take a little break from the ratrace. Maybe I could catch on with one of those little clubs. . . .

A bit later:

VINNIE Why don't you come with me, Auggie? We'll have a blast.

AUGGIE I can't. And besides, I don't want to.

VINNIE I hate to think of you turning into an old man sitting behind that counter.

AUGGIE Don't worry about me. Everybody has to grow old. What difference does it make where it happens?

> This scene was never filmed. Because Dot managed to talk Vinnie into going to Las Vegas with her, the material became superfluous.

12. ONCE MORE, WITH FEELING

Cast: Charles Clemm, Tommy, Jerry, Dennis, Auggie, Jerry, Jimmy Rose.

Charles Clemm enters the store. This time he is dressed in an elegant three-piece suit and speaks with an upper-class Jamaican accent. He asks for pipe tobacco.

Tommy stares at him, recognizing him from the previous scene. "You're no Jamaican," he says. "You're that fence who came in here last week trying to sell those watches." Clemm smiles: "I got tired of that routine. I figured it was time to try out a new one." Dennis is impressed: "Say, you're pretty good. You totally fooled me with that voice." Clemm: "That's nothing. I've got a hundred more where that came from."

For the rest of the scene, Dennis, Tommy, Clemm, and Auggie try out different accents, dazzling each other with their extraordinary mimicry. The whole thing ends in laughter.

> Another near disaster, shot on the first day. The idea for the scene had come to me on the set of *Smoke*. Separately, and on several different occasions, both Steve Gevedon and Malik Yoba had put me in stitches with their ability to do accents—everything from Japanese to Jamaican. It seemed fitting to end the film with everyone in the store impersonating everyone else, but the plan didn't work. We shot two unsuccessful takes, and then Wayne and I went into a corner and frantically tried to come up with a new approach. Then we split up and talked to the actors individually, giving each one fresh guidelines. I remember standing with Giancarlo, throwing out different suggestions for a story he could tell Malik. The one he actually used was completely his own—whether real or invented I don't know. Not only did it settle down the scene and give some shape to the action, but the content of the story touched on many of the same subjects presented in *Philosophers*. Beyond just helping to save this particular scene, his little tale of crime and redemption enriched the film as a whole.

13. INTERVIEW WITH JIMMY ROSE

Because we had to work at top speed, all of the scenes were shot in masters. There was no time to do any of the coverage shots that are standard practice when making a movie—and which prove invaluable when editing material in the cutting room. One of our plans was to use the last hour of the last day to shoot some singles and close-ups of Jimmy Rose (Jared Harris), as well as a number of inanimate objects in the cigar store: the wooden Indian, the cash register, the window, etc. Unfortunately, when the time came to film these bits, the electric generator broke down (because of the heat, I suppose) and we no longer had any lights. We hastily decided to post Jared in a chair outside the store and ask him a number of questions: Jimmy Rose on love, on life, on the various characters who pass in and out of the store. Jared came through with an excellent performance, but after we studied the film the next day, we all agreed that the light was too dim. When we returned to the cigar store in October, we shot the interview again.

14. INTERVIEW WITH LOU REED

I had met Lou Reed the previous year, and in the meantime we had struck up the beginnings of a friendship. When Wayne and I started preparing *Blue in the Face*, it occurred to me to ask Lou to participate. I don't know exactly why. Something to do with his caustic sensibility, perhaps, his appreciation of the ironies of life, or perhaps simply because of his marvelous New York-accented voice. Whatever the reason, Wayne liked the idea as well.

We decided to use Lou as himself, not as an actor: just sit him behind the counter of the cigar store and get him to talk on various subjects. He was to be the resident philosopher of the Brooklyn Cigar Company, a man who just happened to be there, for no particular reason, expounding on this and that. We looked on his presence as a possible way to break up the dramatic scenes and give some variety to the film, but we had no clear idea as to how that might happen.

The interview was shot at the end of the second day, directly after the tumultuous and draining experience of filming *Blackjack* with Roseanne, Harvey, and Vic. I was so tired by then that I could barely open my mouth to ask Lou the questions. We shot twenty-five or thirty minutes of footage, and all during that time I remember thinking that Lou was flat, not at all in good form, and that none of it would make the final cut of the film. Lou was of exactly the same opinion. We walked back to my house together for a drink after the day's work was done, and we both felt disappointed, shaking our heads and trying to shrug it off. "Well, that's show business," we said, and then went on to talk about other things.

As everyone who has seen the film now knows, show business proved us both wrong. At every *Blue in the Face* screening I have attended, Lou's performance provokes the most laughter and the most comments. He steals the movie.

October

1. EXT: DAY. IN FRONT OF THE BROOKLYN CIGAR CO.

AUGGIE and VIOLET are standing in front of the store. AUGGIE seems distracted. As VIOLET talks to him, his eyes scan the street, as if searching for a lost thought.

VIOLET Okay, Auggie, you got it?

AUGGIE Yeah, I got it.

VIOLET Saturday the sixteenth.

AUGGIE Right.

VIOLET It's gotta be then, 'cause that's the only night Ramon and his band are playing in Brooklyn. He's my brother, Auggie, and I'm telling you, he's the best.

AUGGIE Don't worry, sweetheart. It's a date.

VIOLET You gonna be something else, Agosto. Just remember those steps I taught you, and you'll look like Fred fucking Astaire.

AUGGIE (*Smiling*) Okay, Ginger. Whatever you say.

At that moment, coming around the corner to the right of frame, we see a black BOY of about eleven and a white WOMAN in her late twenties. The BOY grabs the WOMAN's purse and starts running, scooting around the corner past AUGGIE and VIOLET and exiting to the left of frame.

WOMAN Thief! Thief! He stole my purse!

AUGGIE (*Under his breath*) Shit. (*He takes off after the kid—exiting the frame*)

In the meantime, the door behind them opens and a number of customers, attracted by the commotion, come out, crowding around the doorway with the WOMAN and VIOLET. Among them are the three OTB MEN (TOMMY, DENNIS and JERRY).

WOMAN I can't believe it! He just ripped it out of my hands! Three hundred dollars in cash and all my credit cards!

DENNIS (*Looking the WOMAN up and down*) Yeah, it's disgusting, ain't it? I mean, an attractive lady like yourself, you can't walk the streets of this city alone no more. What you need—

VIOLET (*Excited, looking down the street*) Look! Look! Auggie, he got him!

DENNIS —is a man to protect you.

TOMMY and JERRY both look disgustedly at DENNIS, appalled by his sleazy come-on.

DENNIS (*Playing the innocent. To TOMMY and JERRY*) What? What I do now?

TOMMY Give it a rest, Dennis. Can't you see she's upset?

AUGGIE and the BOY reenter frame in front of the door. With one hand, AUGGIE is holding him by the collar; in AUGGIE's other hand is the WOMAN's purse. The BOY looks terrified.

AUGGIE (*Handing the WOMAN her purse*) Here's your purse.

WOMAN Thank you. That was . . . that was extraordinary. I don't know how to thank you.

AUGGIE Now go inside and call the cops, and we'll have this little punk arrested.

The WOMAN studies the BOY, who stands there in total silence. The others watch the exchange between AUGGIE and the WOMAN with rapt attention.

WOMAN Arrested?

AUGGIE Arrested. He's a thief, ain't he?

The WOMAN *continues to study the* BOY. *Little by little, we see her resolve crumble.*

WOMAN But he's just a baby.

AUGGIE (*Growing irritated*) What difference does it make? He snatched your purse.

WOMAN I have the purse now. Maybe we should just forget it.

AUGGIE Forget it? What are you talking about?

WOMAN He's just a baby. I can't put a baby in jail.

AUGGIE (*By now genuinely angry*) It's your duty! Is this the kind of city you want to live in? Where little kids rip off people's purses—and get away with it?

WOMAN I can't do it. I just can't do it.

AUGGIE *looks at the* WOMAN; *then he looks at the* BOY; *then he looks at the* WOMAN *again. In a flash, he comes to an impulsive, radical decision: he jerks the purse out of the* WOMAN's *hands and gives it back to the* BOY.

WOMAN (*Shocked*) Hey! What are you doing?

AUGGIE (*To the* BOY, *shooing him away*) Go, kid, go. It's yours.

The BOY, *by now totally confused, stands there mutely with the purse in his hands. He is frozen to the spot.*

WOMAN (*To* AUGGIE, *outraged*) Are you crazy?

The WOMAN *yanks the purse out of the* BOY's *hands. Without hesitating,* AUGGIE *grabs the purse from the* WOMAN *and gives it back to the* BOY.

AUGGIE (To the BOY) Are you deaf? The purse is yours. Now get the fuck out of here! (*He gives the* BOY *a shove, and the* BOY *takes off with the purse, running out of frame*)

WOMAN (*Beside herself*) You son of a bitch! All my money's in there! Are you out of your mind?

AUGGIE (*Boiling over with rage*) No, you are, lady! It's people like you who are turning New York into such a shit-hole. You won't take responsibility! If we don't teach these kids the difference between right and wrong, who's going to do it?

> This time, the notes were written out in traditional script form. We had a much better idea of what we were looking for now, and the October scenes were devised in an altogether different spirit from the ones we shot in the summer: as a way of filling in gaps, tightening narrative threads, and rounding out the earlier material. The experiment was essentially over, and this time our efforts were concentrated on putting together a viable film.
>
> On the other hand, just because we had a script, that didn't mean the actors weren't free to improvise. The entire cast for this new version of *Philosophers* did an excellent job of playing off and around the material as written, immensely improving it, I feel, with every line they spoke. Mira Sorvino was our principal newcomer, and she fit in as if she had been with us from the beginning. Several things are continually happening at once in this scene, and the side argument between Violet and Auggie as well as Dennis's snickering laugh from the front door help make the action unfold with all the multi-level confusion of a real street scene.

2. INT: NIGHT. VIOLET'S BEDROOM

VIOLET is sitting alone, putting on her makeup in front of a mirror.

VIOLET Auggie, you make me so horny. You make my *tripas* . . . tremble. . . . Oh, Auggie, you would be so wonderful . . . if only you were different. (*Pause. She begins opening jars on the table in front of her*) That Auggie, he gonna drive me cuckoo. First he say yes, then he say no. It's on, it's off, it's some other time. But Ramon, he don't know some other time. He play at Freddy's on the sixteenth, and now Agosto, he tell me he busy on the sixteenth. But I tole him: Saturday, the sixteenth. What gives around here, huh? Is somebody deaf or something? I talk myself blue in the face, and still it don't do no good. (*Pause. Fussing with her mascara. Uncaps her lipstick and begins applying it to her lips. Puckers her mouth in the mirror. Growing angrier. As if addressing* AUGGIE) Auggie, I make up my mind. And this is what my mind says. It says: if you don't do the thing you said you would do, then I never say nothing to you no more. You got it? Nothing. Never. No more. (*Pause. Inspects her lips in the mirror. Even angrier: but in a low, quiet, smoldering voice*) You lie to me, Auggie. And people who lie don't deserve no love. You mess with Violetta, and Violetta fight back. (*Almost in a whisper*) I rip your guts out, Auggie. Like a tiger. Like a fucking tiger—with teeth as sharp as the razor blades!

> Violet's monologue is the only interior scene filmed outside the cigar store, but we didn't have far to go: just around the corner to an empty apartment on 16th Street.
> Another departure from the first round of shooting: the close-up. For the first time, we managed to film a scene from two different angles.

3. INT: DAY. THE BROOKLYN CIGAR CO.

AUGGIE and VINNIE are alone in the store, deep in conversation.

VINNIE I don't know, Auggie. It's a lot of money. I'd be crazy to turn it down.

AUGGIE After nineteen years, you're just going to walk away? I can't believe it.

VINNIE It's dollars and cents. This store's been losing money for years, you know that as well as I do. It's a good month when we break even.

AUGGIE But you've got plenty of money, Vin. All those real estate deals out on the Island. You just write this place off on your taxes.

VINNIE It's too late. We're already in contract.

AUGGIE So the Brooklyn Cigar Company gets turned into a health-food store.

VINNIE Times change. Tobacco's out, wheat germ's in. (*Pause*) It might not be such a bad thing for you either, Auggie. I mean, maybe it's time for you to move on, too. I'd hate to see you turn into an old man sitting behind that counter.

AUGGIE Everybody has to grow old. What difference does it make where it happens?

VINNIE (*Lighting up a cigar. Smiling*) No more free cigars, eh, Auggie?

AUGGIE (*Pensive*) You really should think this through before it's too late, Vincent. I mean, sure, it's just a dinky little nothing store, but everybody comes in here. Not just the smokers . . . but the school kids for their candy . . . old Mrs. McKenna for her soap-opera magazines . . . Crazy Louie for his cough drops . . . Frank Sanchez for his El Diario . . . fat Mr. Chen for his crossword-puzzle books. The whole neighborhood lives in this store. It's a hangout, and it helps hold the place together. Go twenty blocks from here, and twelve-year-old kids are shooting each other for a pair of sneakers. You close this store, and it's one more nail in the coffin. You'll be helping to kill off this neighborhood.

VINNIE You trying to make me feel guilty, is that what you're doing?

AUGGIE No. I'm just giving you the facts. You can do whatever you want with them.

> Victor Argo was performing in a play in Los Angeles and could only work with us on Monday, his day off, which was the last day of our three-day shoot. Harvey Keitel, on the other hand, was only available on the first two days, Thursday and Friday. What to do? How to film a conversation between two men who couldn't be in the same room together? The only possible solution was to cheat. We filmed the two halves of the scene on separate days. Peggy Gormley (Sue from *Cowboys and Indians*) read the lines of the missing actor at each session.

4. INT: DAY. THE BROOKLYN CIGAR CO.

VINNIE is sitting alone, agitated, still worrying about his recent conversation with AUGGIE.

VINNIE That Auggie. He's going to drive me crazy. Just when I get the deal together, he comes in and starts playing those fucking violins. Brooklyn, Brooklyn. I'm supposed to care about Brooklyn? I don't even live in this shithole of a town no more.

VINNIE leans forward, elbows on his knees, and puts his head between his hands. He looks down at the ground. Two beats.

A figure enters the frame: a large black man dressed in a Brooklyn Dodgers uniform with number 42 on his back. This is JACKIE ROBINSON. He stops in front of the bench and stares down at VINNIE. The rest of the scene plays on VINNIE's face.

JACKIE ROBINSON Hi, Vinnie. Remember me?

VINNIE (*Awestruck*) Jackie?

JACKIE ROBINSON In the flesh, sport.

VINNIE (*Stammering*) Jackie . . . the greatest player of them all. I used to pray for you at night when I was a kid.

JACKIE ROBINSON I'm the man who changed America, Vinnie. And I did it right here, in Brooklyn. They spat on me, they cursed me, they made my life a never-ending hell, and I wasn't allowed to fight back. It takes its toll, being a martyr. I died when I was fifty-three, Vinnie, younger than you are now. But I was a hell of a ballplayer, wasn't I?

VINNIE The best. You were the best there was, Jackie.

JACKIE ROBINSON And after me, things started to change. I don't just mean for black people, I mean for white people, too. After me, white people and black people could never look at each other in the same way again. And it all happened right here, sport. In Brooklyn.

VINNIE Yeah. And then they had to move the team away. It nearly broke my heart. (*Pause*) Why'd they have to do a dumb thing like that?

JACKIE ROBINSON Dollars and cents, Vinnie. Ebbets Field might be gone, but what happened there lives on in the mind. That's what counts, Vinnie. Mind over matter. (*We see* VINNIE *listening intently, making the connection between the fate of the Dodgers and the fate of the cigar store*) And besides, there are more important things in life than baseball. (*Pause. Looking out the window*) But Brooklyn looks good. More or less the way it was when I last saw it. And Prospect Park over there . . . still as beautiful as ever. (*Pause*) Say, Vinnie. They don't still make those Belgian waffles, do they? Man, what I wouldn't give to sink my teeth into a Belgian waffle. With two scoops of pistachio ice cream on it . . . and maybe a heap of straw-berries and bananas on top of that. Boy, have I missed those things.

VINNIE (*Obligingly*) Belgian waffles? Sure, they still make them. (*Points*) A couple of blocks down, you'll see the Cosmic Diner. Just go in there, and they'll give you all the Belgian waffles you want.

JACKIE ROBINSON Thanks, sport. Don't mind if I do. (*Begins to exit frame. Stops*) A day in Brooklyn just wouldn't be complete without stopping in for a Belgian waffle, would it? (*He exits frame*)

Still sitting on the chair, VINNIE *follows* JACKIE ROBINSON *with his eyes. After a moment, he turns back and looks straight into the camera. His expression is utterly blank. Hold for two beats.*

This scene was written two or three days after the rest of the October material, and the idea came directly from Harvey Weinstein, president of Miramax.

It was 10:00 P.M. when the telephone rang at my house. Harvey was on the other end of the line, calling from his hotel room in London, where it was three o'clock in the morning. He had just had a dream about *Blue in the Face,* he said, and he wondered if it wouldn't make sense to work it into the film: after his conversation with Auggie about selling the store, Vinnie is miserable and confused; he sits down somewhere to weigh the pros and cons of his dilemma, when all of a sudden, out of thin air, a number of the old Dodgers appear to him and begin reminiscing about Brooklyn. What did I think? I thought it was a stroke of genius. First thing tomorrow morning, I would sit down at my desk and see what I could do.

One of the Dodgers Harvey mentioned was Jackie Robinson. He couldn't have known, of course, but I had been thinking about Jackie Robinson all my life. Way back when I was in the ninth grade, everyone in my junior high school was required to participate in a public speaking contest. The subject that year was "The Person I Most Admire." I wrote my speech about Jackie Robinson and wound up winning the first prize. It was 1961, and I was just fourteen years old, but composing that speech was one of the crucial events of my life. After that day, I knew that I wanted to become a writer.

When I sat down to work on the scene, I realized that Jackie Robinson was the only Dodger who had to appear, that his presence would say everything that had to be said. . . .

5. EXT: DAY. IN FRONT OF THE BROOKLYN CIGAR CO.

AUGGIE is standing in front of the door, smoking a cigarette and surveying the street.

A YOUNG WOMAN dressed in a skimpy Las Vegas showgirl outfit and wearing a little bellhop's cap on her head approaches the store. She is holding a yellow envelope in her hand. AUGGIE studies her with a mixture of amusement and curiosity.

YOUNG WOMAN Is this the Brooklyn Cigar Company?
AUGGIE In the flesh. What can I do for you?
YOUNG WOMAN (*Studying the envelope*) I'm looking for Mr. Augustus Wren.
AUGGIE You've found him, beautiful.

YOUNG WOMAN (*Relieved*) Great. I've never been to Brooklyn before. I wasn't sure I'd be able to find you.

AUGGIE Well, Brooklyn's on the map. We even have streets out here. And electricity, too.

YOUNG WOMAN (*Sarcastic*) You don't say. (*Pause*) Well?

AUGGIE Well what?

YOUNG WOMAN I have a telegram for you.

AUGGIE Nobody's dead, I hope. (*Extending his hand*) Let's see it.

YOUNG WOMAN A singing telegram.

AUGGIE (*Grinning*) This gets better and better.

YOUNG WOMAN (*Gearing up for her performance*) Ready?

AUGGIE Whenever you are.

YOUNG WOMAN (*Dancing as she sings. In a throaty, nightclub singer's voice*) .

> The deal is off . . . stop.
> Ba–ba–ba–ba–ba–boom.
> Not selling the store . . . stop.
> Ba–ba–ba–ba–ba–boom.
> See you next week . . . stop.
> Ba–ba–ba–ba–ba–boom.
> I'm sending you love . . . love . . . love
> From Las Vegas!
> Ba–ba–ba–ba–ba–boom.

AUGGIE (*Claps in appreciation*) Dynamite.

The YOUNG WOMAN gives a polite curtsy (in stark contrast to her raunchy performance) and smiles.

AUGGIE (*cont'd*) I'd say that's worth at least a five-dollar tip, wouldn't you? (*Removes his wallet from his pocket*)

YOUNG WOMAN (*Quietly miffed by the small amount*) Five dollars?

AUGGIE *hands her a five-dollar bill; she gives him the yellow envelope.*

AUGGIE Any time you want to deliver some more good news, you know where to find me.

YOUNG WOMAN (*Looking at the money*) Thanks, mister. Now I'll be able to buy that hearing aid my mother's always wanted.

The YOUNG WOMAN *walks off.* AUGGIE *opens the envelope and begins reading the telegram, humming under his breath: Ba-ba-ba-ba-ba-boom.*

> This was the first time I had ever written anything to be sung. Admittedly, the lyrics of the telegram message aren't much to write home about, but still, I had a definite melody in mind when I wrote the words. To my amazement, Madonna sang it precisely as I imagined she would. Beat for beat, phrase for phrase, she delivered the same little tune I had been carrying around in my head. The only difference: there were five ba's before each of my booms, and she used seven.

6. EXT: DAY. IN FRONT OF THE BROOKLYN CIGAR CO.

AUGGIE *is sitting outside the store in his plastic lawn chair, reading* The Philosophical Investigations *by Ludwig Wittgenstein and smoking two cigarettes at once. A boom box sits at his feet.*

VIOLET *comes by in a tight dress and stops in front of* AUGGIE's *chair.*

VIOLET I just wanted to show you what I'm wearing tonight. (*She spins in a circle, modeling her dress*) So you'll know what you'll be missing if you don't do the thing you said you'd do.
AUGGIE (*Admiringly*) Very nice.
VIOLET (*Noticing that* AUGGIE *has two cigarettes in his mouth*) Auggie, you got two cigarettes in your mouth. What do you want to do a thing like that for?
AUGGIE (*Shrugs*) I don't know. It seemed like a good idea at the time. (*Pause*) You want one?

VIOLET *shrugs.* AUGGIE *takes one of the cigarettes out of his mouth and hands it to her.*

VIOLET (*Smoking*) So, what are you going to wear tonight, Auggie?

AUGGIE (*Shrugs*) I don't know. I haven't thought about it yet.

VIOLET I hope you'll be ready, that's all I can say. (*Gesturing to her body*) It would be sad to say good-bye to this, wouldn't it, Auggie?

AUGGIE What do you mean? I'm ready now.

VIOLET You're not even dressed. How can you be ready?

AUGGIE I might not be dressed. But I'm ready.

VIOLET What the hell does that mean?

AUGGIE Watch.

AUGGIE pushes a button on the boom box. Loud salsa music suddenly comes pouring out of the machine. AUGGIE stands up and invites VIOLET to dance.

The camera begins to pull away. VIOLET throws her head back and laughs, then starts dancing in front of AUGGIE. After a few moments, other people enter the frame, all of them dancing to the music. Cut to:

The street from above. Dozens of people have appeared out of nowhere. A wild block party is in full swing. AUGGIE and VIOLET continue to dance, laughing in the midst of the mayhem.

> For reasons still difficult to understand, the first part of this scene did not play well on screen. The performances were good, but the light, perhaps, or the camera angle, or the quality of the sound just didn't work, and we reluctantly dropped it from the film.
>
> The two block-party shots, however, still provide us with our conclusion. The tall blonde dancing in the middle of the crowd is RuPaul.

7. STATISTICS

One by one, different people stand in front of the cigar store and recite the following facts about Brooklyn:

—There are 2.3 million people living in Brooklyn.

—There are 1,600 miles of streets, 4,513 fire boxes, and 50 miles of shoreline in Brooklyn.

—There are 672,569 people living in Brooklyn who were born in foreign countries.

—There are 3,268,121 potholes in Brooklyn.

—There are 605,554 people under the age of 18 living in Brooklyn.

—There were 1,066 forcible rapes committed in Brooklyn last year.

—There are 872,305 African Americans living in Brooklyn.

—There are 412,906 Jewish people living in Brooklyn.

—There are 462,411 Hispanic people living in Brooklyn.

—There are 514,163 people living below the poverty line in Brooklyn.

—There were 32,979 cars stolen in Brooklyn last year.

—There are 90 different ethnic groups, 32,000 businesses, and 1,500 churches, synagogues, and mosques in Brooklyn.

—There were 30,973 robberies, 14,596 felonious assaults, and 720 murders committed in Brooklyn last year.

—Every day, 7,999 Belgian waffles are eaten in the restaurants of Brooklyn.

—Once, there was a major league baseball team in Brooklyn. But that was a long time ago.

In editing the July material (before we knew we would have a chance to shoot again in October) I suggested a number of small elements that could be added to the film without major expense. The map of Brooklyn that appears at the beginning (along with the words "YOU ARE HERE") was one such idea. Another was to flash various facts and statistics about Brooklyn on screen at certain key moments. Once the extra days of shooting were given to us, we decided it would be more interesting to have a cross-section of Auggie's customers recite those figures on the sidewalk outside the store. A casting session was hastily arranged, and more than a hundred people showed up to audition for these briefest of brief roles.

(Among them was Michelle Hurst, who had played Rashid's Aunt Em in *Smoke*.) A video tape was sent to me, and in less than two hours I chose a dozen people to play our Brooklyn "statisticians." A perfect example of the deadlines and pressures we had to deal with in setting up our second round of shooting.

8. VIOLET SINGING "FEVER"

After the first round of shooting in July, Miramax threw a small cast party at Sammy's Rumanian Restaurant on the Lower East Side. The highlight of the evening came when Mel Gorham stood up on the little stage and sang an unforgettable rendition of "Fever." Wayne, who was still fighting the bug in his system, had left the party by then and missed the performance. Just one or two days before we began shooting again, he said to me, "Everyone is still talking about how great Mel was when she sang 'Fever.' Why don't we have her do it for us after she finishes her monologue?" "Why not?" I said. And so we hired a couple of musicians to accompany Mel, and Wayne finally got to see her do the number—in a radically different version.

Later on, when we were putting together the final cut of the film, we brought Mel back to loop the lines she speaks over the song.

9. BELGIAN WAFFLE POSTER

The Waffle Man carries around a Belgian waffle menu that features a succulent, full-color photo of his heart's desire. When we filmed Lily Tomlin's scene in July, there was no time to do an insert shot of the photo, which would have given the audience a clear idea of what her character so desperately craved. To remedy this lack, we prepared a shot of a Belgian waffle poster in October—which turned out to be the last shot of the film. . . .

The poster was taped to a wall inside the cigar store. We planned the shot to last a certain number of seconds (I forget how many), and then the camera started to roll. With just two or three seconds left, the tape suddenly loosened and the poster fell off the wall. It was a typical *Blue in the Face* moment. We thought we were finished, but the god of adhesives had decided to play one last prank on us. So the poster had to be remounted, and the shot had to be done again.

This time it worked. This time the movie was really over.

10. VIDEO MATERIAL

This was the final piece of the puzzle. In discussing ways to open up *Blue in the Face*, Wayne and I became attracted to the idea of going out into Brooklyn and talking to real people, of pushing certain parts of our film into the realm of pure documentary. Yes, the cigar store was an imaginary place peopled by imaginary characters, but so much vital energy had come from the actors' performances that it didn't feel like a contradiction to try to include the actual Brooklyn world that surrounds the store . . . and see what happened when we mixed the two elements.

In an effort to save both time and money, Wayne suggested that we shoot these documentary sequences in High-8 video and then, once we were in the cutting room, transfer the material we wanted to keep onto film. Since we would be too busy on the set to take care of it ourselves, we had to enlist someone else's help. That person turned out to be photographer Harvey Wang, author of *Harvey Wang's New York*.

Given that both our leading actor and producer were

named Harvey, and given that Wayne's last name was Wang, it felt like some kind of weird, cosmic joke that the best man for the job should be named Harvey Wang. To enhance the beauty of the coincidence, Harvey Wang is not Chinese (as Wayne is) but Jewish (as Wayne's co-director is). So, a Chinese-Jewish team making a film about Brooklyn brought in a Jewish man with a Chinese name who just happened to live in Brooklyn. What could have been more appropriate? The three of us laughed about it constantly, and Wayne never tired of introducing Harvey to other people as his brother. But underneath all the horseplay, there was something wonderfully in keeping with the spirit of the project we had undertaken. This was *Blue in the Face* in a nutshell: strange, unpredictable doings set against a backdrop of diversity, tolerance, and affection.

Harvey threw himself into his assignment with great relish. In eight days of work, he amassed over sixteen hours of footage. No more than a few minutes are included in *Blue in the Face*, but having seen every one of the several dozen interviews he recorded, I believe this material would make an excellent film in its own right: a documentary portrait of Brooklyn in all its rough-and-tumble glory. As Harvey himself has written: "There is no one voice for all of Brooklyn. Like an orchestra, each voice contributes an accent, a 'fuck you buddy, that's my parking space' attitude, a cheer, a kvetch. The resulting cacophony is the soundtrack of this one-of-a-kind place."

It's all there in his film.

lulu on the bridge

The Making of

lulu on the bridge

Rebecca Prime: Three years ago, when you were working on the postproduction of *Smoke* and *Blue in the Face*, you did an interview with Annette Insdorf, and the last question she asked you was, "Now that you've caught the bug, do you have any desire to direct again?" You answered her, "No, I can't say that I do." Obviously, you've had a change of heart. Any particular reason?

Paul Auster: I guess it's dangerous to talk about the future, isn't it? The idea for *Lulu* actually came to me around that time, while I was still working on those films. I saw the story as a movie. And because I was feeling burned out by movies just then—postproduction on *Smoke* and *Blue in the Face* dragged on for almost a year—I did everything I could to resist it. But the story kept coming back to me, kept demanding that I do something about it, and eventually I gave in to the impulse. And when I did, I made a fatal mistake.

RP: How so?

PA: I decided to write it as a novel. If the story was good, I said to myself, then it didn't matter how I told it. Book, film, it didn't matter. The heart of the story would burn through no matter what form it took. So I sat down and started writing—and six or seven months later, when I stood up and examined what I had done so far, I realized it was no good. It didn't work. It was a dramatic story, not a narrative story, and it needed to be seen, not just read.

RP: Why?

PA: Because of the stone, to begin with. Because of the film inside the story. Because of the dreamlike structure of events. A whole host of reasons.

RP: And so you went back and started over again . . .

PA: Not right away. I thought the project was dead, and I turned my attention to other things. A year went by, maybe a year and a half, but the story never really left me. When I finally understood that it was something I needed to do, I took a deep breath and started again. But this time I stuck to my original conception and wrote it as a screenplay. So much for trying to force things. I learned a lot from that blunder.

RP: Still, even though you wrote it as a film, the story feels more like a novel than most films one sees. Like one of *your* novels, actually.

PA: Well, habits die hard, as Izzy says at one point. But the fact was that I felt all along that *Lulu* was a continuation of my work, that it's of a piece with everything else I've done.

RP: Most films seem to set out to tell one thing, and they usually proceed in a linear fashion. With *Lulu on the Bridge*, the story works on several different levels at once.

PA: That's what makes it so difficult to talk about. There are a number of threads running through the story, and by the time you come to the end, they're so tangled up with one another, you can't pull one out without disturbing all the others. The most important thing, though, is that at bottom it's a very emotional story, a story about deep and powerful feelings. It's not a puzzle, not some code to be cracked, and you don't have to "understand" it in a rational way to feel the force of the emotions.

RP: Let's talk about the "dreamlike structure of events" you mentioned earlier.

PA: On one level, it's all very simple. A man gets shot, and in the last hour before his death, he dreams another life for himself. The content of that dream is provided by a number of random elements that appear to him just before and after the shooting. A wall of photographs in a men's room featuring women's faces—mostly the faces of movie stars—and a chunk of plaster that falls from the ceiling. Everything follows from those elements: the magic blue stone, the young woman he falls in love with, the fact that she's an actress and lands a role in a film, the title of that film, the director of that film, and so on. That's one way of reading the story—the framework, so to speak. But that's hardly the most interesting way of looking at it. It gives the film some plausibility, I suppose, but it doesn't take the magic into account. And if you forget the magic, you don't have much of anything.

RP: Can you elaborate?

PA: Because, on another level, all these things really happen. I firmly believe that Izzy lives through the events in the story, that the dream is not just some empty fantasy. When he dies at the end, he's a different man than he was at the beginning. He's managed to redeem himself, somehow. If not, how else to account for Celia's presence on the street at the end? It's as if she has lived through the story, too. The ambulance passes, and even though she can't possibly know who is inside, she does, it's as if she does. She feels a connection, she's moved, she's touched by grief—understanding that the person in the ambulance has just died. As far as I'm concerned, the whole film comes together in that final shot. The magic isn't just simply a dream. It's real, and it carries all the emotions of reality.

RP: In other words, you believe in the impossible.

PA: We all do. Whether we know it or not, our lives would make no sense if we didn't. . . . Think of something like *A Midsummer Night's Dream*. Elves and fairies prancing through the woods. Sprinkle pixie dust in a man's eyes, and he falls in love. It's impossible, yes, but that doesn't mean it isn't real, that it isn't true to life. Love is magic, after all, isn't it? No one understands what it is, no one can explain it. Pixie dust is as good an explanation as any other, it seems to me. And so is the blue stone—the thing that brings Izzy and Celia together. Just because a story is told "realistically" doesn't make it realistic. And just because a story is told fancifully doesn't make it far-fetched. In the end, metaphor might be the best way of getting at the truth.

RP: *Lulu on the Bridge* operates on a metaphorical level, but it is also grounded in reality.

PA: Well, you can never stray too far from the world of ordinary things. If you do, you slip into allegory, and allegory doesn't interest me at all. Two or three years ago, Peter Brook did an interview in the *New York Times*, and he said something that made an enormous impression on me. "In all my work," he said, "I try to combine the closeness of the everyday with the distance of myth. Because, without the closeness you can't be moved, and without the distance you can't be amazed." A brilliant formulation, no? *Lulu on the Bridge* is that kind of double work, I think. At least I hope it is.

RP: When all is said and done, *Lulu* could probably be described as a love story, couldn't it? That seems to be the heart of the film, at least for me. What happens between Izzy and Celia.

PA: Yes, I think you're right. Izzy is a man who's led a less than noble life. He's selfish, quick-tempered, incapable of loving anyone. He's cut off from his family, and his marriage to Hannah—a beautiful, good-hearted young woman—ended after just a few years. Probably because he couldn't keep his hands off of other women. Then he's shot, and in the delirium of his final moments, he conjures up a great and overpowering love. In doing so, he reinvents who he is, becomes better, discovers what is best inside him. It's a big love, of course. A love so big he's actually willing to die for it.

RP: Izzy is willing to die for Celia, but Celia also sacrifices herself for Izzy.

PA: Precisely. It works both ways. Celia jumps off the bridge and disappears. You think that might be the end of her. Then Izzy dies, and just as he is pronounced dead in the ambulance, we see Celia again, walking down the street. It's as if his death has resurrected her, as if he's died in order to give her another chance at life.

RP: Tell me about the stone. It's probably the strangest element in the story, and yet the odd thing is that everyone seems to accept it. I've attended several screenings of the film, and not once has anyone questioned it or been confused by it.

PA: To tell the truth, I don't really understand what the stone is. I have ideas about it, of course, many feelings, many thoughts, but nothing definitive.

RP: Each person finds his or her own meaning in it . . .

PA: Yes. It becomes more powerful that way, I think. The less fixed, the more pregnant with possibilities. . . . When I first wrote the story, I suppose I thought of the stone as some kind of mysterious, all-encompassing life force—the glue that connects one thing to another, that binds people together, the unknowable something that makes love possible. Later on, when we filmed the scene of Izzy pulling the stone out of the box, I began to have another idea about it. The way Harvey played it, it began to feel to me as if the stone were Izzy's soul, as if we were watching a man discover himself for the first time. He reacts with fear and confusion; he's thrown into a panic. It's only the next day, when he meets Celia, that he understands what's happened. You find your essence only in relation to others. That's the great paradox. You don't take hold of yourself until you're willing to give it away. In other words, you don't become who you are until you're capable of loving someone else.

RP: The stone is one of the elements in the film that clues the viewer to the fact that you can't read the film as a straightforward narrative, that we're clearly in some sort of altered universe. At the same time, it has a very straightforward narrative function. It's the prime mover in what could be called the "thriller" aspect of the story. What compelled you to make use of this genre?

PA: Because it seemed right, it felt right. Thrillers are very much like dreams. When you strip away the surface details, they begin to function as metaphors of our unconscious. People without faces pursuing you through dark, abandoned streets. Men hanging from the edges of buildings. Fear and danger, risk, the contingencies of life and death.

RP: With *Lulu,* how would you describe the thriller aspect of the plot?

PA: It's fairly rudimentary. Dr. Van Horn is associated with the group that developed the magic stone. Various scoundrels representing other groups are trying to gain possession of this priceless object. Stanley Mar would be one. The three thugs who assault Izzy would be another. They lock him up, thinking he knows where the stone is. Then Van Horn's group tracks down this other group and eliminates them. Van Horn then begins to interrogate Izzy.

RP: But he's interested in more than just the stone, isn't he?

PA: Of course he is. He's interested in Izzy's soul. Van Horn isn't at all what he first appears to be. He's an interrogating angel. He's the figure standing between Izzy and the gates of death. His job is to find out who Izzy is.

RP: In their last conversation, when Izzy refuses to reveal that he knows Celia Burns, Van Horn storms out in a fit of anger. Why?

PA: Because he wants the stone, and he understands that Izzy isn't going to help him. At the same time, I see his anger as a test. He wants to know if Izzy will buckle under the pressure or try to protect the person he loves. Izzy stands firm, and even though Van Horn doesn't get what he seems to want, in the end this might be an even more satisfying outcome for him. Remember, he doesn't rush out. He turns at the last moment and says to Izzy, "May God have mercy on your soul." And he means it. There's tremendous ambiguity in that line, of course, but it also represents a spontaneous outburst of compassion.

RP: And then there's Celia—what might be called the "feminine" side of the movie. In some sense, she's everything Izzy is not.

PA: Her most important quality, I think, is vitality. Celia is *alive*. She's generous, she's fetching, she's desirable—the kind of young woman every man can fall in love with. At the same time, she's not a pushover. She's not some simpering cutie-pie. She has opinions, she's capable of anger, she's willing to stand up for herself.

RP: And she's also an actress. I was particularly struck by the line she says to Izzy about playing a prostitute: "I really liked doing that scene." It gives us a glimpse into how she might be capable of playing Lulu.

PA: Yes. It's a jocular, offhanded kind of line, but it does establish an important link. It's a little fulcrum that connects Celia to Lulu.

RP: Celia is a flesh-and-blood character, but at the same time there's a fascination with female archetypes in the film. Just under the surface, the story seems to be making constant references to myth. When Celia looks up at Izzy after she's taken hold of the stone for the first time and says, "Come on, don't be afraid, it's the best thing, it really is," you feel this is just the kind of thing Eve might have said to Adam in the Garden of Eden. When Izzy opens the three boxes and finds the stone in the last one, you can't help but think of Pandora's box.

PA: All the images in the story are connected; everything bounces off of everything else. To a large degree, the film is about how men invent women. It begins with the very first shot—when we see that wall of photographs of women's faces. All those movie stars! I'm intrigued by the fact that for most of this century images of beautiful women have been projected on screens and have fed the fantasies of men all over the world. That's probably why movie stars were invented. To feed dreams. Izzy invents a new life for himself through the medium of a picture. There's Mira Sorvino's face on the wall—and the movie begins. In a way, it duplicates what we all experience when we watch movies. We walk into a dark place and leave the world behind. We enter the realm of make-believe.

RP: Why Lulu and *Pandora's Box?* What exactly were you trying to do by introducing that element into the story?

PA: It pushes the dream farther, throws Celia from one end of her femininity to the other. From good girl to bad girl. It's Izzy's dream, after all, and in some way you can see Lulu as a female version of who Izzy used to be.

RP: I see what you mean when you say the "everything bounces off everything else."

PA: That's why I was so gripped by the Lulu story. Lulu is a completely amoral, infantile creature, a person without compassion. Men lose their minds over her. She doesn't intend to hurt anybody, but one by one all her lovers are driven to suicide, insanity, debasement—every horror you can imagine. Lulu is a blank slate, and men project their desires onto her. They invent her. Just as men invent the women they see in movies. The Lulu plays were written before the invention of movies, but Lulu is a movie star. She's the first movie star in history.

RP: How did you go about adapting the Lulu material?

PA: I went back to Wedekind's two plays, *Earth Spirit* and *Pandora's Box*. I greatly admire Pabst's film, particularly Louise Brooks's performance, but I didn't make much use of it when writing the screenplay, and I certainly didn't want to refer to it in the film. The two plays tell a continuous story, and they add up to nine long acts. Obviously, I couldn't deal with all that. The most I could do was suggest the arc of Lulu's life, and I tried to achieve that by concentrating on what I felt were a few of the most interesting and pertinent scenes. I also decided not to do it as a period piece, to modernize the details, the settings, and so on. The plays are a hundred years old now, and there's so much dreadful writing in them, so much that creaks and grates, there seemed to be no point in trying to restage them as they were written. In the first scene, I changed the painter Schwarz into the photographer Black. The Pierrot costume became a Charlie Chaplin costume. All in the spirit of the original—but different. In the dressing-room scene, I changed the musical revue into a rock and roll performance. That kind of thing. It's never a word-for-word translation, but at the same time I tried not to stray too far from the gist of Wedekind's dialogue.

RP: Once you started writing the screenplay, were you also planning to direct the film yourself?

PA: Not at first. The original idea was for Wim Wenders to direct it. Wim and I have been friends for a long time now, and we've always talked about doing a project together. For a while, it looked as though *Lulu* would be that project. We even went so far as to have a number of conversations about the story, and when I sent him the finished screenplay, he was very happy with it. I assumed that would be the end of my involvement with the film, that the torch had been passed, so to speak. Then, just a few days later, a funny thing happened. Wim was interviewed by a journalist, and at one point she said to him, "Mr. Wenders, do you realize that the past four or five movies you've made have all been about making movies?" The question caught him by surprise. As a matter of fact, he hadn't been aware of it. *Lulu on the Bridge*, of course, is yet another movie with a movie inside the movie, and Wim called me up the next morning to say that he was suddenly feeling worried. Was that his destiny—to be a filmmaker who could only make films about films? He wasn't backing out of the project, but he wanted to think it over for a while before committing himself. Was that okay? Of course it was okay. So I hung up the phone and realized that the film no longer had a director.

RP: How could you be sure?

PA: Making a movie is such a difficult, exhausting process, you can't go into it with anything less than total enthusiasm. The slightest doubt, the smallest flicker of uncertainty, and you're sunk. If Wim was wobbling about it, then my feeling was that he probably shouldn't do it. . . . He was going to call me back with his decision the following week, and in the meantime I started thinking about who else should do it, who else *could* do it. No names jumped out at me. The script is so strange, I suppose, so particular to me and my own private universe, that I couldn't think of anyone whose sensibility would be compatible with the material. That was when it occurred to me that perhaps I should do it myself. It was my story, after all, and why not see the thing through to the end? At least it would be made exactly the way I wanted it to be made— for better or for worse. So I wrote Wim a fax saying that if he decided not to direct the film, I was inclined to do it myself. I sent the letter through the machine, and one minute later the telephone rang. It was Wim. "I just tore up a letter I was going to fax to you," he said, "trying to persuade you to direct the movie yourself." And that was that. Without really intending to work in the movies again, not only had I written another screenplay, but now I was going to direct as well.

RP: And you weren't scared?

PA: No, not really. I had spent two years working on *Smoke* and *Blue in the Face* and had a very clear idea of what I was getting myself into. No one twisted my arm to do it. It was a decision I made on my own, which means that somewhere, deep down, I'd probably had a real hankering to do it.

RP: You finished writing the script in early February 1997. Now, almost exactly a year later, you're in postproduction. How did it happen so fast?

PA: Two words: Peter Newman. Peter was the producer of both *Smoke* and *Blue in the Face*, and once we started working together, we became great friends. I can't say enough good things about this man. His integrity, his optimism, his sense of humor, his resilience. When I told him about this new project that I wanted to do, he simply went out and raised the money. In record time. It only took about two months.

RP: Peter Newman was also responsible for one of the scenes in the film, wasn't he?

PA: I'm not sure he'd want me to talk about it—but yes, he was. The airplane story that Philip Kleinman tells at the dinner party early in the film came directly from Peter. It's a true story, something that really happened to him. I know it's rather disgusting, and more than a little disturbing, but the fact was that I was very impressed when Peter told it to me—for what it revealed about his moral qualities, his goodness as a human being. That's how it stands in the film: as a moral tale.

RP: How did you go about casting the film? Did you write the script with any specific actors in mind?

PA: Harvey Keitel. He was the only one. It's not that I set out to write a role for Harvey, but once I got into the story a bit, I began seeing him in my mind, and at a certain point it became inconceivable to think of Izzy without also thinking of Harvey.

RP: You'd worked together before, of course.

PA: Yes, and we'd both developed a great deal of respect for each other. It goes without saying that Harvey is a superb actor. But there's something more to it than that. The way he moves, the irresistible qualities of his face, his groundedness. It's as if Harvey embodies something that belongs to all of us, as if he *becomes* us when he's up on the screen. When he agreed to play Izzy, I knew that we were going to have an extraordinary time together. And we did. Working with him on this role was one of the best experiences of my life.

RP: Mira Sorvino plays Celia, but at an earlier stage in the project the part was supposedly offered to Juliette Binoche. Is that true?

PA: Yes. But that was very early, when Wim still thought he would be involved. Juliette was the actress he proposed, and she was interested. But then she won her Academy Award, and in all the uproar that followed, it became difficult for her to decide what to do next. So I moved on. It's not as though this kind of thing doesn't happen every day when you're trying to put together a movie. Early on, I formulated a little phrase to help me get through the inevitable disappointments and hard knocks ahead. "Every person and every thing is replaceable," I told myself, "except the script." I've repeated those words to myself a thousand times since then, and they've helped; they've more or less allowed me to keep my head screwed on straight.

RP: So you lost one Academy Award actress and got another. Not such a bad trade-off!

PA: The gods were smiling on me, there's no question about it. . . . It's such a difficult, complex role—in effect two roles, many roles— and only a very gifted actress could begin to do it justice. I had worked with Mira for one day on *Blue in the Face* and had been impressed with her intelligence and talent. She has a fierce commitment to getting things right, and you can't learn that kind of attitude—it's who you are. Last spring, we both happened to wind up on the jury at Cannes. We saw each other every day for two weeks and got to know each other better, to become friends. When it finally became clear to me that Juliette wasn't going to be in the film, I didn't hesitate to ask Mira. It turned out to be my luckiest stroke, the smartest move I made. I knew she was going to be good, but I had no idea she had it in her to reach the heights she did, to touch such deep emotional chords. Mira is a very brave person, a girl with guts. And yet she's also immensely fragile. Her pores are open to the world, and she feels everything, registers everything happening in the air around her. Like a tuning fork. It's rare to find this combination of strength and sensitivity in one person. Mix that in with a keen mind and a heavy dose of natural talent, and you really have yourself something. And Mira is really something. I loved the whole adventure of working with her.

RP: What about the other actors? There are at least thirty speaking parts in the film.

PA: In many cases, I approached actors I had worked with before. Giancarlo Esposito, Jared Harris, Victor Argo, Peggy Gormley, and Harold Perrineau had all been involved with *Smoke* and *Blue in the Face*. It was a great advantage to be able to turn to them, because I knew that I could trust them—not just as actors, but as people. Gina Gershon is a close friend of one of my wife's sisters, and we've known each other for years. Mandy Patinkin had played the lead in *The Music of Chance*. Vanessa Redgrave was also a friend. And even Stockard Channing, who couldn't be in the film, did me a little favor a couple of weeks ago when she came in and recorded the phone message that Celia receives from her agent telling her she's been given the part. You might not see Stockard in the film, but you hear her voice!

RP: Do-it-yourself casting.

PA: To a small degree. All the other actors came through Heidi Levitt, who was in charge of casting. Auditions, video reels, telephone calls, nail-biting decisions.

RP: What about Willem Dafoe?

PA: That was a different story, a completely different story. Originally, Dr. Van Horn was called Dr. Singh, and the role was going to be played by Salman Rushdie. Salman is another friend, a very good friend, but also—believe it or not—a wonderfully able actor. I asked him to be in the movie just after I finished the script, and he accepted. We were both very excited about it.

RP: What were your reasons for thinking of him?

PA: First of all, as a recognizable figure, his presence would have reinforced the constant overlapping of dream and reality in the film. A man who has been forced into hiding through terrible, tragic circumstances suddenly appears as a man in charge of interrogating someone who is being held against his will. The captive made captor. It was my little way of trying to turn the tables on the world. I wanted to make a gesture in Salman's defense, to reinvent reality just enough for it to be possible to have Salman Rushdie appear in the film—not as himself, but as an imaginary character. Finally— and most important of all—I knew that he would give an excellent performance.

RP: Why didn't it happen?

PA: Fear, mostly. And bad planning on my part, bad planning all around. I've spent so much time with him, have been in so many public places with him—restaurants, theaters, the streets of New York—that I forget that most people think of him as a walking time bomb, that if they get anywhere near him, they're likely to be blown to bits. Nine years have gone by since the *fatwa* was declared, and he's still, mercifully, very much with us, but his name seems to trigger off an irrational panic in many people, and a certain percentage of the crew wanted extra security guarantees if he was going to appear in the film. The cost of doing such a thing would have been prohibitive, and eventually I had to abandon the idea. I fought tooth and nail to make it happen, but it didn't. It was a tremendous disappointment to me. I consider it a personal defeat, a moral defeat.

RP: The film was already in production at that point, wasn't it?

PA: We were in our sixth week, and those scenes were scheduled for the eighth week—the last days of shooting in New York.

RP: It didn't leave you much time, did it?

PA: Our backs were up against the wall. I thought the movie would have to shut down, that we wouldn't be able to finish. It was an awful period, let me tell you.

RP: So Willem stepped in—literally at the last minute.

PA: The very last minute. He received the script on a Sunday, accepted the role on Monday, and when he showed up for a rehearsal with me and Harvey the following Sunday, he had his part down cold. He knew every line perfectly. The next day, Monday, we filmed his first scene. Can you imagine? He's positively brilliant in the role, and he prepared the whole thing in a week. Willem saved the movie. He stepped in and single-handedly rescued us all. It was heroic what he did, and I'm so grateful to him, so deeply in his debt, that I can hardly think about it without getting a little weak in the knees.

RP: You learn to roll with the punches, don't you?

PA: You don't have any choice. Things are going to go wrong. You never know when, and you never know how, but you can be sure it will happen when you're least expecting it. That's why you need to have a good group of people around you, people you can depend on. I was very lucky in that regard. I had a game and cooperative cast, a valiant first assistant director—Bobby Warren—and the people I hired to head the various departments all broke their backs to make the film work. It's not just a matter of knowledge and technical skill. It comes down to character and soul, the way you live your life. Not losing your temper, keeping your sense of humor under trying circumstances, respecting the efforts of others, taking pride in your own work. All the old-fashioned virtues. I can't emphasize how important these things are on a movie set. You have to create a good environment for people to work in, to establish a sense of solidarity. If that doesn't happen, the whole thing can go to hell in about two seconds.

RP: How did you go about choosing the different creative department heads—production designer, costume designer, director of photography, and so on?

PA: I suppose it was similar to the casting. A combination of people I had worked with before, friends, and absolute strangers.

RP: Kalina Ivanov, the production designer, was a *Smoke* and *Blue in the Face* veteran.

PA: Exactly. We had remained friends in the interim, and the truth is that it never occurred to me to ask anyone else to handle the job. Kalina is more than just a designer. She's a real filmmaker, a participant in the whole process. And she also has one of the most energetic, ebullient personalities I've ever encountered—with this great big Bulgarian laugh and a wicked sense of humor. You need people like Kalina with you—people who love challenges, who never take no for an answer, who walk through fire if that's what it takes to get the job done.

RP: And Adelle Lutz, the costume designer?

PA: Known to everyone as Bonny. A friend. But also someone whose work I had admired for a long time. Costumes are an important element in *Lulu*, especially in the *Pandora's Box* sections, and I needed someone with tremendous flair and imagination, a person with original ideas. Just as important, I knew that Bonny was a grown-up and would be able to handle the pressures of the job—which were clearly going to be enormous.

RP: Why enormous?

PA: Because there were so many characters to dress and design costumes for—and so few dollars and days to do it in. A lesser person would have cracked up and jumped out the window.

RP: Surely you exaggerate.

PA: Well, maybe a little—but not as much as you might think. The whole film had to operate on a very restricted budget, but the wardrobe department got the worst of it, I think. One example stands out very vividly in my mind. In the original script, the last segment from *Pandora's Box*—the one that Izzy watches in silence on his VCR—was an elaborate wedding scene that had at least fifty actors and actresses in it. It was supposed to be from an earlier moment in the story, and therefore everyone who had died later on—Peter Shine, Candy, and Lulu—would be seen alive again, in the pink of health, happy, resurrected, with a resplendent Lulu floating among them in her wedding dress. It would have been beautiful, but the hard fact was that we couldn't afford to do it. The extras were one thing, but once Bonny toted up the costs of dressing fifty actors in evening clothes, the expense proved to be too great. At first, I thought about reducing the number of guests at the party, but as I continued to whittle down the list, this compromise began to look rather dismal. What saved the scene was the extraordinary dress that Bonny designed for Mira—the one with the peacock feathers. It was so striking, so sublime, that it allowed me to rethink the scene and do it with no guests at all. Just Lulu alone in her bedroom, right after she's climbed into the dress. It turned out well, I think, and visually it's one of the strongest scenes in the film. But it was motivated by desperation. Without Bonny, I would have been lost.

RP: And what about Alik Sakharov, the director of photography? How did you decide to work with him?

PA: Because I knew the schedule was going to be very intense and grueling, I wanted to hire someone who was rather young—a person with a lot of physical stamina, who still had something to prove to the world. I interviewed quite a few people, some of them very well known. At first, Alik wasn't even on the list. But then Kalina called me up and urged me to meet with him. She talked about his work so enthusiastically, I couldn't resist—even though I was on the verge of hiring someone else. It was a sunny day in late spring, I remember, and Alik came to my house. Not only had he read the script thoroughly, and not only did he understand it and admire it, but he had written out extensive notes about how he would go about filming it. I myself had very definite ideas about how I wanted the film to look and had already thought about how many of the scenes should be shot. For the first thirty or forty minutes, I didn't say much. When you're interviewing someone, it's always more important to hear what the other person has to say. So I asked Alik how he would approach this scene, and then that scene, and then this other scene, and after a while it was as if I were listening to my own thoughts. Shot for shot, look for look, he had almost the same idea about the film that I did.

RP: What kinds of preparations did you and Alik make before filming began?

PA: We worked for weeks, just the two of us, all through the late summer and early fall, talking through every scene again and again, making up shot lists, analyzing the story in visual terms. That was the foundation of the film. Everything grew from those early conversations. Not only did we develop a plan that we both believed in, but we learned to trust each other, to depend on each other's insights and judgments. By the time filming began, we were comrades, partners in a single enterprise. We worked together in a state of tremendous harmony, and I can't tell you how important that was to me on the set. Alik was a rock of dependability, and I could always count on him, could always get my ideas through to him. He's a man of great dignity and depth of soul, and he has the endurance of a marathon runner. We were on the set for at least twelve hours every day, would go to the Technicolor lab in midtown for dailies every night, and often had to squeeze in time to scout new locations before, between, or after the day's work. And from start to finish, Alik kept going at full tilt. He was my closest collaborator on the film, the one person who was with me every step of the way.

RP: What was it like working with the actors?

PA: That's the fun part, the best part of the job. Four years ago, when Wayne [Wang] and I started rehearsing for *Smoke*, I discovered that I felt naturally connected to actors, that I had an innate sympathy for what they do. A startling discovery to make so late in life, no? But when you stop and think about it, there's a definite affinity between acting and writing novels. In both cases, the object of the work is to bring imaginary beings to life, to take something that doesn't exist and make it real, make it believable. A writer does it with his pen, and an actor does it with his body, but they're both trying to achieve the same thing. In writing my books, I always have the feeling that I'm inside my characters, that I inhabit them, that I actually become them. Actors feel the same way about what they do, and because of that I don't have any trouble understanding what they say to me. Nor do they seem to have any trouble understanding what I say to them.

RP: As a director, you're part of a collaborative process. Did you miss the creative control you have as a writer?

PA: When I was a kid, I was very involved in sports. I played on a lot of teams—baseball teams, basketball teams, football teams—and until I was well into high school, it was probably the biggest thing in my life. Then I grew up, and for the next twenty-five years or so I spent most of my time alone, sitting in a room with a pen in my hand. You have to enjoy being alone to do that, and I do enjoy being alone, but that doesn't mean I don't enjoy working with other people, too. When I began collaborating with Wayne on our two movies, it brought back memories of playing on those sports teams as a kid, and I realized that I had missed it, that I was glad to be participating in a group effort again. Yes, as a writer you have total control over what you're doing, and as a filmmaker you don't. But that's like saying oranges taste like oranges, and apples taste like apples. The two experiences are entirely different. When you write a book, you have all the time in the world. If you make a mistake, nobody sees you make it. You can just cross out the sentence and start over again. You can throw out a week's work, a month's work, and nobody cares. On a film set, you don't have that luxury. It's do or die every day. You have to accomplish your work on time, and you don't get a second chance. At least not with a tightly budgeted film like ours. So, needless to say, things can get pretty nerve-racking at times. But that doesn't mean they aren't enjoyable. When things go well, when everyone is doing his or her job the way it's supposed to be done and you pull off the thing you've set out to do, it becomes a beautiful experience, a deeply satisfying thing. I think that's why people get addicted to working in movies—the grips, the gaffers, the camera team, the prop men, the sound people, everyone. They work terribly hard, the hours are long, and no one gets rich, but every day is different from the day before. That's what keeps them at it: the adventure of it, the uncertainty, the fact that no one knows what's going to happen next.

RP: Did you find that the *imaginative* process involved in directing differs significantly from the one involved in writing?

PA: Not as much as you might think. The outward circumstances are utterly different, of course—one person sitting alone in a room as opposed to dozens of people on a noisy set—but at bottom you're trying to accomplish the same thing: to tell a story. *Lulu* was my script; it wasn't as if I was directing someone else's work. And I tried to use all the tools at my disposal to tell that story as well as I could: the actors, the camera, the lights, the locations, the sets, the costumes, and so on. Those elements create the syntax of the story. There were times when I thought: the camera is the ink, the lighting setups are punctuation marks, the props are adjectives, the actors' gestures are verbs. Very strange. But standing there on the set every day with the crew, I somehow felt that they were creating the story with me—with me and for me. It was as if they were all inside my head with me.

RP: Earlier, you talked about things going wrong on the set. Can you give me an example of what you meant?

PA: I could give you dozens of examples. Some big, some small. A lighting setup that short-circuited at the worst possible moment. A prop gun that kept misfiring. A dress that tore. All the usual mishaps. Once, I even ruined a take myself by laughing too hard. Jared Harris was doing something so funny, I just couldn't control myself any-more. . . . The incident I learned the most from, though, would have to be something that happened in the second or third week of shooting. During preproduction, I had had several meetings with Jeff Mazzola, the prop master, and we had made a thorough list of all the things that would have to be on hand for every scene in the film. Jeff was an integral part of what we did every day, and beyond being a pleasant person to be around, he brought a lot of intelligence and enthusiasm to his work. He was the one who helped me design the stone that Izzy finds in the briefcase. He was the one who worked out the pie-in-the-face scene with me—and actually threw the pie at Mira. He was the one who drove the ambulance in the last scene. I mention these things so you'll have an idea of how closely we worked together. Anyway, for the scene in which Celia says good-bye to Izzy and drives off to the airport, we needed a black town car. I had specifically told Jeff that I wanted a car that had a back window that went all the way down—so that Celia would be able to lean out and blow Izzy a kiss as the car drove away. Most cars these days have windows that go only halfway down, and Jeff had given precise instructions to the car rental place that we needed an older-model car. So, the day arrives when we're supposed to shoot the scene, and the car shows up on the set. There was an establishing shot we had to do—the car parked in front of Celia's building—and since Harvey and Mira were still in the hair-and-makeup trailer getting ready for their first scene together, I figured we could knock off the establishing shot first, which would help us save time for more important things later in the day. Just to make sure, though, I told Jeff that we should check to see if the window went all the way down. No point in doing the shot if we had the wrong car, was there? And lo and behold, the window went only halfway down. I was furious. We were working on a very tight schedule, and I knew this little blunder was going to cost us precious time and money. What could I do? I couldn't very well turn on Jeff and start blaming him. It wasn't his fault. He had ordered the right car, and I wasn't about to criticize him for not doing his job. He *had* done his job. But still, you feel this anger surging up inside you, this horrible sense of frustration. Fortunately, Jeff was just as angry as I was. Even angrier, probably. He's so conscientious about his work, and he treated this screwup as an insult to his professional pride. That's when I learned an important lesson about being a director. You can actually live your anger through other people. Jeff called up the car rental place, and as I stood there next to him, listening to him scream and curse at the man responsible for the mistake, I began to feel much better. Jeff's anger was my anger, and because he could express it for me, I was able to stay calm. At least on the outside.

RP: Of all the hundreds of things that happened on the set, what moment are you proudest of?

PA: That's hard to say. In general, I'm proud of everything we did, of everyone's work. Even when we made mistakes, we always managed to fix them—so there's really nothing I look back on with any deep regret. But the proudest moment, I don't know. There's one *happy* moment that jumps out at me, however. I don't know why I think of this one now, but there it is. The pie-in-the-face scene. Maybe because I just mentioned it a few minutes ago. It's such a small part of the film, but it took a lot of careful preparation to get it right, and Mira was a great sport about it. We all had fun doing those four little video scenes. The horror movie, the pie-in-the-face, the nun praying over the dying child, and the hooker bit with Lou Reed in the bar. I gave Mira a different name for each of these parts, just to keep things amusing. The nun, I remember, was Sister Mira of the Perpetual Performance. We probably had such a good time with these things because all the other work we did was so intense, so demanding, and these little clips gave us all a chance to relax a little, to play in a different key. Not just Mira and the other actors, but the crew as well. Anyway, I was very keen to do a pie-in-the-face gag. It's a lost art, an ancient turn that's vanished from films, and no one knows how to do it anymore. I asked a couple of older directors for advice, but they couldn't help me. "Just make it funny," one of them said. Yes, but how? So I had to sit down and figure it out for myself. The problem was that I didn't have any room for flubs. It had to be done perfectly on the first take. Otherwise, we would have needed three or four hours to set up the shot again, and we didn't have that kind of time to spend on such a small thing. If we got it wrong, the whole set would have to be redone, Mira's hair and makeup would have to be redone, and we couldn't afford to do that. The only solution was to devise a fail-proof technique.

RP: What did you use for the cream?

PA: Reddi Wip. We experimented with shaving cream, but it wasn't as good. Once everything was prepared and we'd gone through a couple of dry runs, I turned on some crazy Raymond Scott music to get everyone in the mood, and then I started giving instructions to Mira and David Byrne, who played the escort. The whole crew was watching anxiously, hoping it would work, and when it did, the whole place erupted in wild cheers and laughter. It was a wonderful moment. Not just for me, but for all of us. I remember saying to myself, "Good grief, I think I'm actually getting the hang of this job."

RP: Is it a job you'd like to do again?

PA: This is where we came in, isn't it?

RP: Not really. It's three years later, and you've just finished directing a film. Would you like to do it again?

PA: All things being equal, yes. But things are rarely equal, so I'm not going to speculate about the future anymore. The only thing I can say with any certainty is that I've poured myself into making *this* film, and I'm glad I had the chance to do it. It's been a big experience for me, and I'm never going to forget it.

February 22, 1998

lulu on the bridge

Written and Directed by
Paul Auster

Producers
Peter Newman, Greg Johnson, Amy Kaufman

Director of Photography
Alik Sakharov

Editor
Tim Squyres

Production Designer
Kalina Ivanov

Costume Designer
Adelle Lutz

Music
Graeme Revell

Executive Producers
Sharon Harel, Jane Barclay, Ira Deutchman

Still Photographer
Abbot Genser

CAST

(In order of appearance)

Izzy Maurer	**Harvey Keitel**
Dave Reilly	**Richard Edson**
Young Man	**Nick Sandow**
Young Woman	**Mel Gorham**
Tyrone Lord	**Don Byron**
Man with Gun	**Kevin Corrigan**
Celia Burns	**Mira Sorvino**
Pierre	**Victor Argo**
Dr. Fischer	**Peggy Gormley**
Bobby Perez	**Harold Perrineau**
Hannah	**Gina Gershon**
Sonia Kleinman	**Sophie Auster**
Catherine Moore	**Vanessa Redgrave**
Philip Kleinman	**Mandy Patinkin**
Stanley Mar	**Greg Johnson**
Laughing Man Escort	**David Byrne**
Dying Girl	**Holly Buczek**
Not Lou Reed	**Lou Reed**
Restaurant Man #1	**Tom Gilroy**
Restaurant Man #2	**Paul Lazar**
Restaurant Man #3	**Michael Ceveris**
Russian Thug	**Slava Schoot**
Chinese Thug	**Henry Yuk**
German Thug	**Fred Norris**
Black	**Giancarlo Esposito**
Dr. Van Horn	**Willem Dafoe**
Alvin Shine	**Jared Harris**
Peter Shine	**Josef Sommer**
Molly	**Cara Buono**
Candy	**Karen Sillas**
Jack	**David Thornton**
First Pursuer	**Brian McGuiness**
Second Pursuer	**Neil Donovan**
Paramedic #1	**Socorro Santiago**
Paramedic #2	**O. L. Duke**

What follows is the entire shooting script of *Lulu on the Bridge*. In the final version of the film, a number of scenes were either shortened or eliminated. The complete cast is listed in the credits.

1. INT: NIGHT. NEW YORK JAZZ CLUB. THE MEN'S ROOM.

Crowd noise outside. Two hundred people clapping rhythmically, urging the featured group to come out on stage. Chanting: Kat-man-du. Kat-man-du.

IZZY MAURER, a jazz veteran in his late forties or early fifties, is peeing into one of the urinals. We see him from behind. It is an old place, with crumbling plaster and paint peeling from the walls. On the wall directly in front of him, Scotch-taped above the urinals in haphazard fashion, are photographs of various movie actresses cut out from newspapers and magazines: Louise Brooks, Ingrid Bergman, Jean Harlow, Ava Gardner, Grace Kelly, Vanessa Redgrave, Isabella Rossellini, Mira Sorvino, and others. The camera scans the faces of the movie stars. Reverse angle: close-up of IZZY's face studying the photos as he pees.

DAVE REILLY, a member of the band, opens the door and pokes his head into the men's room. A bit frantic.

DAVE
There you are. Come on, Izzy, let's go. They're waiting for us.

IZZY
(*Still peeing*) Just a second. I can't go on with my dick hanging out, can I? (*Finishes. Zips up his pants*)

Cut to:

2. INT: NIGHT. NEW YORK JAZZ CLUB. HALLWAY.

IZZY steps out of the men's room into the corridor. The crowd noise increases. Two patrons of the club—a YOUNG MAN and YOUNG WOMAN—happen to be walking by. The space is so narrow that IZZY can't get past them. An awkward, indecisive moment: the man accidentally bumps into IZZY.

IZZY

(*Irritated*) Watch it.

YOUNG MAN

Sorry. (*Realizing who it is*) Jesus, you're Izzy Maurer, aren't you?

IZZY

Out of my way, kid. I've got to go on. (*The noise of the crowd swells*) Are you deaf?

YOUNG MAN

I just want you to know that I'm a big fan. I've been following your stuff for years.

YOUNG WOMAN

(*Equally impressed*) It's true. This is like, a big moment for him, you know?

IZZY

Well, it's not a big moment for me.

Both the YOUNG MAN and YOUNG WOMAN react to IZZY's cruelty with hurt, bewildered looks. IZZY begins pushing his way around them.

Noticing that the YOUNG WOMAN is attractive, he pauses for a moment to look her up and down as he slides past.

DAVE

(*From the other end of the corridor*) Izzy! Come on!

Shot of IZZY *from behind, walking quickly down the tunnel-like corridor toward* DAVE, *who is standing at the end, bathed in light. Cut to:*

3. INT: NIGHT. JAZZ CLUB. THE STAGE.

Katmandu performs. There are six musicians in the group. IZZY *plays the saxophone. He is the lead performer.*

It is a large place: high ceiling, murky light, customers sitting at tables with drinks in front of them. Then, just as the tempo quickens, a disturbance is heard in the far corner of the room (off camera). A man is shouting. People are starting to scream.

IZZY, *oblivious to the commotion, goes on playing with his eyes closed—lost in the music. The* MAN *comes into view—lurching, possessed, a gun in his right hand.*

MAN

Nancy! Nancy! God wants it this way, Nancy! We're going to burn in hell, Nancy! You and me and God—all of us together!

He fires off a wild shot. The bullet goes into the ceiling. Chunks of plaster rain down. The MAN *runs past the stage, looking for* NANCY. *The drummer and the pianist stop playing.* IZZY *continues, eyes still closed. Confusion, alarm, people getting up and running headlong for the exits. Chairs are overturned, bodies collide. Fast cuts. Zoom: the* MAN *spots* NANCY, *terrified, getting up from her seat.* ANOTHER MAN *is with her, his arm around her shoulder.*

MAN (cont'd)

(*Taking aim*) God wants it this way, Nancy! You belong to me—not to him—not to anyone but me!

IZZY'S *eyes finally open. An instant later, the gun goes off.* IZZY *is hit. The bullet goes through his left hand and then into his chest. Blood begins to spread across his shirt. We see the* MAN *rush toward* NANCY *in the upper* left-hand corner of the screen. He shoots her, shoots the man she is with, and then, howling, turns the gun on himself and puts a bullet through his own head.

Meanwhile . . . IZZY, gravely wounded, staggers for a moment and then topples off the stage to the floor. TYRONE LORD, the black drummer, leaps off the stage. He crouches beside IZZY and clamps his hands over the wound.

IZZY is lying on his back. IZZY's POV: we see a small chunk of plaster come loose from the ceiling and fall through the air. Close-up of IZZY's face: his eyes close. Cut to:

4. INT: NIGHT. HOSPITAL OPERATING ROOM.

IZZY, breathing through tubes, is lying on a hospital bed, surrounded by black limbo. Sounds of the respirator.

5. EXT: DAY. NEW YORK STREET.

Late afternoon, autumn. An attractive young woman, CELIA BURNS, is walking down the street. She enters a French restaurant: Chez Pierre.

6. INT: DAY. CHEZ PIERRE.

It is an hour or so before dinnertime. Busboys are setting up the tables. PIERRE, the owner, a man in his fifties, is sitting at one of the tables, drinking an espresso and smoking a cigarette. He is reading the New York Post. We see the front-page headline: "IZZY LIVES! Jazzman survives 7-hour operation. Left Lung Removed."

He glimpses CELIA over the top of his paper. Casually, but with affection. He clearly has something of a crush on her.

PIERRE

Hi there, pretty one.

CELIA

(*Stops*) Hi, Pierre. (*Beat*) I was wondering . . . (*Is about to say something, but is distracted by the newspaper headline*) He made it. I'm glad.

PIERRE

(*Momentarily confused, then catches on. Turns the paper around*) Yeah, he made it. But the article says he'll probably never play again. A one-lunged saxophonist with a broken hand. Doesn't sound too hopeful, does it?

CELIA

Did you ever hear him play?

PIERRE

Nah. I'm not too big on jazz. Give me Chuck Berry any day.

CELIA

I hear it's good.

PIERRE

They say there's been a big run on Katmandu's last CD.

CELIA

That's good.

PIERRE

Good? I'd call it pretty ironic. The guy plays for years, and nobody's ever heard of him. Then he gets shot, his career is destroyed, and suddenly he's a success.

CELIA

At least he's alive. You can't do anything unless you're alive. (*Starts walking toward the back of the restaurant*)

Celia.

CELIA

(*Stops*) Yes?

PIERRE

Weren't you going to say something?

CELIA

(*Laughs*) I completely forgot. (*Taps her head*) I have an audition next Tuesday. I wondered if I could work dinner instead of lunch.

PIERRE

Arrange it with Bob or Helen. If they're not willing to switch, the answer's no. If they are, then no problem.

CELIA

Okay. Fair enough. (*Starts walking away again*)

PIERRE

(*Turns back to the newspaper. Then, over his shoulder*) What's the part?

CELIA

A shampoo commercial.

PIERRE

Are you the before or the after?

CELIA

Probably neither. I don't think I'll get it.

PIERRE

Of course you will. It's in the bag.

CELIA

(*Smiles, touches her head*) Not enough hair.

True enough, her hair is rather short.

7. INT: DAY. THE HOSPITAL. A DOUBLE ROOM.

Some days later. IZZY *is in bed, heavily bandaged around the chest. His left arm is in a sling; there is a cast on his left hand.* DR. FISCHER, *a psychotherapist in her forties, is sitting in a chair beside the bed. A pen in her right hand, a yellow legal pad on her lap. The curtain around* IZZY's *bed has been closed, giving the scene a tight, claustrophobic feel.*

DR. FISCHER

So there's no point in discussing it. Is that what you think?

IZZY

How can I discuss something I can't even remember?

DR. FISCHER

That's normal. Memory loss is perfectly normal in cases like these.

IZZY

Fuck normal. Is that the only word you people know around here? I don't give a shit about normal.

DR. FISCHER

You're angry. And why shouldn't you be? A total stranger almost killed you—for no reason at all. If I were in your shoes, I'd be angry, too.

IZZY

You still don't get it. I'm not angry because I was shot. That's the one part of the business I'm willing to accept.

DR. FISCHER

I see. So getting shot was "just one of those things." Is that what you're telling me?

IZZY

Look, it's a crazy world out there, lady. Lunatics on the prowl, a gun in every pocket, and who am I to think that one of them couldn't be turned against my poor carcass? Just read the papers. The American sky is dark with ammo, and every seventeen minutes, another person gets hit.

DR. FISCHER

What are you trying to say?

IZZY

That those are the breaks. If I could go back to my old life, I wouldn't feel so bad. I'd shrug it off, get on with playing my sax, and that would be that. As it is, the moment I leave this hospital, I'm nowhere.

DR. FISCHER

You're alive. Don't ever forget that. You're alive, and by the time you get out of here, you'll be in reasonably good physical shape. Everything else is secondary. It might take a while for you to figure out your next move, but you start with life. And life is a beautiful thing, Mr. Maurer.

IZZY

No it's not. Life is life, and it's only beautiful if you make it beautiful. I wish I could say I've done that, but I can't. The only beautiful thing I've ever done is play music. If I can't have that, I might as well be dead. Am I making myself clear? I'd rather have lost both my legs or both my eyes than my left lung. A lung equals breath. Breath equals music. Music equals life. Without music, I have no life.

DR. FISCHER

You talk like someone who feels he's been punished.

IZZY

Well, maybe I have. A madman fires a bullet into my body, and justice is finally done.

DR. FISCHER

Then what about all that crazy world stuff? If you accept what happened as a random, arbitrary event, then you can't turn around and tell me it was done on purpose. It's got to be one or the other. You can't have it both ways.

IZZY

I can't, huh? And what if I feel like contradicting myself? Who's going to stop me?

DR. FISCHER

All right, contradict yourself. Let's say you were punished. In fact, let's go one step further and say that you deserved to be punished. If that's the case, then my question to you would be: who did the punishing?

IZZY

(*Shrugs. Defensive*) How should I know?

DR. FISCHER

Come, come, Mr. Maurer, you can do better than that. Who did the punishing?

IZZY

God. It has to be God, doesn't it? I mean, who else can punish a person like that?

DR. FISCHER

Are you telling me you believe in God?

No, Frau Doktor, that's not what I'm telling you. I don't believe in anything.

8. INT: DAY. CELIA'S APARTMENT. WEST TWENTY-FIFTH STREET.

CELIA *lives in a simple one-bedroom apartment in Chelsea. She enters with a purse slung over her shoulder and a yellow plastic bag from Tower Records in one hand. She flings her purse onto the sofa and walks over to a small table on which there is an inexpensive portable CD/tape player. She slides her hand into the bag and pulls out the Katmandu CD. She begins trying to remove the clear plastic wrapper and finds it exceedingly difficult. Her fingernails can't get a purchase on it. She mutters under her breath, exasperated. Finally, unable to get the wrapper off with her hands, she puts the CD in her mouth and begins using her teeth.*

After much effort, a slit is opened, and she finishes the job with her fingers, carefully peeling the silver seal from the edge of the jewel box. Once this long comedy of frustration is over, she takes out the CD and inserts it in the machine. She pushes a button and the music begins. The camera moves up to her face. We see her listening. Thoughtful.

9. INT: DAY. IZZY'S APARTMENT. PERRY STREET.

The music continues to play. . . .

We see IZZY *sitting in an armchair in the living room of his small, cramped apartment on Perry Street. His saxophone case lies on the floor, unopened. He stares at it as if it were a dead animal. Under the music, we hear the telephone ring.* IZZY *makes no move to answer it. After a moment, we hear* IZZY'S *voice saying:*

IZZY'S VOICE
Leave a message, and I'll get back to you.

Then, after the beep:

Izzy, it's Dave again. Come on, man, don't do this to me. We gotta
talk. You hear me? Don't be a schmuck, Izzy. (*Beat*) Just remember
who your friends are, okay?

*The receiver clicks. A moment later, the phone rings again. We hear IZZY's
voice ("Leave a message, and I'll get back to you"), a beep, and then another
message. As it plays, IZZY sighs, gets up from his chair, and leaves the
apartment. He moves with great difficulty. He is weak, disoriented, barely
able to put one foot in front of the other without losing his balance.*

FEMALE VOICE

Izzy, pick up the damn phone. It's Hannah, for Chrissakes. Remember me? We used to be married. Back in the old days. When
knights were brave and chicks were bold . . . and bullets weren't
invented. (*Beat*) Give me a call, Maurer, I want to know how you're
doing.

*By the time the message is over, IZZY has already left the apartment. The
empty room and the voice.*

Then, after the click, cut to:

10. EXT: DAY. STREET MONTAGE.

The music continues to play . . .

*We see IZZY stumbling around the streets of the West Village. Handheld
camera. Perceptual wobbles. Tops of buildings, sky, clouds, shuffling feet.
Colors fade in and out. Overexposures, underexposures, glinting light.
IZZY's attention is momentarily caught by isolated objects. The world in
fragments. He gets tangled up in a dog leash, bumps into a trash can. And
yet, through it all, a sense of earnest struggle, no self-pity.*

259

He moves with the determination and courage of a small child learning how to walk—or an old man refusing to give up.

A number of passersby seem to recognize IZZY. *By now, after all, he has become a famous New York figure. We see one shaking his hand and patting him on the shoulder, as if wishing him luck.* IZZY *looks down, nodding vaguely, unable to engage himself in the conversation.*

Finally, he enters the White Horse Tavern. The moment he opens the door, the music stops. Crowd noises from within.

11. INT: DAY. THE WHITE HORSE TAVERN.

An hour or two later. IZZY *is seated at a corner table with a stack of newspapers piled high in front of him: the New York dailies, the* Village Voice, *the* Observer, *the* Amsterdam News. *He is sipping a cold drink and reading a copy of* Newsday. *Utterly absorbed.*

BOBBY PEREZ, *a casually dressed man in his mid-thirties, approaches the table.*

BOBBY

Hi, Izzy.

IZZY *doesn't look up; goes on reading his paper.*

BOBBY (cont'd)

Hi, Izzy. How're you doing?

IZZY *looks up. From his expression, it is clear that he doesn't recognize the man.*

BOBBY (cont'd)

Bobby Perez. I did the sound at your Summer Stage gig last year. (*Still not much of a response. Beat*) We were all rooting for you, Iz. I'm really glad you pulled through.

IZZY

Thanks, Billy. I'm doing much better now. I think I'm a lot younger than I was the last time you saw me.

BOBBY

(*A little confused*) Wow. Yeah, probably. I see what you mean.

IZZY

And I forgot to put on my watch this morning. (*Holds up his left wrist to demonstrate*) See? No watch. I consider that progress, real progress.

12. INT: DAY. IZZY'S APARTMENT. THE BEDROOM.

Seven-thirty in the morning. IZZY is sleeping on his back. He wears boxer shorts, no top. The covers have been kicked off. We see the surprisingly large and still raw scar inscribed across his chest—the result of the emergency operation that saved his life.

The intercom buzzer sounds in the next room. Again. Three, four times. Each ring is longer and more insistent than the one before it.

IZZY's eyelids flutter. He opens his eyes. Cut to:

13. INT: DAY. IZZY'S APARTMENT. THE FRONT DOOR.

A minute later. IZZY, wearing a bathrobe, opens the door. His ex-wife, HANNAH, is standing in the hall. She is an energetic, dark-haired woman in her mid-thirties.

IZZY

(*Taken aback*) Oh. It's you.

HANNAH

(*Stepping past him into the apartment*) You don't pick up your phone, so I figured I'd pay you a visit.

Barely pausing, she marches off in the direction of the kitchen, leaving the frame. We hear the banging of cupboards, the sound of running water, a refrigerator door opening and closing, the rattling of pots and pans. IZZY shuts the front door, follows her to the threshold of the kitchen, and observes her from behind. For once he seems amused. Her energy seems to have lifted him temporarily out of the doldrums.

IZZY

You look nice in those pants.

HANNAH

(*Over her shoulder*) Don't get any ideas, chum. What's inside these pants is strictly off limits.

IZZY

Don't worry. It just brings back memories, that's all. That plump, protruding little ass of yours. For a year or two, it was the most interesting place in the world for me.

HANNAH

My ass and I are doing just fine without you, Izzy. You're not the only man who's ever admired it, you know.

IZZY

So I gathered. You don't get a tan like that hanging around the city. That new boyfriend of yours must be working out okay. (*Steps into the kitchen*) What is it? A house in the Hamptons, or something more exotic?

HANNAH

(*Busying herself with making coffee, pouring juice, popping bread into the toaster*) We'll get to him later. We have other things to talk about first.

IZZY

Like what?

HANNAH

Like you, dumbbell, that's what. I want to know what's happening to you.

IZZY

What for? I mean, you don't even *like* me.

HANNAH

You still don't know who I am, do you? After all these years, you still don't have a clue.

IZZY

Apparently not.

HANNAH

Once I give my heart to someone, it's forever. I might not want to live with you anymore, but that doesn't mean I don't care about you. (*Beat*) You're still a part of who I am, you jerk.

14. INT: DAY. IZZY'S APARTMENT. THE LIVING ROOM.

Half an hour later. IZZY and HANNAH are sitting at a small table in a corner of the living room, eating breakfast. The saxophone case is still on the floor—but in a different spot. Stereo equipment. Hundreds of records, tapes, and CDs. A few dozen books. Posters on the walls.

HANNAH

So what do you do with yourself, Izzy? How do you spend your time?

IZZY

The usual stuff. Breathing, eating, sleeping, trying to keep my head screwed on straight.

HANNAH

And you don't feel . . . lonely?

IZZY

Well, I read a lot of newspapers. That's one way of keeping in touch with your fellow human beings. You'd be amazed how much they can cram into one paper. (*Beat*) So many sad things, Hannah. It can really knock the stuffing out of you sometimes.

HANNAH

That's why I only read the comics.

IZZY

(*Ignoring her comment. Earnestly*) Most of it I can take. The fires, the earthquakes, the plane crashes. Even political horrors . . . wars . . . stuff like that. It's life, after all. It's what people do to each other, and you have to try to understand it.

HANNAH

You sound like you're seventeen years old.

IZZY

(*Still ignoring her*) But then, sometimes, you run across a little story on one of the back pages, and your heart just stops beating. A mother boils her baby in the Bronx. A man sets his girlfriend's daughter on fire in Brooklyn. I mean, it's so easy to turn life into garbage, isn't it?

HANNAH

It's not your life, Izzy. You can't go around tearing yourself apart over every rotten thing that happens.

IZZY

I don't. At least I don't make a big point of it. But these people live in the same city I do. I'd like to forget it, but sometimes I just can't.

HANNAH

Toughen up, sport. Put the chip back on your goddamn shoulder.

IZZY

(*Beat. Reflects*) I'm not the same person I used to be.

HANNAH

(*Studying him*) Don't change too much, okay? (*Beat*) You don't have to be miserable if you don't want to.

IZZY

I'm not miserable. (*Beat*) As a matter of fact, I think I'm doing okay.

HANNAH

(*Smiles*) Good. Then you're well enough to come over for dinner next week and meet Philip.

IZZY

So that's his name, huh?

HANNAH

Philip Kleinman. He's a movie producer.

IZZY

Never heard of him.

HANNAH

Big surprise. When was the last time you went to the movies, Iz?

IZZY

About twelve years ago.

HANNAH

Not since Gene Kelly retired, huh?

IZZY

Now that he's dead, I'll probably never go to the movies again.

HANNAH

(*Changing the subject*) You're going to like him. I guarantee it.

IZZY

And if I don't?

HANNAH

Then you can sit there and eat your food.

IZZY

And watch you be happy.

HANNAH

That's right. And see with your own eyes that I've finally gotten you out of my system.

15. INT. NIGHT. PHILIP KLEINMAN'S APARTMENT. TRIBECA.

We see HANNAH from behind, opening the front door. IZZY has arrived for the dinner party.

IZZY

(*Awkward*) Hi.

HANNAH

(*Ironical*) Excuse me if I'm in shock. (*IZZY steps into the apartment*) I didn't think you'd come.

IZZY

You invited me, remember?

SONIA, KLEINMAN's *ten-year-old daughter, wanders into the entrance hall.*

SONIA

(*To* IZZY) Hi.

IZZY

Hi.

HANNAH

(*To* IZZY) This is Sonia, Philip's daughter.

SONIA

(*Hesitates briefly*) Are you Izzy Maurer?

IZZY

Well, I used to be.

SONIA

Who are you now?

IZZY

(*Smiles*) I don't know. Maybe nobody.

SONIA

Well, nice to meet you, Mr. Nobody. (*Starts walking down the hallway to her room. Stops. Over her shoulder*) See you around.

HANNAH

(*Taking* IZZY *by the arm and steering him toward the living room*) There's been a slight change in plans. Philip's working on a project with Catherine Moore, and she's in New York for a few days, so we invited her to dinner too.

IZZY

The actress?

HANNAH

Former actress. She's a director now. She hasn't acted in ten or fifteen years.

IZZY

Catherine Moore. (*Beat. Remembering*) I used to have a crush on her.

Cut to:

The dining room. Time has passed. PHILIP KLEINMAN, a lively man in his forties, and CATHERINE MOORE, an English woman in her late fifties, are sitting at the table with IZZY and HANNAH. They are coming to the end of the meal.

IZZY

(*To CATHERINE*) So what made you give up acting?

CATHERINE

Vanity, Mr. Maurer. Beauty fades. The flesh gives out. You lose interest in being someone else's idea about who you are. I didn't want to be invented by other people anymore.

IZZY

So now you invent yourself.

CATHERINE

Exactly. I'm the one who controls the images.

IZZY

But no one sees you.

CATHERINE

(*Laughs*) So much the better. (*Beat*) They see what I think.

PHILIP

What they'll be seeing next is a new version of *Pandora's Box*. After a thousand bends in the road, we finally have a deal in place. (*Beat*) All we need is someone to play Lulu.

IZZY

Who's Lulu?

HANNAH

(*A little exasperated*) Come on, Maurer. Enough with the jokes already.

IZZY

No, I'm serious. Who's Lulu?

HANNAH

Lulu. As in Louise Brooks. As in Frank Wedekind. As in the opera by Alban Berg.

IZZY

Oh, that Lulu. Yeah. It rings a faint bell.

PHILIP

The girl who eats men for breakfast. You know, the one who's done in by Jack the Ripper.

CATHERINE

(*Turning to* PHILIP; *referring to a previous conversation*) You see what I mean, Philip? It's not at all obvious. People don't remember anything.

HANNAH

Don't worry, Catherine. It's not people, it's Izzy. Talk to him about anything but music and he's like a little kid.

PHILIP

(*Spotting* SONIA *enter the room*) Speaking of kids . . . (*Beat, as* SONIA *approaches the table*) Hi, sweetheart.

SONIA *gives a little wave to the company, then stops by* CATHERINE, *whose chair is closest to the door.* CATHERINE *studies* SONIA *for a moment, then reaches out and strokes her face gently with her hand. She is clearly taken with the girl's youth and loveliness.* SONIA *smiles and puts her hand on* CATHERINE's *shoulder.*

CATHERINE

(*To* SONIA) And so, my little beauty, are you going to be an actress when you grow up?

SONIA

No. I'm going to be a writer. Books are better than movies, don't you think? You see the pictures in your head.

PHILIP

Ten years old, and she has an opinion about everything.

HANNAH

(*To* SONIA) You getting tired?

SONIA

Yeah. I came out to say good night.

HANNAH

Do you want me to tuck you in?

SONIA

Is that okay?

HANNAH

(*To* PHILIP) You don't mind, do you?

PHILIP

Mind? Why should I mind?

HANNAH

(*Smiles. Gets up from her chair*) Okay. I'll be back in a few minutes.

CATHERINE

Is it all right if I go, too?

SONIA

(*Suddenly playful. Goes into a limp-wristed pose and puts on a broad New York accent*) Of cawse, dawling. I'd be chawmed.

SONIA *leaves the room with a mincing, exaggerated feminine walk.* CATHERINE *and* HANNAH *follow—both imitating her. The two women laugh. A wide shot of the three leaving the room.*

When they are gone, PHILIP *takes two large cigars out of his pocket and extends one to* IZZY.

IZZY

No, thanks.

PHILIP

(*Lighting his own cigar. Thoughtful, studying* IZZY *carefully*) Do you mind if I ask you a question?

IZZY

(*Uncertain about what* PHILIP *is driving at*) A question? Sure. Ask any question you want.

PHILIP

You don't have to answer if you don't want to. But something happened to me a couple of weeks ago, and I'm still trying to figure out if I did the right thing or not.

IZZY

You want to know what I would have done in your place?

PHILIP

Right. If you had been me, how would you have acted. (*Puffs on his cigar*) I was on a plane to London—going to see Catherine, as a matter of fact. Just as we go into our descent, I decide I have to go to the toilet. I go down the aisle, but the door is locked, so I stand there shooting the breeze with one of the stewardesses. (*Puffs on his cigar*) Finally, the door opens and out steps this good-looking girl. Very pretty, maybe twenty-four or twenty-five. She gives me an odd little look—something between a smile and a frown—and then she edges past me and I go into the bathroom. (*Puffs on his cigar*) The toilet seat and the cover are both down, and sitting on the cover is a huge turd. (*Puffs again*) I have no idea what to do. This good-looking girl has dumped her business all over the toilet seat cover, and I can't lift the thing to do *my* business without facing . . . uh . . . certain unpleasant problems. (*Puffs again*) If I complain to the stewardess, she'll think I did it. We've just had this friendly conversation, and I don't want her to think I'm that kind of person. (*Gesturing with the cigar*) Besides, there isn't much time. We're going to land in about seven minutes, and the only thing I'm really interested in is emptying my bowels and getting back to my seat. (*Puffs again*) That's the situation. Now tell me what you would have done if you'd been me.

IZZY

(*Thoughtful*) I don't know. (*Beat*) I would have complained I guess, but I'm not sure: (*Beat*) What did you do?

PHILIP

I took out some paper towels and cleaned up the mess.

IZZY

(*Impressed*) Incredible.

PHILIP

Yeah. Incredibly disgusting.

IZZY

(*Thinking it over*) I think it was a noble thing. You didn't complain. You spared the girl's feelings. You took responsibility for her when you didn't have to. (*Beat*) I don't think I've ever done anything that generous. (*Beat*) You did an admirable thing.

PHILIP

Maybe, maybe not. I'm still not sure. Maybe I was just being a coward. You know, trying to avoid a scene.

IZZY

Maybe. But I still think you acted like a mensch.

SUDDENLY: *a loud blast of rock 'n' roll music is heard from the other end of the apartment. "Big Girls Don't Cry" is playing at full volume. Cut to:*

SONIA's *room.* SONIA, HANNAH, *and* CATHERINE *are dancing to the song and singing the words: laughing, having a great time together. After a moment,* PHILIP *and* IZZY *appear in the doorway and watch.* HANNAH *and* CATHERINE *wave to them.* SONIA *blows a kiss. The dancing continues.*

16. EXT: NIGHT. STREET MONTAGE.

We see IZZY *leaving* PHILIP KLEINMAN's *building. He heads north. Walking is still difficult for him, but his coordination and stamina have improved since his outing in scene 10.*

It is after eleven o'clock. An autumn night in New York. The streets are crowded with pedestrians, traffic. Sound distortions: snatches of conversations, the whoosh of passing rollerblades, the rattling of manhole covers as trucks pass over them—as if IZZY *has entered a state of intense alertness, a zone of rare perceptual sensitivity.*

He winds up somewhere in the westernmost part of lower Manhattan, walking along empty streets lined with old warehouses and converted loft buildings.

Not another soul is in sight. It has become so still that IZZY has become aware of the sound of his own footsteps. They resonate against the pavement. At one point, he stops to listen—suddenly afraid that someone might be following him. He looks around. There is no one. He has been making the sound himself.

Walking west, a block from the Hudson River. Twenty or thirty feet ahead, lit by a glowing street lamp, IZZY catches a glimpse of a man. The man is lying on the ground, his head on the sidewalk and his feet in the gutter— sprawled out like a drunk.

IZZY continues walking, but more slowly now, sensing that something might be wrong. Closer: we can see that the man is dressed in a pinstriped business suit, that he is wearing a white shirt and a tie. Hardly the clothing of a drunk or a man who sleeps in the streets. His neatly polished shoes gleam in the light of the lamp.

Closer still. We hear the mounting panic in IZZY's breath, the shudderings of fear that pass through his body. IZZY approaches.

The man is dead. He has been shot through the middle of his forehead, and his eyes stare vacantly upward, reflecting the light of the street lamp.

IZZY lowers himself to the ground, crouches over the body, and looks at the dead man's face. A moment of horror. The man is thirty-five or forty. Short, sandy hair; a squarish, All-American face. IZZY can't take his eyes off the bullet hole in the middle of his forehead. The camera moves in on the bloody circle, that death hole that stares back like a third eye. Extreme close-up. IZZY feels that he is drowning in it, sinking straight into the center of the dead man's brain.

The man isn't a stranger so much as another version of himself. It is as if IZZY is looking at his own death, the death that almost was.

Finally, he can't take it anymore. He turns away from the dead man, pivoting so abruptly on the balls of his feet that he falls down. As he hits the ground, a terrible noise escapes from his lungs. A breath, an immense outrush of breath—as if he has been too scared to breathe.

He tries to stand up but is still so winded that he stumbles and falls again. He crawls off on all fours, moving away from the gutter toward the shadow of the nearest building. He collapses again, landing on top of a briefcase, which is lying on the sidewalk. No doubt it belongs to the dead man.

Not even aware of what he is doing, IZZY grabs hold of the briefcase and clutches it to his chest. He slowly climbs to his feet. Without turning back to look at the dead man, he staggers off into the darkness.

17. INT. NIGHT. IZZY'S APARTMENT. THE LIVING ROOM.

IZZY is sitting at the table, drinking a glass of bourbon. The bottle is beside him. In front of him: the briefcase. He studies it for a long time, reluctant to open it, yet unable to turn his eyes away.

At last: he undoes the latch. He reaches his hand inside. One by one, he pulls out: a credit card receipt slip (slightly crumpled, as if it has been thrown into the briefcase and forgotten); a paper napkin with a telephone number written on it; a pale blue Tiffany box, sealed up with ample amounts of Scotch tape, measuring about five inches along each side. He puts his hand back into the briefcase and feels around for something more. Nothing. He turns the briefcase upside down and shakes it. Nothing.

He examines the credit card slip. Insert shot. The name of the cardholder is STANLEY MAR. The purchase was for a seventy-five-dollar necktie at Barney's on 4-12-96.

Next, he examines the napkin. Insert shot: Scrawled in blurry ink from a felt-tip pen, we read: 555-0192.

Then, and only then, the box. He tries to tear off the tape with his fingers. It is stubborn, and it takes some time for him to remove it. Inside the box there is another box—this one made of sturdy brown cardboard and taped even more securely than the first.

IZZY tries to tear off the tape with his fingers, but with no success. He gets up from the table and leaves the frame. The camera stays on the box. We hear noises from the kitchen. IZZY comes back into the frame holding a paring knife. He sits down at the table and slits open the tape with the knife. Inside the second box there is a third box. This one is black and shiny and quite small—about three inches along each side. IZZY slits the tape and removes the top. There are small strips of shredded newspaper inside—a nest of packing excelsior. Hidden inside the papers there is a small stone. It is an irregular lump of hard material approximately two to two-and-a-half inches in diameter. It easily fits inside IZZY's palm.

He puts the stone down on the table. Insert shot. The stone is a stone only in the loosest sense of the term. It clearly doesn't come from the ground, and it clearly isn't precious or beautiful or any of the other things one might have expected it to be. It looks like a clump of construction material that has fallen off a building: a jagged shard of cement studded with gravel and glittering fragments of glass or mica. It is a homely, forlorn thing, a bit of late-twentieth-century detritus.

Around the edges of the frame during the insert shot, we see some of the strips of the shredded newspapers. The papers are written in different languages: Russian, Chinese, Hebrew, Arabic. Sound: all through this shot, a vague murmuring of different voices can be heard, male and female alike, each one speaking a different language.

Nothing can be heard distinctly. Every now and then, a word emerges from the confusion, but only for the smallest flicker of a second.

Shot of IZZY, sitting at the table. The murmurs continue. He picks up the stone, puts it down again, and stares at it. He pours himself another drink. Takes a sip, puts the glass down on the table, and continues to look at the stone.

18. INT: NIGHT. IZZY'S APARTMENT. THE BEDROOM/THE LIVING ROOM.

Later. IZZY, *dressed in a T-shirt and boxer shorts, enters the bedroom with the stone in his hand. He puts it down on the bedside table, climbs into bed, and turns out the light.*

Obscurity. We see IZZY *lying in bed, his eyes open, staring up at the ceiling. After a moment, a glowing blue light can be seen to his right, coming from the area of the bedside table. The source of the light, however, is not visible, since* IZZY'S *body and head are blocking the view.*

After another moment, IZZY *notices the blue glow and is wrenched from his thoughts. He sits up suddenly, turns his head, and looks at the stone.*

Shot of the bedside table. The stone has utterly changed. It is smooth now, and all around it the air is bathed in a rich blue light.

IZZY *lets out a gasp of alarm. He quickly gets out of bed and rushes to the door. He flicks on the overhead light. Just like that, everything returns to normal. Shot of the bedside table. The stone looks as it did before. Shot of* IZZY. *He is breathing hard, panicked. He has no idea what is going on. He turns off the overhead light again. Obscurity. For a moment, nothing happens. Perhaps it was all a dream. Three, four beats. Then, just as* IZZY *is about to turn on the light again, the stone begins to glow once more. The same blue, the same mysterious light. After a few moments, the stone begins to levitate, rising three or four inches off the surface of the table. It hovers in the air for several moments, the blue light steadily intensifying. Beside himself with confusion and fear,* IZZY *turns on the light again. Shot of the bedside table. The stone as before. Cut to:*

The living room. IZZY *enters, turns on the light, and stumbles into the saxophone case. He kicks it aside. Goes to a chest of drawers. Opens the top right drawer and rummages inside, desperately sifting through various objects. Gives up; slams the drawer shut. Opens the top left drawer.*

Same desperate rummaging. Finds an old pack of cigarettes and a book of matches. Shakes a cigarette out and lights up. Takes a drag. It causes intense pain. He grabs hold of his chest and doubles over for a moment. Gradually pulls himself together. Sits down in the armchair. Cautiously takes another puff. The camera slowly moves in on IZZY's face. His hand trembles as he brings the cigarette to his mouth.

19. INT: DAY. IZZY'S APARTMENT. THE BEDROOM.

The next morning. IZZY, *looking haggard and unshaven, dressed in his bathrobe, stands by the bedside table, where the stone still sits from the previous night. Holding the napkin in his hand, he checks the telephone number that is written on it. He reaches for the telephone, then hesitates. He studies the phone for a moment. Reaches again, hesitates again. Takes a deep breath. Reaches a third time and picks up the receiver. Sound of the dial tone. Beat. Reluctant to dial, he looks at the number on the napkin again.*

Then, very quickly, he begins to dial the numbers . . .

20. INT: DAY. CELIA'S APARTMENT. THE KITCHEN.

The Katmandu CD is playing softly. CELIA *sits at the table wearing her bathrobe and drinking coffee. She has just woken up. The phone rings. She reaches for the phone (which is mounted on the wall) and lifts the receiver off the hook.*

CELIA

Hello . . . (*Listens*) Who? . . . You're kidding . . . Believe it or not, I'm listening to your record now . . . My name? How can you call me if you don't know my name? . . . Oh. I see . . . Celia Burns. (*Listens. Pronounces name more clearly*) Celia Burns. . . . All right. If it's that important . . . Okay . . . Two-fifty-eight West Twenty-fifth Street. Second floor . . . Fine. I'll see you then. (*Hangs up, completely perplexed*)

21. INT: DAY. CELIA'S APARTMENT. THE LIVING ROOM.

An hour later. CELIA, *dressed in casual clothes, opens the door.* IZZY *is standing in the doorway, holding a plastic bag in his left hand.*

IZZY

(*Hesitates*) Celia?

He studies her face. A brief moment of confusion—as if he recognizes her from somewhere.

CELIA

It *is* you. I recognize you from your picture. (IZZY *steps into the apartment and she shuts the door*) After I hung up, I thought someone might be playing a trick on me.

IZZY

No tricks. Just one question. Do you know a man named Stanley Mar?

CELIA

(*Puzzled*) Stanley Mar?

IZZY

M-A-R.

CELIA

I don't think so.

IZZY

(*Agitated*) Thirty-five, forty. Looks like a businessman, maybe a lawyer. Wears nice suits. Shops for his ties at Barney's.

Little by little IZZY *is backing* CELIA *into the apartment. He is so upset, so consumed by his need to understand, that he scarcely takes any notice of her. She, on the other hand, is becoming a little frightened.*

CELIA

(*Backing away from him*) I don't know. Maybe. I had a drink with someone named Stanley about a year ago. He never told me his last name.

IZZY

(*Very agitated*) Maybe? What's this maybe. (*Takes the napkin with her address and phone number on it out of his pocket and thrusts it at her*) What's this? What the fuck is this?

CELIA

(*Studies the napkin*) This isn't my handwriting. (*Looks at* IZZY) How did you get this?

IZZY

He had it on him. And you're going to stand there and tell me you saw him only once?

CELIA

If it's the same Stanley we're talking about—yes. I work in a restaurant. I served him dinner one night, and he asked me out. I found him boring. All he talked about was money.

IZZY

(*Holding up the plastic bag. Adamant; nearly hitting her in the face with it*) And what about this? I suppose you don't know anything about this, either.

CELIA

(*Backing away; peeved; slowly gaining the upper hand*) I don't know what you're talking about. (*Beat*) Look, I really like your music, and I'm sorry about what happened to you, but you're acting like a crazy man. If you don't calm down, I'm going to have to ask you to leave.

IZZY

(*Reaches into the bag, pulls out the black box, and holds it up*) You don't understand.

He puts the box on the coffee-table, lifts the top off the box and takes out the stone. He shows it to her, holding it between two fingers.

CELIA

(*Unimpressed, puzzled*) What is it?

IZZY

You tell me.

CELIA

(*Laughs*) Me?

IZZY

Mar was carrying two things with him. The napkin with your number on it—and this.

IZZY hands the stone to CELIA. She examines it.

CELIA

It doesn't look like anything. It's just . . . shit . . . a little piece of shit. (*She hands it back to him*)

IZZY

I know. That's what it looks like, doesn't it? (*Beat*) Close the blinds.

CELIA

(*Thrown*) What?

IZZY

We have to make it dark in here. (*Puts the stone down on the coffee table, walks to a window, and pulls down the shade*) The darker the better.

CELIA

I don't like it when people order me around.

IZZY

(*Walks to another window; pulls down another shade*) Just humor me.
I'm not going to hurt you. (*Pulling down another shade*) You don't
mean anything to me—

CELIA

(*More and more peeved*) That's pretty obvious, isn't it?

IZZY

—I just have to show you this.

CELIA

(*Firm*) Five minutes. And then I want you out of here. Got it? I
have better things to do than play games with you.

IZZY

(*Ignoring her; pulling down the last shade*) Okay. Now turn out the
light.

CELIA *walks over to the light switch by the door. She flicks the switch, and
the overhead light goes off. Obscurity.*

IZZY

Now watch.

A few beats. Nothing happens.

CELIA

(*Cynical*) I'm watching.

IZZY

(*Impatient*) Just wait. Give it a little time.

Close-up of the stone on the coffee table, barely visible in the darkness. Little by little, it begins to glow, to become smooth, to emit the same blue light it did in IZZY's *apartment.*

A close-up of CELIA's *face, bathed in the blue light. She is astonished, filled with wonder.*

CELIA

Oh my God.

IZZY

You see?

CELIA

(*Awed*) It's beautiful. It's the most beautiful thing I've ever seen.

IZZY

And Mar never said anything to you about it?

CELIA

(*Transfixed by the light; not wanting to be interrupted*) Sshh!

CELIA *begins walking toward the coffee table, approaching the stone, which is now hovering a few inches above the surface. The nearer she gets, the more intense and radiant the light becomes.*

IZZY

(*Alarmed*) What are you doing?

CELIA

(*Standing near the stone; studying it; amazed*) Be quiet.

IZZY

Don't touch it!

CELIA

Why not?

IZZY

Because . . . because we don't know what it is.

CELIA

Don't be silly. Of course I'm going to touch it. (*Beat*) How could I not touch it?

She sits down on the sofa next to the coffee table, leans forward, and cups the glowing stone in her two hands. For a moment or two, she just sits there, absorbing the feel of it. Then, very slowly, she begins to smile. The stone seems to have produced some unexpected, happy effect. Another moment goes by, and she begins to laugh—softly, as if to herself, as if some daunting inner puzzle had suddenly been clarified. It is a laugh of knowledge, of understanding.

IZZY

What does it feel like?

CELIA

(*Not wanting to interrupt the experience—yet playful, teasing*) I'm not going to tell you. (*Beat, concentrating on the feel of the stone*) I don't share secrets with cowards.

IZZY

(*A little defensive*) I'm just not stupid, that's all.

CELIA

(*Looking up at him. Her face full of life, joy*) Oh, come on. Don't be afraid. It's the best thing. It really is. It's like nothing else.

She starts laughing again, swept away by the power of what is happening to her.

Reluctantly, IZZY *walks over to the sofa and sits down beside her. He looks at* CELIA *suspiciously. After a moment, she reaches out with the stone, her arm fully extended.* IZZY *finally opens his hand, and she places the stone carefully in his palm. IZZY sits back and holds the stone in both hands. After a moment, he laughs nervously, surprised by what he is feeling.*

CELIA

(*Studying him carefully*) It's amazing, isn't it?

IZZY

(*Sinking more deeply into the feeling*) Jesus . . . (*After a moment, hands the stone back to her. A long silence. Studies her intently*) You feel more alive, don't you?

CELIA

Yes. (*Beat. Thoughtful. Looking straight ahead*) More . . . connected.

IZZY

Connected to what?

CELIA

I don't know. (*Beat. Thinks. Still looking ahead*) To myself. To the table. To the floor. To the air in the room. To everything that's not me. (*Another beat*) To you.

Several more beats. She hands the stone back to IZZY. He holds it for a while before speaking. CELIA watches him.

IZZY

(*Looking ahead*) When I woke up this morning, I didn't know who you were. The way I'm feeling now, I think I could spend the rest of my life with you. I think I'd be willing to die for you.

CELIA

(*Growing upset*) Don't . . .

IZZY

I'm sorry. I'm just telling you the truth. (*Hands her the stone. Another beat*)

CELIA

Do you know what it means to die for someone? (*Long beat. Almost to herself*) It's not fair.

IZZY

Why not?

CELIA

Turn on the light. Please turn on the light.

A moment passes. IZZY gets up, walks to the nearest light switch, and turns it on. The room returns to normal. The blue stone returns to its original state. As IZZY walks around the room, opening the curtains and blinds, CELIA puts the stone back in the box. IZZY watches carefully.

IZZY

I think I should go now.

CELIA

I'm sorry.

IZZY

I'll come back tomorrow.

CELIA

Yes. Come back tomorrow.

He looks at her tenderly. She gives him a weak, confused smile. Hands him the box. He puts it in his pocket, touches her face with his hand. She kisses his hand gently.

Then he turns, walks to the door, and leaves the apartment. She continues to sit on the sofa. Watches the door close.

She leans back her head, arching her neck over the top of the sofa, puts her hands over her eyes. When she removes her hands, we see that she is blinking back tears. Close shot.

She stands up, fighting against her feelings, struggling not to break down. She begins tidying the living room—opening the curtains more, adjusting the blinds.

Suddenly, without coming to any apparent decision, she rushes across the room, opens the door, and leaves the apartment.

22. EXT: DAY. WEST TWENTY-FIFTH STREET.

IZZY is walking slowly down the street. Over his shoulder, we see CELIA running to catch up with him. She moves on past him, stops, and then turns to face him.

CELIA

(Out of breath. A moment) I have some shopping to do. I thought maybe you'd like to come with me.

IZZY

(Studying her. A smile slowly forming) Sounds good.

CELIA

Eggs, oranges, those kinds of things.

IZZY

You can't live if you don't eat, right?

23. INT: DAY. CELIA'S APARTMENT. THE BEDROOM.

Several hours later. IZZY and CELIA are in CELIA's bed, under the sheets. Daylight pours through the window. The stone is nowhere in sight. CELIA is awake, her head propped in one hand, watching IZZY, who is lying on his back. He has just opened his eyes.

CELIA

(*Smiling, tranquil, and yet totally puzzled*) I don't even know who you are.

IZZY

(*Reaching out and gently touching her face*) Yes you do. You know everything about me.

He sits up. We see the scar.

CELIA

(Laughs) Not really.

IZZY

But it doesn't matter, does it?

CELIA

No. As long as you don't get up and leave now, I don't suppose it does.

IZZY

(*Taking her in his arms; settling in*) You don't see me rushing to get out of here, do you?

CELIA

(*Her head on his chest, smiling. Beat*) Tell me, Izzy, are you an ocean or a river?

IZZY

What?

CELIA

It's a game I used to play with my sister. You have to answer.

IZZY

(*Catching on*) An ocean or a river. (*Thinks for a moment*) A river.

CELIA

Are you a . . . match . . . or a cigarette lighter?

IZZY

A match. Definitely a match.

CELIA

Are you a car . . . or a bicycle?

IZZY

A bicycle.

CELIA

Are you an owl or a hummingbird?

IZZY

Hmm. I used to be a hummingbird. But now I'm an owl.

CELIA

Are you sneakers or boots?

IZZY

That's not fair. You have to give me a chance now.

CELIA

(*Holding firm*) Sneakers or boots?

IZZY

Boots. (*Pulling her up so that he can see her face*) Now it's my turn.

CELIA

It's fun, isn't it? We used to do it for hours.

IZZY

(*Puts his fingers to his lips, as if to say no more talking*) All right now, concentrate. (*Beat. Entering a different register; very serious*) Are you a real person . . . or a spirit?

CELIA

(*Long beat; studying him; gradually becoming more emotional*) A real person.

IZZY

Do you understand what's happened, or are you in the dark like me?

CELIA

(*Trembling slightly*) In the dark.

IZZY

Are you in love . . . or just going along for the ride?

CELIA

(*With tears gathering in her eyes*) In love.

IZZY

Are you with the person you love . . . or not with the person you love?

CELIA

(*Begins to cry in earnest; overcome*) With the person. (*Close-up of her face. She repeats the line—almost inaudibly*) With the person.

24. EXT: DAY. CELIA'S BUILDING. THE ROOF.

IZZY and CELIA are sitting on a blanket on the roof. CELIA is dressed now; IZZY as before. The city sprawled out around them. We catch them in mid-conversation.

IZZY

There was a hole . . . right in the middle of his forehead . . . like a huge blind eye. I thought I was going to drown in it. Once I looked in there . . . I thought I'd never get out.

CELIA

(*Long beat. Absorbing what he has said. Touches him tenderly*) He must have been killed for the stone.

IZZY

Then why didn't they take it?

CELIA

(*Thoughtful*) Maybe something went wrong.

IZZY

I wish I could give it back.

CELIA

Back? Back to who?

IZZY

To the person who owns it. I don't know . . . to the place where it belongs.

CELIA

Do you know what it reminds me of?

IZZY

What?

CELIA

The Berlin Wall.

IZZY

Not big enough.

CELIA

Remember when the wall came down in eighty-nine? Little pieces of it were floating around all over the place. A friend of mine was given one in Germany. It looked exactly the same . . . exactly like the thing you found.

IZZY

A cruddy little chunk of cement.

CELIA

Just like that.

IZZY

So you're saying that Russian scientists planted some mysterious substance in the Berlin Wall?

CELIA

No. I'm just telling you what it reminds me of.

IZZY

I'll tell you what it reminds me of. A piece of some building you see on a New Jersey highway. You know, a bowling alley, or a warehouse . . . or maybe some fly-by-night topless bar.

CELIA

(*Amused*) Why not?

IZZY

(*Beat. More serious*) Celia?

CELIA

(*Taking a sip of her drink. The pleasure of hearing him say her name*) Say it again.

IZZY

Celia.

CELIA

I love hearing you say that. (*Beat*) Say it again.

IZZY

Celia.

CELIA

(*As if melting*) Yes?

IZZY

(*Smiling*) Are you happier on this roof . . . or happier downstairs in bed?

Cut to:

25. INT: DAY CELIA'S APARTMENT. THE BEDROOM.

Same as scene 23. IZZY *and* CELIA *are in bed. They have just finished making love. Light pours through the windows.*

IZZY *is lying on his back.* CELIA *is touching and examining his scar.*

CELIA

It's a beautiful scar. Without this scar, you wouldn't be alive. Without this scar . . . you wouldn't be here with me now. . . . Do you understand? It's a good and precious thing . . . (*Her eyes drift over to the alarm clock on the bedside table. It's five-thirty. Sudden panic*) Oh, my God! I have to go to work. (*Jumps out of bed and begins getting dressed*)

IZZY

(*Still lying in bed*) Why don't you call in sick?

CELIA

(*Rushing around*) I can't. I really can't. I've earned twelve hundred dollars as an actress this year. If I didn't have this job, I wouldn't eat.

IZZY

I don't want to let you out of my sight.

CELIA

I'll be back by midnight. You can wait for me here.

IZZY

(*Thinking*) Maybe I could work with you.

CELIA

What do you mean?

IZZY

I don't know. Maybe they need another waiter or something.

CELIA

(*She laughs at the absurdity of the proposal*) But you're a musician.

IZZY

Not anymore. My job is to be with you. That's my work now.

CELIA *sits down on the bed and takes hold of his hand. Moved by what he has said.*

CELIA

Are you real . . . or did I make you up?

IZZY

(*Pursuing the question*) Well?

CELIA

We could talk to Pierre.

IZZY

Pierre? What is it, a French restaurant?

CELIA

Not really. It's sort of fake French. Just like Pierre. I think he's from the Bronx. (*Beat*) There might be an opening for a busboy.

IZZY

I'll wash dishes if I have to.

CELIA

(*Leaning over and kissing him*) You'd better get dressed, then.

IZZY

(*Climbing out of bed. Touching his face*) I should shave, don't you think? Don't want to make a bad impression.

CELIA

Don't worry. If Pierre doesn't hire you, I'll tell him I'm going to quit.

26. INT: NIGHT. CHEZ PIERRE.

Close-up of a glass. We see ice water being poured into it. The camera backs up to reveal IZZY, *dressed in a white jacket, working as a busboy at Chez Pierre. It is dinnertime, and the place is crowded. Hustle, bustle, colliding conversations. We see* PIERRE *behind the bar, serving drinks to customers who are waiting for tables. Across the room,* CELIA *is taking orders at a table for four. She looks up and sees* IZZY *clearing away dishes from a table. Their eyes meet; they exchange a warm, complicitous smile.* PIERRE, *in between at the bar, notices their secret communication. He appears to be none too pleased. The camera lingers on* PIERRE'S *face for a moment. A blood-curdling scream is heard. Cut to:*

27. INT: NIGHT. CELIA'S APARTMENT. THE TV SCREEN/THE LIVING ROOM.

A close-up of CELIA'S *face: an expression of absolute terror. She is screaming her lungs out. From behind, we see a man walking toward her, backing her into a corner. Pounding music. Her arm is raised, and a butcher knife gleams in his hand.* CELIA *has run out of space. She sinks to her knees in despair.*

The camera backs up. The scene has been playing on the TV set in CELIA's *living room.* IZZY *and* CELIA *are watching together on the sofa, eating ice cream out of a container. It is a video reel of samples of* CELIA's *work.*

CELIA

That was the first part I got. Three years ago—just after I came to New York. *Horror Machine VI.* You take what you can get, right? (*Watching screen. Her expression changes; brightens enthusiastically*) Oh— watch this. It's a little bit I did in *The Laughing Man.*

Cut to the screen. CELIA, *wearing an elegant 1920s dress, is in a restaurant, sitting at a table with a man in a tuxedo. Jaunty music. She looks radiant, beautiful. She studies the menu, looks up, smiles at the man. An instant later, a cream pie hits her in the face.*

CELIA (*off*)

Pow!

IZZY (*off*)

(*Laughs*) That's terrible.

The TV screen goes black for a few moments.

CELIA

Now for some pure corn.

Next clip. CELIA, *dressed in a nun's habit, is sitting beside a hospital bed. A ten-year-old girl is lying there with her eyes closed—on the point of death, perhaps already dead. A religious choir sings in the background. Hands clasped together,* CELIA *prays for the child, her voice filled with conviction and suffering.*

CELIA ON SCREEN

. . . Yea though I walk through the valley of the shadow of death, I will fear no evil, for thou art with me . . .

The screen suddenly goes silent. We see the word MUTE *in the upper left-hand corner.*

                    CELIA *(off)*
You don't want to hear this.

                    IZZY *(off)*
Yes I do.

                    CELIA
It's awful.

                    IZZY
No it's not.

The MUTE *sign disappears.*

                CELIA ON SCREEN
Surely goodness and mercy shall follow me all the days of my life,
and I shall dwell in the house of the Lord forever.

After the clip ends, the screen goes black for a few moments, as before.

                    CELIA
This is something I did last year.

Next clip. CELIA, *wearing a blond wig, is sitting at a bar, smoking a cigarette
and nursing a drink in front of her. She is clearly a prostitute.*

After a moment, a MAN *appears and sits down beside her. Sultry music
plays in the background.*

                    IZZY
Hey, that's Lou Reed.

                    CELIA
No it's not. It just looks like him.

                    MAN ON SCREEN
Hi, Sweetheart.

CELIA ignores him, goes on smoking her cigarette.

                  MAN ON SCREEN (*cont'd*)
Looking for some fun?

                    CELIA ON SCREEN
(*Cynical*) Fun? What's your idea of fun, big guy?

                    MAN ON SCREEN
I don't know. You tell me.

                    CELIA ON SCREEN
(*Long beat, deciding whether or not to answer him*) It'll cost you fifty
bucks to get me off this stool. You want me to walk through that
door with you (*gestures with her head to the front door*), it'll cost you
another fifty bucks. The motel charges seventy-five, and my rates
start at a hundred and twenty per half hour. That's with my clothes
on. You want me to take them off, it's another fifty. (*Beat*) Still
interested?

                    MAN ON SCREEN
Yeah, I'm interested.

                    CELIA ON SCREEN
(*Sighs*) All right, be a good boy and go outside and wait for me. I
want to finish my drink.

*The MAN hesitates for a second, then gets up and leaves. CELIA takes a
drag of her cigarette and stares ahead, then lifts the glass to her lips. The
screen goes black for a few moments, as before.*

                         IZZY
Jesus, you're one tough cookie.

CELIA

Scary, isn't it? (*Beat*) I really liked doing that scene. (*Clicks off the TV with the remote control*) Not much to show for myself so far.

IZZY

Nun . . . whore . . . murder victim . . . and a pie in the face. I'd say you're off to a good start.

CELIA

Movies are tough. I've always had better luck with plays. (*Beat*) I got an agent two months ago. She's the one who put together this tape.

IZZY

Has it helped?

CELIA

Yes and no. I've had more auditions—but no work yet. (*Beat*) I have another audition Monday afternoon.

IZZY

What's the part?

CELIA

Lulu. There's going to be a new version of *Pandora's Box*.

IZZY

(*Stunned*) You're kidding.

CELIA

(*Not understanding*) No, it's really happening. They're looking for someone completely unknown. (*With self-deprecation*) So maybe I have a chance. (*Beat*) I'd love to do that part. It's one of the best roles ever written for a woman.

IZZY

I know the people making that movie. Catherine Moore—she's the
director, right? And Philip Kleinman's the producer.

CELIA

You know them?

IZZY

(*Enthusiastic*) Know them? I just had dinner with them a few days
ago. I'll call them up, put in a word for you . . . get the ball rolling.
(*Laughs. Claps his hands, rubs them together*) I'm going to get you that
part, Celia. You watch. With me around, you don't need an agent.

28. EXT: DAY. NEW YORK STREET CORNER.
CORNER OF PRINCE AND LAFAYETTE.

IZZY *is talking to someone from a pay phone on the corner, watching the
entrance of the building at 225 Lafayette Street.*

IZZY

I just wanted to thank you, Hannah. You've been great. (*Listens*)

Shot of CELIA *leaving the building*

IZZY

There she is now. I'll catch you later. (*Hangs up*)

CELIA *is standing in front of the door, looking around.*

IZZY (*still not at normal speed, but less hobbled by his injuries than before*)
rushes into the frame, puts his arm around CELIA's *shoulder, and kisses her
on the cheek.*

IZZY

How did it go?

CELIA

(*Looking uncertain*) I don't know.

They begin walking down the street.

CELIA (*cont'd*)

I don't think I was very good.

They walk for a moment in silence

CELIA (*cont'd*)

But it was a good experience. I got to talk to Catherine Moore, anyway. She's fantastic. An incredible woman.

The camera pulls back. We see CELIA and IZZY walking down the street together from behind. We no longer hear what they are saying.

29. INT: NIGHT. CHEZ PIERRE.

Another crowded dinner hour at the restaurant. IZZY goes about his job, pouring ice water into glasses at various tables. He glances up and sees CELIA taking orders at a table occupied by three businessmen in their thirties. This time, the bar is manned by someone other than Pierre—who is off in the kitchen.

Closer shot of CELIA with the three men. They all appear to be rather drunk. Each one studies CELIA with lust in his eyes, looking her up and down. She stands there with her order pad, pretending not to notice.

FIRST MAN

You wouldn't be free later tonight, would you?

CELIA

(*Matter-of-factly*) Sorry, I'm busy. (*Beat*) Have you decided on your orders?

SECOND MAN

She's just playing hard-to-get.

THIRD MAN

We'd be happy to . . . uh . . . make it worth your while.

CELIA

The duck is very good tonight. The chef is recommending it.

FIRST MAN

Fuck the duck. (*Laughs at his own witless joke*) I'm interested in other kinds of meat.

Reaches out and pats CELIA *on the behind. She swats his hand away.*

Shot of IZZY. *He has seen what has just happened. He puts down the pitcher of ice water on the table he is serving and rushes over to the table with the three men.*

IZZY

(*Addressing the* FIRST MAN. *Angry*) Hey, stupid. Keep your hands to yourself.

CELIA

It's all right, Izzy. I can handle it.

FIRST MAN

(*To* IZZY) Mind your own business, (*spitting out the next two syllables with contempt*) bus-boy.

SECOND MAN

Yeah. Go and clear away some dirty dishes.

IZZY

(*To* FIRST MAN) This is my business, asshole.

CELIA

(*Growing alarmed. Trying to push* IZZY *away*) It's nothing. Believe me, it's nothing.

IZZY

(*Boiling into a rage*) Nothing? This schmuck starts feeling you up, and you call it nothing?

He pushes CELIA *aside. Goes after the* FIRST MAN *and grabs him violently by the lapels. Pain shoots through his left hand. He drops his left arm but continues holding on with his right. With one hand, he pulls the* FIRST MAN *out of his chair.*

IZZY

Come on, wise guy—do it again! I dare you. Do it again!

IZZY *throws the* FIRST MAN *backwards—straight into a nearby table. Clattering plates, silverware, overturned wine glasses. A woman shrieks. A general commotion breaks out in the restaurant.* IZZY *goes after the* FIRST MAN *again. The* SECOND MAN *and the* THIRD MAN *get up from their seats and go after* IZZY. PIERRE *comes running from the kitchen. He is beside himself with fury.*

PIERRE

Stop it! Stop it!

He pushes aside the SECOND MAN *and* THIRD MAN, *then wraps his arms around* IZZY *in a powerful bear hug from behind—just as* IZZY *is about to punch the* FIRST MAN *in the face.*

PIERRE

(*To* IZZY) How dare you! How dare you!

Wrestling him away from the others, he pushes IZZY *toward the bar, then—releasing him—throws him roughly against it.* IZZY *bangs his back against the panel and falls to the ground. A sense of* IZZY'*s weakness, of the physical toll this outburst has caused him.*

PIERRE

Are you trying to ruin this business! Is that what you want—to destroy me!

IZZY slowly climbs to his feet. PIERRE grabs him again.

PIERRE

I'll kill you, you son-of-a-bitch! Do you hear me! I'll kill you!

CELIA tries to pull PIERRE away from IZZY.

PIERRE

(*Shrugging her off*) I never should have hired this maniac. I never should have let you talk me into it.

Suddenly returns to his senses a little bit. Sees the THREE MEN and other CUSTOMERS starting to leave the restaurant. In gracious, accommodating tones.

PIERRE

Please, everyone, please go back to your seats. I'm sorry for the disturbance. (*Chasing after the THREE MEN*) Please, gentlemen, please return to your table. Dinner is on the house tonight.

The departing customers return. BUSBOYS, WAITERS, and WAITRESSES begin clearing up the mess caused by the fight. PIERRE turns his attention back to IZZY, who is still standing by the bar. With calm and bitter determination.

PIERRE

You—I want out of my sight. Get your things and leave. You're fired.

CELIA

Pierre, please . . . it won't happen again.

PIERRE

(*Ignoring her appeal*) You're damned right it won't. If he ever sets foot in my place again, I'll tear him apart.

CELIA

(*Standing firm; defending* IZZY) If he goes, I go.

PIERRE

Then go. I don't care. You brought this bum in, you can take him out.

CELIA

(*Upset. To* PIERRE) You don't know what you're saying . . .

PIERRE

(*To* CELIA) I used to be the only friend you had. . . . (*Looks at* IZZY; *shakes his head*) Bad move, Celia. Very bad move.

PIERRE *turns to leave, stops, is about to address one last line to her but thinks better of it and walks away.*

30. EXT: NIGHT. MANHATTAN STREETS.

A few minutes later. CELIA *and* IZZY *are walking along slowly, side by side.* CELIA *is very agitated.*

CELIA

(*On the point of tears*) How could you do that? Do you know how much I need that job? Two-and-a-half years I've been working there—and in one night you ruin everything.

IZZY

(*Not defending himself. Contrite, ashamed*) I'm sorry. That's how I used to be. All crazy and wild. I'm sorry. I don't want to be that person anymore. I swear to you, I'll never act that way again.

31. INT: NIGHT. CELIA'S APARTMENT.

CELIA and IZZY enter the apartment in silence. They are both out of sorts, grumpy, not finished with their quarrel. IZZY heads straight for the bathroom and bangs the door shut. CELIA goes into the bedroom. A light is flashing on the answering machine. She sits down on the bed and plays the message.

> WOMAN'S VOICE

Celia, this is Maggie. I've just had two calls. One from Philip Kleinman and one from Catherine Moore—and you've got the part. You're the one they want. It's fantastic. Call me tomorrow morning, and I'll fill you in on the details. Congratulations, darling. I'm just over the moon for you.

CELIA is stunned. She sits on the bed without moving. At that moment, IZZY walks into the bedroom. She looks up and smiles at him, a strange expression on her face.

> IZZY

Are you all right?

> CELIA

I got the part. I'm Lulu.

32. INT: DAY. ODEON RESTAURANT.

A celebratory Sunday brunch. Five people are present, sitting at a round table: IZZY, CELIA, PHILIP KLEINMAN, HANNAH, and CATHERINE MOORE. Begin with a close shot of IZZY's face. He is happy, enjoying himself, pleased to have played such an important part in getting CELIA the role. To one side of him, PHILIP and HANNAH are talking to each other; to the other side, CELIA and CATHERINE are engrossed in conversation. IZZY alone says nothing, listening to both pairs of speakers at once, turning his attention now to one pair, now to the other. We hear bits of what each pair is saying.

PHILIP and HANNAH are studying CELIA across the table. IZZY watches them as they watch her. After a moment, he abruptly turns his attention to CELIA and CATHERINE.

CATHERINE

"We are all lost creatures," he said. "It is only when we admit this that we have a chance of finding ourselves."

CELIA

But Lulu doesn't admit anything. She doesn't know anything. She just is.

CATHERINE

Wedekind said that Lulu isn't a real character, that she's an embodiment of primitive sexuality . . . and whatever evil she causes comes about by accident—because she's passive, because she plays a purely passive role.

CELIA

(*Thinks again*) No . . . I don't agree. She's impulsive, but she's not a destroyer. . . . She doesn't care what people think of her. That's what gives her her power. She has no pretensions. She doesn't play by the same rules as everyone else.

CATHERINE

(*Testing her*) But Wedekind wrote the play. He created her.

CELIA

It doesn't matter. He was wrong.

CATHERINE

(*Smiles. As if to herself*) We'll see.

Cut back to HANNAH.

HANNAH

So, Izzy, I hear you're going to be hanging around Dublin with us.

IZZY

(*Jolted from his thoughts*) Huh?

CELIA

(*To* HANNAH) He'll be getting there a few days after I do.

IZZY

(*To* HANNAH) Yeah. I'm getting rid of my apartment . . . putting my things in storage. When the movie's over, Celia and I are going to look for a new place together.

HANNAH

(*Happy for them, but with a slight pang*) Sounds cozy.

CELIA

(*Sure of herself*) It will be.

Shot from under the table. We see CELIA's *hand reach out and begin to touch* IZZY's *thigh. He takes hold of her hand in his.*

PHILIP (*off*)

Catherine, did you talk to Max about using bigger speakers for the rock 'n' roll scene?

CATHERINE (*off*)

He's taking care of it. I still haven't figured out how we'll light it, though.

PHILIP

Well, you'll be there the day after tomorrow. You can discuss it with George at the soundstage.

Cut to close-up of CELIA, *whispering into* IZZY's *ear.*

CELIA

Meet me downstairs. I have to talk to you.

IZZY looks around at the others, then stands up.

IZZY

(*To no one in particular*) Excuse me. I'll be back in a minute.

The camera follows IZZY as he walks away from the table and heads for the stairs. Just as he is about to go down, he turns around for a parting glance at CELIA. Cut to:

IZZY'S POV: Long shot of CELIA sitting at the table with the others.

She turns surreptitiously toward IZZY, meets his gaze, and smiles.

33. INT: DAY. ODEON RESTAURANT. DOWNSTAIRS.

An open area with a sofa, a couple of chairs, a potted plant, a pay telephone, the rest room doors. IZZY is standing there, waiting.

A moment later, he sees CELIA coming quickly down the stairs. She rushes straight into his arms and begins kissing him—passionately, tenderly, not caring who sees her.

34. INT: DAY. WEST TWENTY-FIFTH STREET.
OUTSIDE CELIA'S BUILDING.

A black town car is parked in front of CELIA's door. The driver sits behind the wheel, waiting.

35. INT: DAY. CELIA'S APARTMENT.

IZZY

(*Looking through the window*) The car is here.

CELIA's packed bags are in front of the door. She walks over to the window and looks down at the street with IZZY.

CELIA

I wish you were going with me now.

IZZY

It's better this way. You can settle in, and I'll take care of things here. It's just a few days.

CELIA

(*Hugging him*) I don't want to let you out of my sight. I need you with me.

IZZY

(*Wrapping his arms around her*) You're going to knock their socks off.

CELIA

(*She smiles but is not really comforted. Putting her head against his chest*) I love you, Izzy.

IZZY

(*Holding her tight*) What did I do to deserve you? (*Beat*) You're my angel, Celia. My miracle. My whole life. (*Several beats. Disengages his right arm from her and reaches into his pocket. Pulls out the little black box and gives it to her*) Here, take this. Maybe it will help.

CELIA

(*Taking the box with one hand, still holding him closely with the other*) What for?

IZZY

Every time you look at it, you'll think about me.

CELIA

And what about you? Aren't you going to think about me?

I don't need the stone for that. I'll be thinking about you every minute.

36. EXT: DAY. WEST TWENTY-FIFTH STREET. OUTSIDE CELIA'S BUILDING.

IZZY slams the back door of the car shut. The car pulls away. IZZY stands there and watches. After a moment, CELIA sticks her head out the window and looks back at him. She blows him a kiss. The car continues to move down the street. She blows another kiss.

Close-up of IZZY's face, the palm of his right hand open beside it in a farewell gesture. A couple of beats. He lets his hand drop. A sense of loneliness, isolation.

37. EXT: DAY. MANHATTAN STREET.

IZZY walks downtown, heading toward his apartment in the Village.

38. EXT: DAY. PERRY STREET. OUTSIDE IZZY'S BUILDING.

IZZY approaches the building, walks up the front steps, opens the door, and goes inside.

39. INT: DAY. IZZY'S APARTMENT.

IZZY steps into the apartment, shuts the door (without locking it), and turns on the light. He looks around for a few seconds, trying to get his bearings. He hasn't been there in weeks, and it's as if he's walked in on a stranger's life.

Suddenly, out of nowhere, three THUGS *(one Russian, one German, one Chinese) burst into the apartment. Before* IZZY *can say a word, the* GERMAN THUG *grabs him from behind and the* CHINESE THUG *punches him in the stomach.* IZZY *doubles over in pain.*

RUSSIAN THUG

(*Heavy accent*) You're a slippery fellow, Mr. Maurer. Don't you like your apartment anymore?

IZZY

(*Gasping for breath, still aching from the punch*) Who are you? . . . What do you want?

RUSSIAN THUG

No, Mr. Maurer, who are you, and what do *you* want? What gives you the right to meddle in our business?

CHINESE THUG

(*Heavy accent. To the* RUSSIAN) Again, boss?

RUSSIAN THUG

Absolutely.

The CHINESE THUG *punches him again.* IZZY *falls down. The* GERMAN THUG *kicks him in the back.* IZZY *howls.*

GERMAN THUG

(*Heavy accent*) Who are you working for, and why did you kill Stanley Mar?

IZZY

(*Sprawled out, struggling against the pain. Gets up on one knee*) I didn't kill him.

RUSSIAN THUG

It's too late for lies, my friend.

The GERMAN THUG *grabs hold of* IZZY *and pulls him to his feet.* IZZY *totters for a moment. Then the* CHINESE THUG *punches him in the face, and* IZZY *falls down again.*

40. EXT. DAY: DUBLIN AIRPORT.

Morning. An Aer Lingus plane lands on the runway.

41. INT: NIGHT. A ROOM SOMEWHERE.

IZZY, *badly beaten, wakes up to find himself lying on a cement floor. He seems to be in a basement room somewhere. Gray cinder-block walls, utterly bare and empty. A thick metal door. One small window at the top of one wall. Opaque, wire-reinforced glass. Dimness.* IZZY *rolls over and groans, still barely conscious.*

42. INT: DAY. IZZY'S APARTMENT.

The telephone is ringing in the living room of IZZY's *apartment. The place is in turmoil: overturned furniture, books and records scattered across the floor, torn clothes. The camera slowly pans the room. The phone stops ringing and* IZZY's *voice comes on.*

IZZY'S VOICE
Leave a message, and I'll get back to you.

After the beep, we hear:

CELIA'S VOICE
Izzy—I've missed you again. I'll be in tonight, so you can call me when you get back. Everything is fine here, but I miss you so much, I can't wait to see you. Just three more days. *Just!* (*Laughs*) It feels like forever. I love you, Izzy. I kiss you. I send you a thousand hugs.

Cut to:

43. INT: NIGHT. DUBLIN. CELIA'S HOTEL ROOM.

CELIA *hangs up the phone. She is sitting beside a table. In front of her we see the little black box. She removes the lid, takes out the stone, and holds it in her palm—studying it carefully.*

44. INT: DAY. THE ROOM.

IZZY *wakes up in the bare, mysterious room. Dull light slants through the window. The bruises on* IZZY's *face have healed somewhat—suggesting that he has been there for several days.*

Once he returns to consciousness, he notices a box of crackers near the door. It has apparently been some time since he has eaten.

IZZY *crawls toward the door, takes hold of the crackers, and greedily rips open the box.*

He eats a cracker, chewing hard, desperate to satisfy his hunger. Then another cracker; then another—shoving them into his mouth like an animal. His cheeks fill up. The difficulty of swallowing.

He stops. Sorrow and fear overwhelm him. Struggling to rein in his emotions and stay calm, he begins to break down and cry. A series of choked-off, broken sobs. Little bits of cracker powder fly out of his mouth as the air leaves his lungs.

There is, of course, no water anywhere.

45. EXT: DAY. DUBLIN. ST. STEPHEN'S GREEN.

Sunday afternoon. CELIA *and* HANNAH *are strolling through the park. It is a bright tranquil day, and numerous other people are roaming about: young couples, families, children. The contrast between this setting and the atmosphere of the room in the previous scene should be made as stark as possible. An emphasis on the beauty of the surroundings, nature as opposed to the harshness of* IZZY's *cell. Green grass, trees, flowers, shrubs, sparrows, ducks bobbing on the surface of the pond.*

HANNAH

When will he be here?

CELIA

The day after tomorrow.

HANNAH

How does he sound?

CELIA

I don't know.

HANNAH

You don't know?

CELIA

He hasn't called. And I haven't been able to reach him.

HANNAH

Well, you know Izzy. Just when you think you know what he's going to do, he turns around and does something else.

CELIA

I'm starting to get worried.

HANNAH

He has a plane ticket, doesn't he? And an up-to-date passport?

315

CELIA

Yes.

HANNAH

Then don't worry. He'll be on that plane. I've seen how he looks
at you—and believe me, there's no way he's not going to show up.

*The camera cuts away to a young couple kissing under a tree, a toddler
running across the grass, a bird hopping from a branch and taking off into
the air.*

CELIA

The funny thing is, I wouldn't be here if I hadn't met Izzy. He's
the one who got me the part.

HANNAH

Not really. He made the phone call, but you got yourself the part.

CELIA

(*Thoughtful; struggling to express herself*) But it's all connected. I'm
Lulu because Izzy loves me. Doing this role is part of our story
together. I'm convinced of that.

HANNAH

But that's good, no?

CELIA

Yes, it's good. But Lulu scares me. She's a monster, really.

HANNAH

It's a tough role. I mean, Pandora opens the box, and all the evils
of the world come flying out. (*Beat*) What I want to know is, who
decided that Pandora is a woman?

CELIA

(*Smiles*) Men.

HANNAH

That's the trouble. It's a man's story. And men—excuse the expression—don't know shit. (*Beat*) Anyway, it's only a movie, right? Don't worry. You'll be fine.

CELIA

Well, there's no turning back now, is there?

46. INT: DAY. SOUNDSTAGE. THE SET OF *PANDORA'S BOX*.

What follows is a contemporary version of the last part of Act I of Earth Spirit. *It is set in a loft space.* BLACK, *the painter Schwarz from Wedekind's play, has been turned into a photographer. He has been taking pictures of* LULU. *She is dressed in a Charlie Chaplin costume: baggy trousers, tuxedo jacket, bowler hat, small fake mustache. Photography devices: screens, umbrellas, reflectors, standing lamps.*

The entire set is visible. Film crew, equipment, adjustable walls, etc. The scene begins with an overhead shot of CATHERINE *sitting in a chair and studying the monitor.*

She is flanked by the SCRIPT SUPERVISOR *and the* DIRECTOR OF PHOTOGRAPHY. *As the camera sweeps past her, she leans to her left and whispers something to the* D.P. *The camera continues to move, taking in the* SOUNDMAN, *the sound cart, and the* FIRST ASSISTANT DIRECTOR; *then, the* CAMERA OPERATOR, *the* FOCUS PULLER, *the* SECOND ASSISTANT CAMERAMAN *(clapper), and two* STAGEHANDS.

Close-up of the clapper. It reads: "PANDORA'S BOX. *Scene 3, Take 1.*"

One by one, at the appropriate moments, we hear offscreen voices pronounce the following instructions:

FIRST ASSISTANT DIRECTOR (*off*)

Roll speed.

317

SOUNDMAN (*off*)

Speed.

FIRST ASSISTANT DIRECTOR (*off*)

Roll camera.

FIRST ASSISTANT CAMERAMAN (*off*)

Marker.

SECOND ASSISTANT CAMERAMAN (*off*)

Scene 3. Take 1. Mark.

Once the clapper has been lowered, we hear:

CATHERINE

(*Calmly*) Action.

A close-up of LULU's *face. She begins twitching her nose.*

BLACK (*off*)

Hold still.

LULU

(*Referring to the mustache*) It itches. (*She wiggles her nose again*)

BLACK (*off*)

(*Irritated*) Stop it!

LULU

(*Beat*) I'm bored.

BLACK

Look, it wasn't my idea to take these dumb pictures.

LULU

It wasn't mine either, was it? Thank Peter Shine and his magazine for this. (*Beat*) At least you're getting paid.

She begins twitching her nose again. Impish, playful—perversely sabotaging the pose.

Master shot. BLACK *walks out from behind his tripod and approaches* LULU. *He is intensely irritated.*

BLACK

Can't you be good—just once?

LULU

(*Shrugs*) I'm good. I'm always good.

BLACK

We'll be here all day if you don't settle down.

LULU

You don't want to take my picture. You want to get inside my pants. (*Smiles*) You want to stick your tongue down my throat.

BLACK

(*Tormented, wavering*) Don't talk like that.

LULU

Why not? It's the truth, isn't it? If I'm wrong, then why aren't there any assistants around? (*Looks left; playfully*) Nobody there. (*Looks right*) Nobody there. (*Laughs*) It's just you and me, honey-pie.

BLACK

(*Losing control*) You're impossible.

LULU *grins at him, as if egging him on, daring him to make a move.* BLACK, *finally breaking down, impulsively grabs hold of her and kisses her on the mouth. She neither resists nor shows any enthusiasm.*

LULU

(*Teasing*) Oh, you bad man. (*Smiles, pulls off the face mustache*) Can't you wait until I turn back into a girl again? (*Tosses the mustache aside*)

319

They kiss again. LULU *is more passionate this time. After a moment, however, she begins giggling. She disengages from* BLACK *and begins smacking her lips, as if trying to identify a taste.*

LULU

Hmm. Garlic. (*Smacks her lips together again*) Or maybe . . . sausage. Hot sausage!

BLACK, *deeply upset by now, looks at her with a mixture of horror and lust.*

BLACK

Who the hell are you, anyway?

LULU

I'm me. That's who I am.

She takes off the bowler hat and tosses it aside. She runs her hand through her hair, shakes her head.

BLACK

What do you want?

LULU

(*Unbuttoning the jacket, taking it off, and tossing it aside*) I don't know.

BLACK

What do you believe in?

LULU

(*Sliding off her suspenders, undoing the button of her trousers*) I don't know. (*Beat*) Don't ask so many questions. I don't like it.

BLACK

Do you have a soul?

LULU

(*Lets the trousers drop, kicks them aside*) I don't know.

BLACK

Have you ever been in love?

LULU

(*Unbuttoning her shirt*) I don't know.

BLACK

(*Appalled*) You don't know?

LULU

(*Emphatic*) I don't know.

The camera moves in for a close-up of LULU*'s face. She continues unbuttoning the shirt. In the background we hear:*

CATHERINE

And . . . cut.

CELIA*'s face relaxes as she comes out of character and returns to herself.*

47. INT: NIGHT. THE ROOM.

IZZY, *wide awake, is sitting on the floor with his back against a wall, hugging his knees. Dimness. To the degree that it is possible to make them out, his facial wounds appear to be much better.*

After a few moments, sounds can be heard coming from outside the door. At first, an exchange of unintelligible voices, speaking in various foreign languages. The voices grow louder. Shouts are heard; an increasingly argumentative, violent tone. Then, followed by the sound of blows, bodies being thrown against the door.

Grunts, yelps, ever-mounting commotion. IZZY, *afraid, confused, watches the door.*

A line of bullets sweeps across the door, denting the metal surface. After that, all goes silent again.

IZZY *crouches in the far corner of the room, terrified. We hear him breathing. A few moments go by. Then, with a great clattering of locks and bolts, the door abruptly swings open. A man enters: mid-forties, dressed in an elegant suit. This is* DR. VAN HORN. *As soon as he steps across the threshold, the door slams shut behind him. More clatter of locks and bolts. He is carrying a brown paper bag. He puts it down next to the door.*

DR. VAN HORN
(*Calmly*) Hello, Mr. Maurer. I'm Dr. Van Horn.

IZZY
(*Slowly getting to his feet*) I can go now, right? (DR. VAN HORN *says nothing*) I mean, you're the good guys, aren't you? Isn't that what just happened? The good guys got rid of the bad guys?

DR. VAN HORN
Yes, we're the good guys.

IZZY
(*Beat. Not sure of what is going on*) I want to go home.

DR. VAN HORN
You will, I promise you. But we have to talk first. It's very important.

IZZY
(*Studying* DR. VAN HORN) I don't believe you.

DR. VAN HORN
(*Ignoring* IZZY's *remark. Begins sniffing the air*) It doesn't smell very good in here, does it?

IZZY

A man has to shit. If he doesn't have a toilet, what do you expect?

DR. VAN HORN casts his eyes about the room. Finally settles his gaze on one shadowy corner—undoubtedly the spot where IZZY relieved himself.

DR. VAN HORN

(*Thoughtful*) Montaigne once wrote: "Let us not forget that philosophers and kings—and even ladies, too—must defecate."

IZZY

(*Harking back to his wish to go home*) Well?

DR. VAN HORN

(*Referring to the excrement*) Don't worry. I'll have it cleaned up. (*Beat. Walks around a little*) You must be hungry. When was the last time you ate?

IZZY

I don't want food. I just want to get out of here.

DR. VAN HORN

(*Sighs*) We're the good guys, Mr. Maurer, I can assure you of that. What I want to know is whether you're good, too. (*Beat*) Are you good, Mr. Maurer? Are you worthy?

IZZY

Worthy of what?

DR. VAN HORN

(*Pursuing his own line of thought*) I thought you could help us, you see. I had such high hopes for you. But I was wrong to trust you, wasn't I? (*Beat*) Am I right or wrong, Mr. Maurer?

IZZY

I don't know what you're talking about.

DR. VAN HORN

(*Firmly*) Yes you do. (*Beat. Looking* IZZY *in the eyes*) Stanley Mar, for one thing. And a little box he was carrying with him. Do you know how precious that stone is? (*Beat. Trying to control his emotions*) It took years to achieve that light. Do you have any idea of the good it can do? (*Falls silent, meditative. After a moment, he looks up again*) I'm so disappointed in you. (*Goes over to the paper bag and picks it up. Hands it roughly to* IZZY) Here. Change your clothes. You stink.

48. INT: DAY. SOUNDSTAGE. THE SET OF PANDORA'S BOX.

Unlike the previous extract from Pandora's Box *(scene 45), we do not experience the action as a movie within a movie but as the movie itself.*

A reworking of Act III of Earth Spirit, *combined with references to the theater scene in Pabst's film.*

(*Background:* LULU *is performing in a rock 'n' roll concert. The other characters who appear in this section of the story are* PETER SHINE *[based on Dr. Schoen from the play], his fiancée* MOLLY, *and his son* ALVIN *[based on Alwa].* SHINE, *in his late fifties or early sixties, is the publisher of a successful rock 'n' roll magazine. He has been involved with* LULU *for several years—at once irresistibly attracted to her and repulsed by her. For* LULU, SHINE *is the only man who counts, in spite of her numerous other conquests and liaisons. Finally, in an effort to break away from* LULU *once and for all and end their secret, on-again, off-again affair,* SHINE *has gotten himself engaged to* MOLLY, *an attractive but unremarkable young woman in her late twenties. Simultaneously, he has begun promoting* LULU'S *career as a pop singer.* ALVIN, *his twenty-five-year-old son, has written and arranged her material.*)

The scene takes place in LULU'S *dressing room—in a break between sets.*

The dressing room is empty. The door opens. We hear loud cheering, clapping—a large audience giving an enthusiastic reception to the first part of

324

LULU's concert. ALVIN rushes in, excited. A moment later, LULU enters as well. She looks flushed, happy, pleased with herself, nearly out of breath. She flops down in a chair.

ALVIN

Unbelievable. (*Uncorks a bottle of champagne*)

LULU

(*Catching her breath. Smiles*) They liked it, didn't they?

ALVIN

(*Pouring her a glass of champagne*) They went crazy. Where did you learn those moves?

LULU

(*Shrugs, as if to say she has no idea. Takes a sip of the champagne*) Is the other dress ready?

ALVIN

Relax. You have thirty minutes.

In the background, we hear music from another rock band coming from the stage. This music continues throughout the rest of the scene, punctuated by applause and cheering. An intense, chaotic atmosphere infuses the action.

LULU

(*Thinking*) This is just what Peter wanted, isn't it?

ALVIN

What do you mean?

LULU

He turns me into a success, and then, the more I succeed, the farther he can push me away from him. (*Beat*) It's his way of getting rid of me.

ALVIN

(*Sipping his champagne*) You don't know what you're talking about.

LULU

(*Slight pause*) Give me a cigarette.

ALVIN *dutifully shakes out a cigarette from a pack on the table, lights it, and then hands it to* LULU. *She takes a drag.*

ALVIN

He came tonight, you know. He's in the audience.

LULU

(*Feigning indifference*) He did? That's nice.

ALVIN

Just because he's marrying Molly, that doesn't mean he doesn't care about you.

LULU

He thinks he wants to marry her, but I'm the one he wants.

ALVIN *shrugs, growing tired of the conversation. He looks at his watch. Just then, a knock is heard at the door. Alvin walks across the room and opens it. It is* PETER SHINE: *hip, well-dressed, at ease with his own power.*

ALVIN

Hi, Dad.

ALVIN *leaves the door open and* PETER *pokes in his head.* LULU *looks up and gives him a blank stare. She doesn't greet him.*

PETER

(*Smiling, to* LULU) What can I say? It's a breakthrough performance, Lulu. They'll be talking about it for months.

LULU

(*Coolly*) Let's hope so. If I danced any harder, I'd probably go into orbit.

The door opens a little wider and LULU *catches sight of* MOLLY, *a pretty brunette, standing in the doorway with* PETER.

LULU

(*Suddenly agitated, distraught*) What's she doing here?

PETER

She came to wish you luck for the second half.

MOLLY

(*Taking a step or two into the room, waving shyly to* LULU) Hi.

LULU

(*Ignoring* MOLLY; *boiling over with rage. To* PETER) You mean you actually brought her here? You mean she's actually been sitting next to you, watching me perform?

PETER

Why not? What difference does it make who sees you?

MOLLY

(*Beginning to grow upset; plucking up her courage*) I thought you were great, Lulu. I loved it.

LULU

(*Still addressing* PETER *and ignoring* MOLLY. *Exploding into a tantrum*) Get her out of my sight! Do you hear me! Get her out of here!

PETER

(*Trying to calm her down*) Take it easy. . . . You're getting all worked up over nothing . . .

ALVIN

(*Upset; to* PETER) Good work, Dad. Couldn't this have waited until after the show?

LULU

(*Hysterical*) I want her out of here! Out of my dressing room! Out of the theater! If she stays, I'm not going on! I'll cancel the rest of the show!

PETER

(*Shooing* ALVIN *and* MOLLY *out the door*) It's all right. I'll take care of it. (*Shutting the door firmly once they leave. Turning to* LULU) Stop acting like a baby. You disgust me. You're so incredibly . . . vulgar. (*Takes out a cigarette and puts it in his mouth*)

LULU

No smoking. (*Points to a* NO SMOKING *sign posted in the room*) Can't you read? I thought you owned a magazine.

PETER

(*Throws down the cigarette in disgust*) You signed a contract. You can't just walk out.

LULU

(*Long pause. The tension goes out of her; she slumps in her chair and closes her eyes. Wearily*) I'm so tired.

PETER

You'll go back on, then?

LULU

(*Eyes still closed; waving him off. As if to herself*) Yes, yes . . . I'll go back on. Now leave. I don't want you here anymore.

PETER

(*Wounded by her indifference*) Just like that?

LULU

(*Opens her eyes; gives him a cold, hard look*) Yes. Just like that.

PETER *doesn't move.* LULU, *understanding that she has just won an important victory, persists in the game she is playing.*

LULU

(*With a shooing gesture*) Go . . . go . . . go back to your sweet little Molly. (*Smiles knowingly*) Is that girl in for a surprise or what?

PETER

What's that supposed to mean?

LULU

When she finds out who you really are.

PETER

Stop it! (*Increasingly upset*) I'm finished with you.

LULU

You are, huh? And what happens six months from now when you've used that little girl up and start wanting me again? What happens when you pick up the phone in the middle of the night and dial my number? Do I answer it . . . or just let it ring?

PETER

(*Losing control. Raising his hand*) I should smack you. Right across the face!

LULU

(*Walking right up to him; brazenly; thrusting out her jaw*) Go ahead. Hit me. Come on, punch me as hard as you can. If that's what it takes for you to touch me again, then knock the living daylights out of me.

PETER, *overcome, realizes that he is lost, damned forever. He takes hold of* LULU's *face with his two hands, draws her toward him, and begins covering her with kisses.*

LULU, *luxuriating in her triumph, closes her eyes and leans back her head. A small inward smile spreads across her mouth as* PETER *kisses her neck.*

A moment later, the door opens. LULU *hears the sound and opens her eyes. Shot of the door:* ALVIN *and* MOLLY *are standing there, aghast. Pounding rock 'n' roll pours in from the stage.*

Shot of PETER'S *back as he goes on kissing* LULU. *He stops, turns around, and looks* MOLLY *straight in the eyes. She begins to cry. Whatever hopes he had of breaking away from* LULU *have now been permanently destroyed.*

Then, suddenly breaking the spell, the background music goes silent. A voice calls out:

CATHERINE (*off*)

Cut!

Wide shot of the set. We see the crew and the equipment as we did in scene 45. The actors begin to relax.

CATHERINE

(*To the* SCRIPT SUPERVISOR) Let's print that one. But I want to have another go at it. Just give me a few minutes.

CATHERINE *walks away from the crew and enters the set. Long shot. We see her walk up to* CELIA, *who is leaning against a table, speak to her for a moment, and then lead her out of the dressing room. Once they leave the frame, cut to:*

CATHERINE *and* CELIA, *standing on the other side of the set partition wall.*

CATHERINE

It's still a little too broad . . .

CELIA

I was trying to hold back, but it's such an emotional scene . . .

CATHERINE

I know. It's all so over the top. But it's about real things. Hidden things, maybe, but things that are there. (*A beat, letting her words sink in*) You don't have to work so hard, Celia. Let the camera do it for you.

CELIA

(*Thinking, working it out for herself*) It's like turning dreams inside out, isn't it?

CATHERINE

We all have them in us. It's just a matter of how you let them go.

CELIA

(*Gently opening her hand—as if releasing a butterfly*) Like that?

CATHERINE

Exactly. And the camera will be there to show it.

Cut to:

49. INT: DAY. SOUNDSTAGE. A HALLWAY.

We see CELIA walking quickly down the corridor to her dressing room.

50. INT: DAY. CELIA'S DRESSING ROOM.

Frantic, CELIA sits down at the table, picks up the phone, and punches the keys for an international call. We hear the phone ringing. Eventually, an answering machine message comes on.

IZZY'S VOICE

Leave a message, and I'll get back to you.

CELIA

(*After the beep*) Izzy, where are you? They sent someone to the airport this morning to pick you up, and you weren't on the plane. Izzy, darling, what happened to you?

51. INT: DAY. SOUNDSTAGE. SOMEWHERE BEHIND THE SET.

A few moments later. BILLY (ALVIN) *is standing alone against a wall, smoking a cigarette.* CELIA, *still in her* LULU *costume, walks into frame.*

BILLY

Hi, Celia.

CELIA

(*Distracted*) Hi.

BILLY

Are you okay? (*Offers her a cigarette from his pack*)

CELIA

(*Stops, still distraught*) I'm fine. (*Pulls out a cigarette from the pack and puts it in her mouth*)

BILLY

(*Lighting the cigarette for her*) There's been a lot of talk, you know.

CELIA

Oh? About what?

BILLY

About you. (*Beat*) The word is that you have man troubles.

CELIA

Who said that?

BILLY

I can't remember. But I just wanted to say that—

CELIA

(*Interrupting him*) Don't believe everything you hear—

BILLY

Yeah, maybe so, but I just wanted to say that if there's any . . . any truth to the story, I just wanted to say—

CELIA

(*Cutting him off*)—Say what?

BILLY

That you don't have to be alone if you don't want to.

CELIA

What's that supposed to mean?

BILLY

That I'm here for you. Any time, any place . . . I'm here.

CELIA

(*Trying to control her emotions*) Fuck off, Billy. Just do your job, okay?

52. INT: DAY. THE ROOM.

Daylight slants through the window. A table has been set up in the middle of the room. DR. VAN HORN *sits in a chair on one side;* IZZY *is in a chair on the other side. A desk lamp with a single bulb burning harshly between them.*

IZZY *is wearing a fresh set of clothes. Blue jeans, T-shirt, etc. A suggestion of prison garb.*

In the far corner, a chamber pot. As promised, improvements have been made, but IZZY *is still not free.*

DR. VAN HORN *has several folders in front of him. Every now and then, he opens one of them and scans the papers within. He is also equipped with a notepad and a pen. For reasons never made clear, he occasionally jots something down while* IZZY *talks. At other times, he appears to be doodling.*

Everything about this scene escapes understanding. An air of mystery, doubt, disequilibrium. The same holds true of scenes 54 and 57.

DR. VAN HORN'S *purpose is never defined. At times, he appears to be conducting a police interrogation. At other times, he sounds like a psychiatrist. At still other times, he resembles the Grand Inquisitor.*

> DR. VAN HORN
> Momentous things have happened, and whether you like it or not, you're in the middle of them.

> IZZY
> I don't have it. I told you that before. I don't have it, and I don't know where it is.

> DR. VAN HORN
> (*Changing the subject*) How long have you been here, Izzy?

> IZZY
> (*Shrugs*) What difference does it make? (*Beat*) Too long.

> DR. VAN HORN
> Answer the question. Days? Weeks? Months?

> IZZY
> I don't know. Days, I suppose. I can't remember how many.

DR. VAN HORN

What if I told you seven? What would you say to that?

IZZY

Nothing. I wouldn't say a thing.

DR. VAN HORN

When did you start using the name Izzy?

IZZY

(*Lets out a sigh*) This is ridiculous.

DR. VAN HORN

Your real name is Isaac, isn't it?

IZZY

So?

DR. VAN HORN

How old were you? Six? Eight? Fourteen?

IZZY

I don't remember.

DR. VAN HORN

But you do remember the fireflies, don't you?

IZZY

The what?

DR. VAN HORN

Maybe you called them lightning bugs. It doesn't matter. You know what I'm talking about, don't you?

IZZY

No.

DR. VAN HORN

Those little things that fly around at night. In the summer, when the weather is hot. Tiny pinpricks of light . . . going on and off . . . darting through the air . . . now in one place, now in another. Very beautiful, no?

IZZY

What is this, *Welcome to the World of Insects*?

DR. VAN HORN

No, it's called *Going Back*, or *Delving into the Past*. (*One or two beats; prolonging* IZZY'S *confusion*) Remember Echo Lake? How many summers did you and your family go there?

IZZY

(*Taken completely by surprise. A little frightened. Several beats*) How do you know about that?

DR. VAN HORN

I know about a lot of things. (*Beat*) Do you remember the fireflies now?

IZZY

Yes. (*Beat*) Vaguely. (*Beat; coming clean*) Yes, I remember them.

DR. VAN HORN

You and your big brother would go out in the backyard at night, wouldn't you? Carrying jars with little holes punched in the top. (*Beat*) What was his name again?

IZZY

(*Very quietly; as if filled with dread*) Franz.

DR. VAN HORN

Yes, Franz, that's it. An interesting name. Franz. Franz and Isaac. How many years apart were you?

IZZY

(*With difficulty, barely able to get the word out of his mouth*) Three.

DR. VAN HORN

(*As if to himself*) Right. Three. Three years apart. (*Addressing* IZZY *again*) And so you and your big brother Franz, who was three years older than you, would go out at night to catch fireflies in the back-yard. Your father punched the holes in the tops of the jars, didn't he? With a hammer and an eighth-inch nail. Tap, tap, tap. He was a doctor, your father, wasn't he? Not a pretend doctor like me, with my Ph.D. in anthropology, but an honest-to-goodness medical doctor, the kind who actually cures the sick and helps people get well. Stocky fellow, wasn't he? With strong upper arms, and one of those barrel chests. Bald, too, if I'm not mistaken, and even out there at the lake in the summer, when he had his one, measly week of holiday a year, he walked around in his white shirt, didn't he? No tie, of course, and he'd roll up his sleeves when the weather was particularly hot, but still, that's how you see him in your mind, isn't it? Your father in his white shirt.

IZZY

(*Suffering. Almost inaudible*) Stop it. Don't do this to me.

DR. VAN HORN

(*Ignoring him*) So there you'd be, you and Franz, running around the backyard of the house by Echo Lake trying to catch fireflies and put them in your jars. It was so magnificent, holding that jar in your hand with all those flickering lights inside, and of course the more fireflies you caught and put in the jar, the more impressive and beautiful the lantern would be. The problem was that you weren't very good at catching fireflies. Every time you reached out for one, it would suddenly go dark, and then another would light up somewhere else, distracting you from the first one just long enough to lose track of where it was. So you would go after the second one, and the same thing would happen all over again. And again; and again. Meanwhile, your big brother Franz, who was three years older than you, would be snaring one incandescent bug after another. His jar would be glowing like

337

a small temple of dreams. And again and again you would come up empty-handed. It drove you into spasms of frustration, and the more you continued to fail, the more desperate you became. Finally—in your sniveling, abject little way—you would resort to tears, raising such a fuss that your mother would have to come running outside, your poor mother who was spending a few tranquil moments with your father in the house, your father drinking his one nightly beer in his white shirt with the sleeves rolled up, and nine times out of ten she would settle things by forcing a reluctant, belligerent Franz to part with a few of his fireflies so you'd have something to put in your jar, too. Anything to keep the brat quiet. Right, Izzy? Anything for a few moments of peace.

IZZY

(*On the point of tears*) What kind of a man are you?

DR. VAN HORN

(*Ignoring* IZZY's *question*) When was the last time you saw Franz?

IZZY

I don't want to talk about this.

DR. VAN HORN

Answer the question. (*Beat*) You have to answer the question.

IZZY

(*Beginning to cry*) I don't know.

DR. VAN HORN

Seven years ago, that's when. He asked you to play at your father's funeral, and you refused. Why did you do a thing like that? Who the hell do you think you are? Your brother hates you so much, he didn't even bother to visit you in the hospital after you were shot. (*Beat*) You've burned a lot of bridges in your day, haven't you?

IZZY, *cracking under the verbal assault, buries his face in his hands and sobs.*

53. INT: DAY. SOUNDSTAGE. THE SET OF *PANDORA'S BOX*.

The scene takes place in SHINE *and* LULU's *bedroom. They have been married for a year. On one wall, we see a photograph of* LULU *in the Charlie Chaplin costume.*

CATHERINE *is blocking out the scene with* CELIA, TOM *(the actor who plays* PETER SHINE*), and* BILLY *(*ALVIN*), going through a last rehearsal before attempting the first take.* CELIA *is wearing a skimpy white dress.* TOM *(*SHINE*) is wearing elegant dress clothes—a tuxedo, or some suitable variation.* BILLY *(*ALVIN*) is dressed casually.*

> CATHERINE
>
> All right, that was good. Let's do it one more time, just to make sure you have the blocking down. Remember, Tom, the scene begins with the door swinging open—and then the shove. Celia gets thrown onto the bed, and you . . . *(she walks to a spot in the room and points to the floor)* . . . and you stop here, right where this tape is *(points down to the tape)*. That will make it simpler for you to go to the bureau *(points to the bureau)* and take out the gun. *(Turning to* BILLY*)* Billy, I'll give you a signal when you're supposed to knock. Right after Tom says, "Now do what you have to do. Do it." Okay? Everything clear?

CELIA, TOM, *and* BILLY *nod. As they go to their places on the other side of the bedroom door, the* FIRST ASSISTANT DIRECTOR *whispers something in* CATHERINE's *ear. She nods. Then, once the actors are in their positions:*

> CATHERINE
>
> *(As soon as things seem quiet)* Action.

The scene unfolds primarily from CATHERINE's *POV, with occasional reaction shots of* CATHERINE *watching the actors. The scene feels more like theater than film, and the artificiality of the environment is felt throughout.*

The door flies open. PETER, *holding a resistant, angry* LULU *by the arm, flings her onto the bed.*

LULU

(*Protesting*) But I want to go!

PETER

We're not going anywhere!

LULU

But you promised!

PETER

For what? So you can go and pick up somebody else to sleep with?

LULU

(*Denying everything*) You're out of your mind. (*Getting off the bed*)

PETER

You think I don't know? You think I don't know about that doped-up drummer—and the hockey player—and that dyke painter you've been hanging around with? (*Exploding*) You think I don't know?

LULU

(*Calmly*) I married *you*, didn't I? If I wanted them, why would I marry you?

PETER

(*Ignoring her question; pursuing his own argument*) I could forget all that—pretend to ignore it—but when you start messing around with my own son—then that's—going—too—far!

LULU

I can't help what Alvin feels, Peter . . .

PETER, *continuing to ignore what she says, goes over to the bureau, opens the top drawer, and takes out a pistol.*

LULU

He came on to me, but I turned him down, and that's the god's honest truth. If you don't believe me, go ask him yourself.

PETER

(*Turning around and pointing the gun at her. On the brink of hysteria*)
Do you see this?

LULU, *not taking him seriously, does not answer.* SHINE *repeats the question at the top of his voice.*

PETER

Do you see it!

LULU

Yes, I see it.

PETER

(*Forcing the gun into her hand*) Take it!

LULU

(*Resisting*) Stop it, Peter.

PETER

(*Redoubling his efforts*) Take it.

She finally relents, takes hold of the gun.

PETER

I want to cure myself. Do you understand? And this . . . this is the medicine.

LULU

(*Laughs nervously*) I'm not going to shoot you.

PETER

Not me, darling—you. There's no other way. If you don't do it, then there's no hope for me . . . no hope for Alvin . . . no hope for any of us.

LULU

(*Pointing the gun at him*) It's not loaded.

PETER

Oh no?

LULU points the gun at the ceiling and pulls the trigger. CELIA, providing the sound effect, says "Bang."

LULU

(*Growing scared*) Look Peter, if you've had enough, we can split up . . . get a divorce.

PETER

(*Laughs bitterly*) We're so far beyond divorce, I don't even know what that word means anymore. (*Beat. With madness in his eyes*) Till death do us part, Lulu. (*Furious at her refusal to go along with him. Tries to tear the gun out of her hands*) Here, give it to me. If you won't do it yourself, I'll do it for you.

LULU

(*Struggling to hold on to the gun*) No, Peter. Stop it.

PETER

(*Out of his mind*) Do you think I care? Do you think I give a damn anymore? (*Lunges at her*)

LULU backs away from him. When she is at a safe distance, she lowers the gun.

LULU

(*In a decisive, self-confident tone*) I can't help what other people do, Peter, but I've never been anyone but myself. You know that, and everyone else knows that. Don't turn me into something I'm not. I can't stand all these lies.

PETER

(*Rushes at* LULU, *grabs hold of her shoulders, and forces her to the ground*) On your knees . . . monster! (*Points the barrel of the gun, which is still in* LULU's *hand, at* LULU *herself*) Now do what you have to do! Do it!

Suddenly—a frantic knocking is heard at the door.

ALVIN (*off*)
Dad. Are you all right?

PETER, *distracted by his son's voice, wheels in the direction of the door. His back is turned to* LULU.

PETER
Alvin . . .

LULU *points the gun at* PETER's *back. Again,* CELIA *provides the sound effects. Close-up of her face as she pretends to fire off the five bullets left in the chamber.*

LULU/CELIA
Bang. Bang. Bang. Bang. Bang.

Cut to:

54. INT: DAY. SOUNDSTAGE. SET OF *PANDORA'S BOX*.

The day's shooting is over. CELIA, *out of costume, is sitting in the* SHINE/ LULU *bedroom with* PHILIP, HANNAH, *and* CATHERINE. *She is clearly in distress over* IZZY's *failure to appear.*

> HANNAH
>
> Izzy's unpredictable, yes, but he wouldn't do a thing like this.

> CELIA
>
> Something's happened to him. I know it. He's in trouble.

> PHILIP
>
> Or else he changed his mind. I mean, you never know, do you?

> HANNAH
>
> Shut up, Philip.

> PHILIP
>
> (*To* HANNAH) I'm just trying to look at all the possibilities. (*To* CELIA) If you want, I'll call New York in the morning and get someone to start looking for him.

CATHERINE, *who has been listening to the others with growing concern, finally enters the conversation.*

> CATHERINE
>
> (*To* CELIA) Tomorrow's Sunday. What are you going to do with yourself?

> CELIA
>
> I don't know. I haven't been able to think that far ahead.

CATHERINE

Don't sit around and sulk. Will you promise me that? We have some demanding scenes on Monday and Tuesday, and you need to have a clear head.

CELIA

I'll be all right.

CATHERINE

(*Studying* CELIA) Love affairs come and go, but the work is what lasts. You know that, don't you?

CELIA

(*Defiantly*) No, I don't think I do. I don't think I know anything.

55. INT: DAY. THE ROOM.

The room, as before. Dusk slants through the window.

IZZY and DR. VAN HORN sitting at opposite sides of the table, as before. In the background, we see that certain improvements have been made. There is a cot, for example, and a washstand with a basin of water on it, and a peg on the wall with an extra pair of pants hanging from it.

The scene begins in midconversation. DR. VAN HORN is looking through one of the folders in front of him.

DR. VAN HORN

. . . and on June fourteenth of the following year, ten dollars were missing from your mother's purse. May twenty-ninth, the year after that, you cheated your way through an algebra exam by copying the answers from a girl who sat next to you. Susan Morse—that was her name, wasn't it? She had a crush on you, and so you led her along to make sure you wouldn't flunk the course and have to go to summer school. Nice work, my friend. Susan must have felt quite happy when you stopped talking to her the day after the test.

IZZY

(*Almost inaudible*) I hated school. I was a terrible student.

DR. VAN HORN

(*With a wave of the hand. Closing the folder; opening another*) These are
paltry things . . . hardly worth mentioning . . . but they show a certain pattern, don't they? (*Flipping through the contents of the second
folder*) Out of little seeds do mighty trees grow. (*Studying an entry on
one of the pages*) Ah. (*Taps his fingers on the page*) This little piece of
nastiness interests me. December fourth, six years ago. The Paradise
Lounge, Milwaukee, Wisconsin. You and your band performed
there that night, didn't you? Do you remember a man named Jack
Bartholemew?

IZZY

(*Defensive*) We settled out of court.

DR. VAN HORN

I know that. But you didn't have to break his arm, did you?

IZZY

The guy stiffed us. He begs us to play his lousy club in Milwaukee
in the middle of the goddamn winter, and the night we go on there's
a snowstorm and nobody shows up. So the son-of-a-bitch decides
not to pay us. We didn't even have enough money to get back to
New York. (*Beat*) So I lost my temper.

DR. VAN HORN

You loved playing with that band, didn't you?

IZZY

It was my whole life.

DR. VAN HORN

You shouldn't have given up music, Izzy.

IZZY

I didn't. It gave me up. (*Beat*) I got shot, remember? (*Another beat. Gets up from his chair and walks toward the cot*) I'm tired of this. (*Sitting down on the cot*) I don't want to be here anymore.

DR. VAN HORN

(*Unfazed. Changing the subject*) What else do you care about, Izzy? Besides yourself, that is.

IZZY

Care? What do you mean, care?

DR. VAN HORN

I don't know. Anything. Art. Literature. Collecting stamps. French wines. Astrology.

IZZY

I'm not interested in these questions.

DR. VAN HORN

Come on, Izzy. Indulge me.

IZZY

(*Shrugs. Thinks for a moment. Then, slyly*) Women. Women's bodies. Having sex with women.

DR. VAN HORN

(*Smiling*) Good. (*Beat*) What else?

IZZY

Nothing. Besides music, that's it.

DR. VAN HORN

(*Thoughtful*) What's your favorite book?

IZZY

I don't have a favorite book.

347

DR. VAN HORN

What's your favorite movie?

IZZY

I don't like movies. I never go to them.

DR. VAN HORN

I thought every American loved the movies.

IZZY

Not me. I used to go . . . when I was a kid. But then Gene Kelly retired, and the joy kind of went out of it for me. He's dead now, you know.

DR. VAN HORN

(*For the first time a little surprised*) You're not pulling my leg, are you? You really like Gene Kelly?

IZZY

(*Thinking about it*) Yeah. As a matter of fact, I do.

DR. VAN HORN

Which film? Which song?

IZZY

I don't know. Most of them, I guess. But my favorite number would have to be *Singin' in the Rain*. I never get tired of it. Every time I see it, it's just as great as the time before.

DR. VAN HORN

(*Smiling, sympathetic*) For once I agree with you. I love it, too. In fact, I would even go so far as to say it's one of the finest, most beautiful things ever created by an American. As good as the Declaration of Independence. As good as *Moby Dick*.

IZZY

Shit, it's better than that stuff. *Singin' in the Rain* is forever.

DR. VAN HORN *gets out of his chair and walks toward* IZZY's *cot, smiling. Stops in the middle of the room. Then, in a dignified, almost nostalgic manner, he begins to do a soft shoe dance and to sing in a quiet voice.*

DR. VAN HORN
I'm singin' in the rain / I'm singin' in the rain / What a glorious feelin' / I'm happy again . . .

The scene ends with a close shot of his face.

56. INT: NIGHT. DUBLIN. CELIA'S HOTEL ROOM.

Sunday. Early evening. CELIA *has spent her day off alone, hiding out in her apartment.*

The scene begins with CELIA *entering the living room with the small black box in her hands.*

She walks around the room, pulling down shades and closing curtains, then switches off the overhead light. One lamp is still on next to the sofa. She sits down on the sofa, puts the black box on the coffee table in front of her, takes the stone out of the box, puts the stone on the table, and switches off the lamp. Obscurity.

After a few moments, the stone begins to glow with the same blue light as before. Little by little, the light intensifies, grows more beautiful. CELIA *watches. After a few more moments, the stone rises a few inches off the table. Then, a few moments after that, the stone divides in two.*

Two glowing blue objects hover above the table.

In the radiant blue light that has flooded the room, we see tears rolling down CELIA's *cheeks.*

CELIA

(*Barely above a whisper*) What happened, Izzy? Where are you?

She begins crying in earnest, overwhelmed by sorrow. After a few moments, no longer able to bear it, she reaches out abruptly and turns on the lamp. The room fills with light. The humble, ordinary stone is sitting on the table. Sobbing now, CELIA *gently puts the stone in the box and covers it. It is as if, in this solemn gesture, she has just buried* IZZY. *She looks at the box for a moment. Then, still sobbing, she stands up, opens all the curtains and blinds, and turns on the overhead light.*

A few moments later, unable to contain her misery, she puts on her coat, picks up the black box from the coffee table, and leaves the apartment. The door closes behind her.

57. EXT: NIGHT. DUBLIN STREETS.

Various shots of CELIA *walking through the city. The streets are utterly deserted. The sound of her footsteps ringing against the pavement.*

After a time, CELIA *walks through Merchants' Arch and comes to the Ha'penny Bridge, a pedestrian bridge that spans the Liffey. She goes up the steps and begins to walk across. At the exact center of the bridge, she stops. Wide shot, from a distance. Close shot of* CELIA's *face. Shot of the river below from* CELIA's *POV.*

CELIA *takes the stone out of the box, then looks around to make sure that no one is watching. Holding the stone in her right hand, her arm fully extended, she leans over the edge.*

Two, three beats. She opens her hand and lets the stone fall into the water.

58. INT: NIGHT. THE ROOM.

The room, as before. IZZY *is sitting on his cot, reading a paperback copy of Tolstoy's* Resurrection. *A small lamp burns beside him. On the floor, a tray with dishes on it: the remains of* IZZY's *dinner.*

The sound of locks and bolts being turned. IZZY *looks up.* DR. VAN HORN *enters.*

DR. VAN HORN
(*Taking his seat at the table. Sternly*) Come here, Izzy.

IZZY
(*Reluctant*) Don't you ever sleep?

DR. VAN HORN
We don't have much time. (*Pointing to the chair opposite him*) Sit.

IZZY *dog-ears a page in the Tolstoy novel, closes the book, and puts it down on the pillow. He stands up and walks to his seat.*

IZZY
(*Taking his seat. Warily*) Is something wrong?

DR. VAN HORN
Everything is wrong. (*Beat*) Because of you.

IZZY
(*Sarcastically*) And I thought you were beginning to like me. (*Beat*) Silly me.

DR. VAN HORN
I was. But feelings have nothing to do with this. I can't trust you.

IZZY
Why not? I've been telling you the truth. Every word I've said . . . is true.

Reverse angle shot from over DR. VAN HORN's *shoulder. We see him writing the letters of* CELIA's *name: C-E-L-I-A.*

DR. VAN HORN

So you say. But the words of a liar don't mean anything. They have no credibility.

IZZY

Look, I'm not stupid. You know too much about me for me to lie to you.

DR. VAN HORN

(*Shaking his head*) You're not worthy. You've led a bad, dishonest life.

IZZY

I'm not going to argue with you. (*Beat. In a more somber register*) But then I got shot. You'd think that would be the worst thing that could have happened to me, but it wasn't. I've changed since then. I've let go . . . of my rottenness. I've been trying to be different.

DR. VAN HORN

(*Sarcastically*) A new man.

IZZY

(*Sincerely*) Maybe. I don't know what to call it. But I feel more connected to things now. More connected to other people. Responsible, somehow.

DR. VAN HORN

(*With deep bitterness*) Then why haven't you helped me? (*Long beat, staring at* IZZY) Why haven't you told me about Celia Burns?

IZZY

(*Completely thrown*) Who?

DR. VAN HORN

You heard me.

IZZY

I don't know that person. (*Beginning to recover his wits. Understanding that he must protect* CELIA *at all costs*) What did you say her name was?

DR. VAN HORN

(*With quiet determination*) I could have you killed, you know. All I have to do is bang on the door, and a man will come in here with a gun and put a bullet through your head.

IZZY

(*Sighs*) Been there, done that.

DR. VAN HORN

Sounds like the old Izzy to me.

IZZY

Well, habits die hard.

Reverse angle shot from over DR. VAN HORN'*s shoulder as he speaks. We see him writing on his pad: Celia—Celia—Ce-li-a—S'il y a.*

DR. VAN HORN

If you'd told me right away, the whole situation could have been saved. Now it's probably too late. (*Beat. Making one last appeal*) What if I told you that this is your one chance to do some good in the world? (*Beat. No response from* IZZY. *Tries a new approach*) Tell me about her, Izzy, and I'll let you go. I'll unlock the door, and you'll be free.

IZZY

I wish I could . . . but I don't know this person you're talking about.

DR. VAN HORN

(*Exploding with rage. Slamming his palm down on the table*) Of course you do! You're in love with her!

IZZY

(*Still playing dumb*) I am?

DR. VAN HORN

(*Abruptly standing up. Beside himself*) That's it. I have nothing more to say to you. (*Begins walking to the door. Stops*) You won't be seeing me again. (*Beat*) And without me, you're lost. (*Continues walking. Bangs on door. Turns to* IZZY *one last time*) May God have mercy on your soul.

The door opens. DR. VAN HORN *walks out. The door shuts. The clatter of locks and bolts being turned.*

59. INT: NIGHT. LULU'S APARTMENT. THE SET OF PANDORA'S BOX.

CATHERINE, *the crew, and the equipment are not visible. We experience what happens as unmediated action.*

A variation on Act III of Wedekind's Pandora's Box. *The scene has been shifted from London to the Lower East Side of Manhattan. Following the killing of Peter Shine, Lulu and Alvin have run away. They are destitute, living in the most squalid conditions. Alvin has become addicted to cocaine; Lulu occasionally resorts to prostitution in order to feed them—and to feed Alvin's habit. Alvin does not approve, but he is too weak to stop her.*

Night. It is raining outside. We are in the living room of a tawdry slum apartment. Plaster cracks in the wall; peeling paint; a few pieces of battered, second-hand furniture. There are several leaks in the ceiling. Basins and kitchen pots have been placed on the floor to catch the water, but they are all full, about to overflow. The only light comes from a single bare bulb hanging on a string from the ceiling.

ALVIN, *looking disheveled, with long stringy hair, a motorcycle jacket, and his shirt tails hanging out of his pants, is sitting at a table, trying to gather his few last bits of cocaine into a pile big enough to snort. He appears to be on the edge of desperation.*

The front door opens, and LULU *enters the room. She looks wet, ragged. She is dressed all in black: miniskirt, tights, boots, and a motorcycle jacket similar to* ALVIN's. *She shuts the door with her foot, shaking out a cheap, partly torn umbrella as she walks in. She tries to close the umbrella, can't get the catch to work, and tosses it on the floor.* ALVIN *studies her intently but doesn't say a word.*

She walks over to the table, reaches into her jacket pocket, pulls out a wad of bills, and tosses it onto the table in front of ALVIN.

ALVIN

Where'd you get it?

LULU

You don't want to know. (*Walks away from the table and starts removing her jacket. When it is half off, she puts it back on*) Christ, it's cold in here.

ALVIN

Up to your old tricks again, huh?

LULU

What do you care? You don't have to watch.

She walks in the direction of a bright red plastic armchair, sees a bottle of bourbon sitting on the floor, and picks it up. Drinks straight from the bottle. After a couple of swigs, a knock is heard at the door.

LULU

Who's that?

ALVIN

How should I know? (*Beat. As an afterthought*) One of your admirers, maybe.

LULU goes to answer the door. She opens it on CANDY *(based on Countess Geschwitz from the play), a Lower East Side lesbian painter with a crush on* LULU. *She is dressed in black leather; several facial piercings.*

LULU

(*To* CANDY; *without much enthusiasm*) Oh, it's you.

ALVIN

See? What did I tell you?

CANDY

(*To* LULU) Hi, sweetheart. Can I come in for a minute? I have a present for you.

LULU lets her in without saying anything. CANDY *is carrying a poster tube under her arm. As she takes off her coat, she eyes* ALVIN *with a sarcastic smile.*

CANDY

Well, if it isn't Alvin Shine, Captain Inertia himself.

ALVIN

(*Unfazed. With humor*) Hey there, Butch. Take a load off.

CANDY

(*Sliding a poster out of the tube*) I went into one of those poster stores today, and look what I found.

She unrolls the poster and holds it up. It is a picture from the Charlie Chaplin photo shoot with BLACK *in scene 45. In this shot,* LULU *is without the mustache. The bowler hat is pushed to the back of her head, the jacket is open, the shirt is partly open, and* LULU *is smiling a broad, fetching smile.*

LULU

(*Under her breath*) Oh, Jesus. Get that out of here.

ALVIN

(*Getting up from his seat*) Ah, the good old days. (*Walks toward* CANDY)

CANDY

(*Still holding up the poster*) I think it's beautiful.

ALVIN

(*Looking from the poster to* LULU *and back to the poster*) And just look, she hasn't changed a bit! (*Grabs hold of* LULU's *chin—a little too brusquely—and turns it toward the poster*)

LULU

Stop it.

ALVIN

(*Still holding her chin*) Think of all she's lived through, and the child-like expression in her eyes is still the same.

CANDY

Leave her alone, Alvin.

ALVIN

(*Getting excited*) We have to hang it up! (*Snatches the poster from* CANDY) That's what we need around here—some decoration! A picture like this . . . will inspire us! The goddess . . . of the temple of flesh! (*Laughs*)

He rushes over to a wall, sees a nail sticking out of it, and tries to pin the poster to the nail. The poster falls to the ground.

ALVIN

Shit.

CANDY

Take the nail out of the wall, stupid.

Just then, the light goes out. The room is plunged into darkness.

We can dimly make out the shapes of the three figures.

ALVIN

Great. Now I can't even see.

LULU

I'll go get a candle. (*Disappears into the bedroom*)

CANDY

(*To ALVIN*) You're such a clown, Alvin.

LULU comes back carrying a short, lighted candle on a saucer. The camera moves toward her as she moves toward the camera. A close-up of the light flickering against her face, her eyes. Cut to:

60. EXT: NIGHT. THE STREET BELOW. THE SET OF *PANDORA'S BOX.*

Standing across from LULU's building is JACK. Mid-thirties; leather jacket; dead eyes. He stands there looking up at the building across the street. An addict stumbles by . . . a pair of punk kids.

Shot of the third floor window. A candle is burning on the sill.

Shot of JACK, waiting. He opens his jacket, checks the inside pocket, pats it with his hand.

Shot of the building across the street. We see ALVIN come out, look around, and walk left out of frame.

Shot of JACK. *He follows* ALVIN *with his eyes for a moment, then folds his arms across his chest and leans his back against the wall. Cut to:*

61. INT: NIGHT. LULU'S APARTMENT. THE SET OF *PANDORA'S BOX.*

LULU *and* CANDY *are sitting in chairs, talking, waiting for* ALVIN *to return with a lightbulb. In the meantime, the candle provides the only light.*

CANDY

I don't know why you stay with him.

LULU

I made a promise, that's why. (*Beat*) You wouldn't understand.

CANDY

I understand. I also understand that the night we spent together was the happiest night of my life.

LULU

What happened that night doesn't mean anything. I was curious, that's all. But now it's over.

CANDY *begins to cry at the bluntness of* LULU's *statement.*

LULU (cont'd)

Just pretend it never happened. (*Beat. As* CANDY *continues to cry*) I'm just telling the truth. It's better that way.

CANDY

(*After a moment. Sniffing back her tears*) That's why I love you, Lulu. There's never any bullshit with you, is there?

A knock is heard at the door.

LULU

Alvin. He probably forgot his key. (*Gets up and walks to the door*)

CANDY

(*Trying to put up a brave front. Still tearful*) How many morons does it take to screw in a light bulb?

LULU

(*Laughs. Over her shoulder*) He probably forgot the light bulb, too.

LULU *opens the door.* JACK *is standing in the hall.*

LULU

(*Recovering from her surprise. Smiling*) Hello. And who are you?

JACK

I saw you down on the street before. I followed you here.

LULU

Do you have a name?

JACK

Jack. (*Beat*) You can call me Jack. (*Steps into the apartment.* LULU *closes the door. Then, seeing* CANDY) Who's that?

LULU

My sister. She's a little crazy. I can't get her to leave.

JACK

(*Looking at* LULU) You have a beautiful mouth.

LULU

(*Smiling*) A gift from my mother.

JACK

How much? I don't have a lot of money.

LULU

I don't know. . . . Fifty dollars.

JACK

(*Turning to the door. As if about to leave*) So long. I'll be seeing you.

LULU

No, don't go. (*Putting her hand on his arm. He looks down at her hand with a curiously remote expression on his face*) Please stay.

JACK

How much?

LULU

Half, then. Twenty-five dollars.

JACK

That's still too much.

CANDY

(*Watching and listening to them with growing astonishment and disgust*) Christ, I don't believe this. Pretty soon, you'll be paying him.

LULU

(*To* CANDY) Shut up.

JACK

(*Walking over to* CANDY. *Studies her. They exchange a long look. Then, to* LULU) That's not your sister. She's in love with you. (*Pats* CANDY'*s head*) Nice doggy. (*Then, walking back toward* LULU, *studying her intently*)

LULU

Why are you looking at me like that?

JACK

The first thing that caught my eye was your walk. I said to myself, "That girl has a great body."

LULU

How can you know that?

JACK

And I saw that you had a pretty mouth. (*Beat*) I have only ten dollars.

LULU

All right, what's the difference?

JACK

I'll need some of it back, though. For subway fare.

CANDY

(*Getting up from her seat and walking to the far end of the room*) I can't stand this, Lulu. I really can't stand this. (*JACK and LULU ignore her*)

LULU

I don't have change for a ten. I don't have anything.

JACK

Look in your pockets. You must have something.

LULU

(*Plunges a hand into each pocket of her jacket and fishes around inside. Pulls out a crumpled five-dollar bill*) This is all I have.

JACK

Give it to me.

LULU

I'll get change later. After we're done.

JACK

No, I want it all.

LULU

All right, all right. For God's sake—take it. (*She gives it to him*) But
let's go into the bedroom now. (*Walks over to the candle and picks it
up*)

JACK

We don't need that. It's bright enough.

LULU

(*Putting down the candle*) All right. Whatever you say. (*Walks over to
JACK and puts her arms around him*) I won't hurt you. I really like
you. Don't make me beg anymore.

JACK

Okay. Let's go.

*JACK follows LULU into the bedroom. CANDY lights a cigarette and walks
around the living room—agitated, disturbed. After a few moments, terrible
piercing screams are heard from the bedroom.*

LULU (*off*)

Help! . . . Help!

CANDY rushes to the bedroom door.

CANDY

(*Desperately*) Lulu! Lulu!

*JACK rushes out of the bedroom with a long, bloodstained knife in his right
hand. He plunges it into CANDY's belly. She lets out a grunt of surprise
and pain and then totters backward. JACK catches her with his left hand and
holds her up. With his right hand, he sticks the knife into her again—and
then again.*

Traveling shot. The camera moves in on JACK *and then, slowly, sweeps past him into the bedroom.* LULU *is sitting on the floor, her back against the bed, clutching her stomach.*

LULU

Oh Jesus . . . Oh Jesus.

The life is quickly draining out of her. The camera moves in on her face. A far-off look. A look deep within. The look of a person about to die.

62. INT: DAY. THE ROOM.

The room, as before. It is morning.

IZZY *is pounding on the metal door with his right hand. No one comes.*

IZZY

(*Shouting*) Help! Please—someone—help me!

Nothing happens. After a while, he stops pounding on the door and sinks to his knees. Two or three seconds; breathing hard. Then, mustering his strength, he stands up and staggers over to the table. He grabs hold of the table and pushes it against the wall under the window. He climbs onto the table, stands up, and reaches for the window. He can touch it with his hand, but he isn't high enough to see it. He climbs down from the table, picks up one of the chairs, and puts it on the table. Then he climbs back onto the table himself, pushes the back of the chair against the wall, and climbs onto the chair. This time, he is high enough. He pounds the window with his fist. The glass is thick, unbreakable. He climbs down again, carefully lowering himself from the chair to the table to the floor, and gathers up the silverware from his food tray. He climbs back onto the table, then onto the chair, holding a knife, fork, and spoon in his hand. He takes the knife and begins stabbing at the edges of the window. Cut to:

364

63. EXT: DAY. DUBLIN. OUTSIDE CELIA'S HOTEL.

It is early morning. We see CELIA *leave the building dressed in casual clothes, a bag slung over her shoulder. She turns left and begins walking. After a few moments, as if appearing out of nowhere,* DR. VAN HORN *suddenly enters the frame from the opposite direction.*

> DR. VAN HORN
>
> Celia Burns?

> CELIA
>
> (*Startled. Stops walking*) Yes?

> DR. VAN HORN
>
> May I have a word with you, please?

> CELIA
>
> (*Starts walking again*) I'm sorry. I have to be at the set in fifteen minutes.

DR. VAN HORN *walks quickly beside her, trying to keep up with her. Until now, we have seen them from the side.*

The angle changes at this moment and we see them from the front, walking briskly down the pavement. Behind, at a distance of about ten feet, TWO LARGE MEN *in windbreakers are following them.*

> DR. VAN HORN
>
> It's about Izzy Maurer. He wants to see you.

> CELIA
>
> (*Stopping dead in her tracks. The* TWO MEN *following also stop. Astonished, delighted*) Izzy? You know where he is?

> DR. VAN HORN
>
> I do. If you come with me now, I can take you right to him.

CELIA

(*Laughing; full of hope; confused*) They're expecting me. Let me call first. I don't want them to worry.

DR. VAN HORN

(*Taking her by the elbow and turning her around*) There's a phone in the car.

CELIA

(*Seeing the* TWO LARGE MEN *for the first time*) Who are they?

DR. VAN HORN

Don't worry. They're with me.

CELIA *suddenly grows suspicious, afraid. A series of very quick close-ups of* CELIA's *face,* DR. VAN HORN's *face, and the faces of the* TWO MEN. *At one point, trying to put her at ease, the* TWO MEN *smile at her. One of them is missing his front teeth; the other one is wearing metal braces. The effect is gruesome.* CELIA *begins to back away from them.*

CELIA

I get it. (*Backing away some more*) I know what you want now. (*Removing her purse from her shoulder as she continues to back away*) It's in here.

She throws the bag at one of the MEN, *and takes off running as fast as she can.*

DR. VAN HORN *and the* TWO MEN *rummage through the bag for a few moments, flinging objects onto the ground: a makeup bag, a magazine, a paperback book (Lulu in Hollywood by Louise Brooks), tissues, hairbrush, the Katmandu CD. This gives* CELIA *a small head start on them.*

Long shot: CELIA *runs down the street and out of frame. As* DR. VAN HORN *sifts through the contents of the bag, the* TWO MEN *chase after her.*

64. EXT: DAY. THE CITY STREETS.

Following the same route that CELIA *took in scene 56 on her way to the bridge, the chase continues through the streets of the city. Alternating long shots and close shots. It is six o'clock in the morning. The streets are not very crowded—but nevertheless, some traffic, some pedestrians, a number of physical obstacles.*

Finally, CELIA *reaches the Ha'penny Bridge. She runs up the steps. She is only twenty or thirty feet in front of the* MEN. *She begins running down the walkway; the* MEN *run up the steps. Halfway across, at the same spot from which she dropped the stone into the water,* CELIA *stops running. Exhausted, out of breath. The* TWO MEN *are gaining on her by the second.*

Not knowing what else to do or how else to escape them, she climbs up onto the railing just as they are about to catch her. A long moment. She hesitates. A shot of the water below. A shot of CELIA's *face. A shot of one of the* MEN. *He reaches out his hand, as if to help her down.*

> MAN
> Don't do it, miss. We're not going to hurt you.

Nevertheless, CELIA *jumps.*

The scene ends with a long shot of CELIA *flying through the air and landing in the water. We see the splash—and then she goes under.*

65. INT: DAY. THE ROOM.

The room, as before. IZZY, *still standing on the chair, is hammering away at the handle of the knife with one of the legs from the other chair. Most of the glass in the window is now missing. Just one jagged piece remains. Grunting with each blow he strikes,* IZZY *finally knocks a large chunk free. Then, very carefully, he uses his fingers to slide the last shard from the window frame. Without hesitating or looking back, he hoists himself up and begins to climb through the hole.*

66. EXT: DAY. WAREHOUSE BUILDING/BROOKLYN.

From the outside of the building, we see IZZY *climb through the window. It is just above ground level. Pebbles, dirt, weeds. He pulls himself through by clutching at the ground, groaning as he squeezes through the narrow space. Blazing, blinding sunlight.*

Panting, he finally stands up. A three-or four-day beard. Ragged, disheveled, utterly spent.

Wider shot. The building he has escaped from is a three-story cinder-block warehouse or manufacturing site. The sign on the building reads: BARTHOLDI CASKET CO.

IZZY *begins hobbling away from the building. He begins to run.*

As IZZY *exits frame, we see the Statue of Liberty looming up in the distance.*

67. INT: DAY. PHILIP KLEINMAN'S APARTMENT.
OFFICE SPACE.

A smallish, simple room: the office of a hard-working, independent producer. There are three movie posters hanging on the walls. The first one is The Incredible Shrinking Man. *The second:* Singin' in the Rain. *The third:* La Grande Illusion.

PHILIP
It's a disaster, the worst thing I've ever lived through. She just vanished into thin air. Twelve days of shooting, and on the thirteenth day, she doesn't show up. We had to shut down and send everyone home. The insurance company has three detectives looking for her, and not one of them has found a lead. Nothing. Not even a whiff.

Cut to:

IZZY, shaved and dressed in clean clothes, is sitting in a chair on one side of PHILIP's desk.

IZZY

(*Barely able to speak*) I should have been there with her. (*Beat*) I never should have waited.

PHILIP

(*After a moment*) To tell you the truth, I still have trouble believing what happened. The whole thing's like a dream . . . like she was never really there.

IZZY

(*As if drained of force*) Was she good?

PHILIP

Better than good. (*Beat*) She was extraordinary.

They sit in silence for a few moments, each one lost in his own thoughts. Eventually, IZZY tries to stand up. He is terribly weak, almost unable to move. He gets halfway out of his chair when his knees buckle and he begins to fall. He grabs hold of the desk to steady himself.

PHILIP rushes around from the other side and puts his arm around IZZY to prop him up.

PHILIP

Are you okay?

IZZY

(*Holding on to the desk; trying to maintain his balance; very weak*) Yeah. (*Beat*) Yeah, I'm okay.

PHILIP

Do you want a doctor?

IZZY

No. I'm all right.

With PHILIP's *arm still around him, they advance toward the door. To one side of the doorway, pushed against the wall, there is a small table with a pile of videocassettes on it.*

PHILIP

(*Seeing the cassettes*) I almost forgot. You should have one of these. (*Hands a cassette to* IZZY, *who doesn't say anything*) This is what there is. The editor put together a rough cut of the scenes we shot, and I had them transferred to video. Keep it.

IZZY

(*Taking the video. After a moment; softly*) Thank you.

PHILIP

(*Studying* IZZY) Go home, Izzy. You don't look so good. You need some rest. (*Beat*) Okay?

IZZY

(*Looking down; barely audible*) Okay.

PHILIP

I'll call you if I hear anything.

68. INT: DAY. WHITE HORSE TAVERN.

IZZY *is sitting in the back room of the tavern with* DAVE REILLY *and* TYRONE LORD, *two members of Katmandu. (We have seen them earlier: in scenes 1 and 3.)*

The room is nearly empty. Afternoon light slants through the window. They are sitting in a booth: IZZY *on one side;* DAVE *and* TYRONE *on the other. All three have drinks in front of them. It appears that they have been there for some time.*

IZZY

(*With more vigor than in the previous scene*) You don't believe me, do you?

DAVE *and* TYRONE *exchange a brief private glance, as if to say they don't.*

DAVE

Sure, we believe you, Izzy. Why shouldn't we believe you?

TYRONE

(*Nods*) Definitely.

IZZY *watches them closely. He understands that they are humoring him.*

IZZY

(*Leaning forward*) Tell me. Am I a stone or a tree?

DAVE

Huh?

IZZY

Just answer the question. Am I a stone or a tree?

DAVE *and* TYRONE *ponder for a moment, trying to play along. They answer simultaneously.*

DAVE

A stone.

TYRONE

A tree.

DAVE *and* TYRONE *exchange another glance.* DAVE *shrugs.*

IZZY

(*Not giving up*) Am I a dog or a bird?

TYRONE

(*More into it than Dave*) You're both, man. You're a dog with wings.

DAVE *smiles.*

IZZY

(*More intense, taking hold of* TYRONE's *hand; an arm-wrestling position*) Am I a good person or a bad person?

DAVE

(*Interrupting*) Cut it out, Izzy. You're going to drive yourself crazy.

TYRONE

(*Taking* IZZY's *question seriously. Still gripping his hand; looking him straight in the eye*) You're good, Iz. You're good with some bad stuff mixed in. Just like everyone else.

IZZY

(*Letting go of* TYRONE's *hand. Slumps back in his seat. After a moment: very quietly, as if talking to himself*) Am I here . . . or not here?

Again, DAVE *and* TYRONE *exchange a meaningful glance. The camera turns back on* IZZY. *He is looking down.*

DAVE (*off*)

What difference does it make? Life is just an illusion anyway—right? (*Beat*) Don't worry about it.

Fade out. Music begins to play: slow, deep, sonorous. A piece for full orchestra.

69. INT: NIGHT. IZZY'S APARTMENT. THE BEDROOM.

The music continues.

The scene begins with a close-up of IZZY's *face. He is sitting on the floor, his back leaning against the bed, watching television. No sound—only the music, which slowly and steadily builds in fullness and volume during the course of the scene.*

It is a videotape of Pandora's Box. *The scene, which plays in silence throughout, shows* LULU *walking across her bedroom in her wedding dress. The camera never leaves* LULU *during the scene. Various close-ups of her face. She is at the height of her beauty here, and she gives off an air of innocent, almost virginal joy.*

Intercut between the video and IZZY's *face. He becomes increasingly anguished as the film continues. Eventually, he begins to cry. A bit later, he closes his eyes, unable to watch anymore. With his eyes still closed, cut to:*

70. INT: NIGHT. THE JAZZ CLUB FROM SCENE 3.

The music continues, the volume steadily building.

Another shot of IZZY's *face, his eyes still closed. The camera backs up. We see him lying on the floor of the jazz club from scene 3. The shooting has just taken place. The camera continues to back away from him. We see the confusion of the frightened, stampeding crowd.* TYRONE *tends to* IZZY, *clamping his palms over the wound. Blood seeps out onto his hands. With his head, he gestures frantically for help. Cut to:*

71. EXT: NIGHT. THE STREET IN FRONT OF THE JAZZ CLUB.

The music continues.

With a large crowd of gawkers milling around the entrance of the club, IZZY *is carried out of the building on a stretcher by two paramedics. We see the back doors of the ambulance slam shut.*

72. INT/EXT: NIGHT. INSIDE THE AMBULANCE/THE STREET.

The music continues.

As the ambulance speeds down the street, we see IZZY *lying on his back, attended to by the two paramedics. An IV tube is in his arm. A wire connects his body to a monitor. Cut to:*

Outside. We see CELIA *walking down the street, alone. She is perhaps fifty feet ahead of the ambulance. She turns back at the sound of the siren. Cut to:*

Inside the ambulance. The monitor is registering a flat line. IZZY's *heart has stopped beating. One of the paramedics shakes his head.*

FIRST PARAMEDIC
He's gone. We lost him.

SECOND PARAMEDIC
(*To the driver up front*) Cut the siren, Frank. The guy's dead.

Cut to:

Outside. CELIA *has stopped walking. She is watching the ambulance, which has almost caught up to her. The siren is turned off: a series of strange, stuttering, popping sounds; the noise diminishes to silence. The ambulance slows down.* CELIA, *understanding that the person inside is dead, makes the sign of the cross on her chest with her right hand. She stands there watching the ambulance as it passes by and continues on its way through the traffic. A closeup of her face. A long moment.*

The screen goes black. A few seconds of total silence. The credits come on, accompanied by a female voice performing "Singin' in the Rain."